Sri Lanka Education Sector Assessment

DIRECTIONS IN DEVELOPMENT
Human Development

Sri Lanka Education Sector Assessment

Achievements, Challenges, and Policy Options

Halil Dundar, Benoît Millot, Michelle Riboud, Mari Shojo, Harsha Aturupane, Sangeeta Goyal, and Dhushyanth Raju

© 2017 International Bank for Reconstruction and Development / The World Bank
1818 H Street NW, Washington, DC 20433
Telephone: 202-473-1000; Internet: www.worldbank.org

Some rights reserved

1 2 3 4 20 19 18 17

This work is a product of the staff of The World Bank with external contributions. The findings, interpretations, and conclusions expressed in this work do not necessarily reflect the views of The World Bank, its Board of Executive Directors, or the governments they represent. The World Bank does not guarantee the accuracy of the data included in this work. The boundaries, colors, denominations, and other information shown on any map in this work do not imply any judgment on the part of The World Bank concerning the legal status of any territory or the endorsement or acceptance of such boundaries.

Nothing herein shall constitute or be considered to be a limitation upon or waiver of the privileges and immunities of The World Bank, all of which are specifically reserved.

Rights and Permissions

This work is available under the Creative Commons Attribution 3.0 IGO license (CC BY 3.0 IGO) http://creativecommons.org/licenses/by/3.0/igo. Under the Creative Commons Attribution license, you are free to copy, distribute, transmit, and adapt this work, including for commercial purposes, under the following conditions:

Attribution—Please cite the work as follows: Dundar, Halil, Benoît Millot, Michelle Riboud, Mari Shojo, Harsha Aturupane, Sangeeta Goyal, and Dhushyanth Raju. 2017. *Sri Lanka Education Sector Assessment: Achievements, Challenges, and Policy Options.* Directions in Development. Washington, DC: World Bank. doi:10.1596/978-1-4648-1052-7. License: Creative Commons Attribution CC BY 3.0 IGO

Translations—If you create a translation of this work, please add the following disclaimer along with the attribution: *This translation was not created by The World Bank and should not be considered an official World Bank translation. The World Bank shall not be liable for any content or error in this translation.*

Adaptations—If you create an adaptation of this work, please add the following disclaimer along with the attribution: *This is an adaptation of an original work by The World Bank. Views and opinions expressed in the adaptation are the sole responsibility of the author or authors of the adaptation and are not endorsed by The World Bank.*

Third-party content—The World Bank does not necessarily own each component of the content contained within the work. The World Bank therefore does not warrant that the use of any third-party–owned individual component or part contained in the work will not infringe on the rights of those third parties. The risk of claims resulting from such infringement rests solely with you. If you wish to re-use a component of the work, it is your responsibility to determine whether permission is needed for that re-use and to obtain permission from the copyright owner. Examples of components can include, but are not limited to, tables, figures, or images.

All queries on rights and licenses should be addressed to World Bank Publications, The World Bank Group, 1818 H Street NW, Washington, DC 20433, USA; fax: 202-522-2625; e-mail: pubrights@worldbank.org.

ISBN (paper): 978-1-4648-1052-7
ISBN (electronic): 978-1-4648-1053-4
DOI: 10.1596/978-1-4648-1052-7

Cover photo: © Deshan Tennekoon/World Bank. Used with permission; further permission required for reuse.
Cover design: Debra Naylor of Naylor Design

Library of Congress Cataloging-in-Publication Data has been requested.

Contents

Foreword		*xiii*
Acknowledgments		*xv*
About the Authors		*xvii*
Abbreviations		*xix*
	Overview	**1**
	Introduction	1
	Performance of the Education Sector: A Mixed Success	2
	Critical Issues by Level of Education	7
	Crosscutting Issues	14
	Strategic Priorities and Policy Actions	15
	Conclusion	21
	Notes	22
	References	22
Chapter 1	**Why a Comprehensive Assessment of Education Performance in Sri Lanka?**	**25**
	Introduction	25
	The Economy and the Labor Market	26
	Sri Lanka's Education in the Global Context	28
	The Government's Education Reform Program	29
	Approach, Methodology, and Data Sources	30
	Note	34
	References	34
Chapter 2	**Systemwide Performance: Achievements and Challenges**	**37**
	Introduction	37
	Overview of the Education and Training System in Sri Lanka	37
	Schooling and Training Opportunities	39
	The Quality and Relevance of Education and Training	49
	Labor Market Outcomes	57
	Trends in Sri Lanka's Public Spending on Education	60
	Summary	62

		Notes	62
		References	63
	Chapter 3	**Early Childhood Development: A Missed Opportunity**	**65**
		Introduction	65
		Overview of Early Childhood Development in Sri Lanka	66
		Supply of Early Childhood Development Services	69
		Lessons from International Experience	76
		Conclusion and Policy Options	78
		Notes	79
		References	79
	Chapter 4	**Primary and Secondary Education: The Quality Challenge**	**81**
		Introduction	81
		Education Offerings	82
		Public School Teacher Management in Sri Lanka	84
		Supporting and Monitoring Student Learning	96
		Governance and Accountability	106
		Cost and Financing of Schools in Sri Lanka	110
		Conclusion and Policy Options	113
		Notes	115
		References	116
	Chapter 5	**Technical and Vocational Education and Training: The School-to-Work Transition**	**123**
		Introduction	123
		The Workforce for a Middle-Income Sri Lanka	124
		The TVET Sector: Organizational Structure and Shortcomings	131
		Sri Lanka's Skills Supply System: Areas for Potential Reform	136
		Conclusion and Policy Options	144
		Notes	145
		References	145
	Chapter 6	**Higher Education: From Intakes to Outcomes**	**149**
		Introduction	149
		Overview of the Higher Education Sector	149
		Access to Higher Education	150
		Performance: Inputs, Processes, Outputs, and Outcomes	160
		Financial Resources	181
		Stewarding the Higher Education Sector	191
		Conclusion and Policy Options	195
		Notes	198
		References	201

| Appendix A | Sri Lanka Education Sector Assessment: Main Issues, Strategic Directions, and Policy Actions | 203 |

Boxes

1.1	Skill Types	31
2.1	Characteristics of the Poor in Sri Lanka	47
3.1	Sri Lanka's National Policy of Early Childhood Care and Education, 2004	68
3.2	Features of the Open Approach to Early Childhood Education Curricula	73
4.1	Examination Reforms in Other Economies	100
4.2	Using National Assessment Results	102
4.3	International Assessments and Education Reform	105
4.4	School Internal Quality Assurance in Scotland	108
4.5	Charter Schools and Effective School-Based Management	109
5.1	The Republic of Korea: How Economic Development Changed Investment in Skills	125
5.2	Why Educated Youth Are Unemployed	128
5.3	Industrial Sector Skills Councils	134
5.4	The Efficiency of Vouchers	140
5.5	Examples of Employer Involvement in Training	142
5.6	Benefits of Information Sharing	144
6.1	University of Moratuwa UNI Consultancy Services	178

Figures

O.1	Sri Lanka's Access to Education, by Level	3
O.2	Enrollment, Secondary and Higher Education, Sri Lanka and Selected Countries	4
O.3	Educational Attainment in Sri Lanka, Malaysia, and the Republic of Korea	4
O.4	Enrollment Rates, Ratio of Richest to Poorest Quintile, 2006–12	5
O.5	Mean Scores in National Assessment for Grade 4, 2013	5
O.6	Mean Scores in National Assessment for Grade 8, 2012	6
O.7	Employer Perception of General Education, TVET, and University, 2013	7
O.8	Preschool Enrollment, an International Perspective	8
O.9	Inequality in Access to Preschool by Economic Group, 2012	8
O.10	Tertiary Education Outcomes, an International Perspective, 2012–13	13
O.11	Education Spending, 2007–12	14
O.12	Spending on Public Education, an International Perspective	15
1.1	Educational Attainment in Sri Lanka, Malaysia, and the Republic of Korea, 1960–2010	29
1.2	Skills Formation across the Worker Life Cycle	32

2.1	The Education and Training System in Sri Lanka	38
2.2	Sri Lankans Who Have Passed GCE O-Levels, by Age Group, 2002 and 2012	39
2.3	Student Flow in the Education and Training System, 2013–14	40
2.4	Gross Enrollment Rates, by Education Level, 2006–12	41
2.5	Net Enrollment Rates, by Education Level, 2006–13	41
2.6	Early Childhood Education Net Enrollment Rate, by GNI per Capita, Middle- and High-Income Countries	42
2.7	Enrollment in Secondary and Higher Education, Selected Countries, 2014	43
2.8	Enrollment Rates, by Gender	44
2.9	Access to Education, by Income Quintile	44
2.10	Enrollment, Ratio of Richest to Poorest Quintile	45
2.11	Access to Education, by Level and Location, 2012–13	46
2.12	Access to Education, by Level and Province, 2012–13	46
2.13	Completion Rate, by Gender, 2006 and 2013	48
2.14	Completion Rate, by Location, 2006 and 2013	49
2.15	Completion Rates, Poorest and Richest Quintiles, 2006 and 2013	49
2.16	Mean Scores, National Assessment for Grade 4, by Subject and School Type, 2013	50
2.17	Mean Scores, National Assessment for Grade 8, by Subject and School Type, 2012	51
2.18	Pass Rates, GCE O-Level Examination, 2005–12	51
2.19	Pass Rates, GCE A-Level Examination, 2005–12	52
2.20	Grade 8 Learning Outcomes, by Province, 2012	52
2.21	Standardized Test Scores, Grade 8, 2012	53
2.22	Sri Lanka's Learning Outcomes, an International Perspective	54
2.23	Student Performance Measured by the 2012 National Assessment	55
2.24	Employer Perceptions of General Education, TVET, and University	55
2.25	Skills Most Important for Retention Decisions	56
2.26	Firms Identifying Lack of Skilled Workforce as a Major Problem	57
2.27	Labor Force Participation, Selected Countries	58
2.28	Returns on Education, by Level, 2006–12	60
2.29	Education Spending, 2007–12	61
2.30	Spending on Public Education, an International Perspective	61
3.1	Early Childhood Development Net Enrollment Rates Disaggregated, 2012–13	67
3.2	Early Childhood Development Centers, by Ownership Type and Province	69
3.3	Quality of Preschool Infrastructure, 2013	71
3.4	The Learning Environment in Sri Lankan Preschools, 2013	71
3.5	Teacher Qualifications, by Province, 2002	72
3.6	Registered Early Childhood Development Centers, by District	74

4.1	Densities of School Student-Teacher Ratios	87
4.2	Teachers with Any Training and Year of Entry into Teaching, by Academic Qualification	89
4.3	Assessment System Structure	96
4.4	Developing-Country Participation in International Assessments	103
4.5	Public Spending on Primary and Secondary Education, 2004–13	111
4.6	GCE O-Level Pass Rates and Provincial Investment in Education, 2012	112
B5.1.1	How Economic Development Drove Changes in TVET in the Republic of Korea	125
5.1	Changes in Skills Needs, 1970–Present	126
5.2	Female Labor Force Participation in Developing Countries, 1990–2012	127
5.3	Skills Shortages, by Job Category	129
5.4	Labor Force Skills Stock and Employer Requirements	129
5.5	Labor Force Cognitive, English, and Computer Skills and Employer Requirements	130
5.6	Structure of the TVET Sector, 2016	132
5.7	Wage Premiums in Sri Lanka, by Education and Skill Type	135
5.8	Spending by the Ministry of Skills Development and Vocational Training	139
6.1	Paths to Higher Education in Sri Lanka, 2014	151
6.2	Tertiary Education Gross Enrollment Rate, Selected Countries and Groups of Countries, 2013	153
6.3	Higher Education Gross Enrollment Rate and GDP per Capita, International Comparisons, 2012	153
6.4	Tertiary Education Gross Enrollment Rate, Sri Lanka and Countries Grouped by Income, 1999–2013	154
6.5	GCE A-Levels: Pass Rates and Distribution, by Discipline Groups, 2014	156
6.6	Female Enrollment in Higher Education, Selected Economies and Groups, 2013	158
6.7	Tertiary Education Gross Enrollment Rate, by Province and Gender, 2012–13	159
6.8	Tertiary Education Gross Enrollment Rate, by Quintile and Gender, 2012–13	159
6.9	Higher Education Student-Teacher Ratios and International Gross Enrollment Rates, 2012 or Closest Year	160
6.10	Public Higher Education Faculty Members, by Academic Qualification and Discipline, 2012	161
6.11	Structure of Student and Faculty, 2014	162
6.12	Students Admitted and Graduated, by Gender, 2014	167
6.13	Tertiary Education Graduates, by Gender, Selected Countries, 2013 or Closest Year	167

6.14	Youth Unemployment, Selected Countries and Groups, 2013	170
6.15	Monthly Earnings, by Level of Education, 2009–10	171
6.16	Employment of Graduates Six and Three Months after Graduation, 2014	173
6.17	Graduates and Employment Rate, by Discipline, 2012	173
6.18	Citable Documents per Million Inhabitants, Selected Economies, 1996 to 2014	176
6.19	Spending on General and Higher Education, 2003–13	183
6.20	Tertiary Education Spending as a Share of Total Government Spending and GDP per Capita, Selected Countries, 2012/13	184
6.21	Gross Enrollment Rate and Tertiary Education as a Share of Total Government Spending, 2012–13	185
6.22	Recurrent Block Grant per Student and University Enrollment, 2016	187
6.23	Revenues Generated by Public Universities, 2014	189
6.24	Average Monthly Household Spending per Student in Higher Education, by Quintile, Location, and Gender, 2012–13	191

Tables

1.1	Social Indicators for Sri Lanka and Comparator Economies	27
B2.1.1	Profile of the Poor and Nonpoor	47
2.1	Labor Market Outcomes, by Demographic Characteristics, Education, and Training	59
3.1	Enrollment of 3- to 5-Year-Olds in Preschool or School	66
3.2	Estimated Public Financing Required to Reach 80 Percent Early Childhood Development Enrollment	75
3.3	How to Achieve Early Childhood Development Program Goals	78
4.1	Government Schools, Enrollment, and Teachers, by School Type, 2013	82
4.2	Descriptive Statistics for Public School Teachers	85
4.3	Distribution of Professional and Academic Qualifications of Teachers	89
4.4	Differences between Assessment Types	97
4.5	TIMSS, PIRLS, and PISA Compared	104
6.1	Enrollment in Higher Education, by Institution, 2014	150
6.2	Tertiary Education: Changes and Shares of Enrollment, by ISCED Levels, Selected Countries, 2010–12	152
6.3	Undergraduate and Postgraduate Enrollment, by Discipline, Public Universities and Institutions, 2014	155
6.4	Student Distribution, by Discipline Groups, 2014	155
6.5	Higher Education Enrollment, by Discipline Groups, Selected Countries, 2012 or Closest Year	157
6.6	Female Participation in Higher Education, by Level, 2014	157
6.7	Female Undergraduate Admissions, by Discipline, 2014	158

6.8	Distribution of Faculty Members, by Academic Status, 2007 and 2014	163
6.9	Undergraduate Admissions, Graduation, and Ratios, 2011–14	166
6.10	University Tests for Student IT Competency and Teaching of English, 2012–13	168
6.11	Labor Force Participation and Unemployment Rates, Selected Countries and Groups, 2013	170
6.12	Labor Force Participation, Unemployment, and Underemployment, by Education Level and Gender, 2012–13	171
6.13	Graduates by Discipline, Selected Countries, 2013 or Closest Year	172
6.14	The Importance of Various Skills to Employers, 2014	174
6.15	Agreement of Graduates with Statements about Their Instruction, 2014	175
6.16	University-Industry Collaboration: Constraints and Perceptions, 2015	177
6.17	Number of Resident Patents Submitted, Selected Countries, 2013	179
6.18	Universities Represented in Three International Rankings, Selected Countries, 2014–15	180
6.19	Webometrics Rankings, Selected Countries, 2014–15	181
6.20	U21 Rankings, Selected Countries, 2014 and 2015	181
6.21	Government Spending on Tertiary Education, Selected Economies, 2012 or Closest Year	183
6.22	Per-Student Expenditures on Higher Education, Sri Lanka, 2012 and 2013	186
6.23	Government Spending per Tertiary Student, Selected Economies, 2012 or Closest Year	186
6.24	Staff Compensation in Public Higher Education Institutions as a Share of Total Spending, Selected Economies, 2012	187
6.25	Capital Spending in Tertiary Public Institutions, as a Share of Total Spending, Selected Economies, 2010–13	188
6.26	Expenditures by Category, Public Universities and Institutes, 2012	190

Foreword

Sri Lanka's solid economic growth for more than a decade has helped reduce poverty and promote shared prosperity. Sri Lanka is a lower-middle-income country and was one of the fastest-growing economies in South Asia, with an average growth rate of over 6 percent. High growth and shared prosperity have resulted in the national poverty headcount ratio declining sharply, from 15.3 percent in 2006–07 to 6.7 percent in 2012–13.

Human development indicators in Sri Lanka are impressive by regional and lower-middle-income standards: The country outperformed nearby country comparators on most of the Millennium Development Goals (MDGs). About 96 percent of its citizens have completed primary school, 87 percent have finished secondary school, and there is gender parity in school completion at primary and secondary levels. Although Sri Lanka is well-known for fast progress in educational attainment, it lags behind other middle-income countries in terms of early childhood education, higher education participation and quality, private sector orientation of the technical education and vocational training system, and learning outcomes and socioemotional skills. The result is that Sri Lanka faces an acute shortage of the high-level human resources that are needed for the advanced industrial and service sector activities of a globally competitive upper-middle-income country. Recognizing these issues, the government of Sri Lanka has already set goals for reforming education. The findings of this study could provide inputs for the government agenda.

This study is the first comprehensive and systematic review of Sri Lanka's education sector, covering the stages from early childhood education through higher education. It assesses the performance of the education system in Sri Lanka, analyzes the most critical constraints on performance, and identifies strategic priorities and policy options to improve it. It attempts to answer the following questions:

- How is Sri Lanka's education and training system performing? What are its main achievements to date and what are the main challenges confronting it?

- How can the country address constraints and respond to challenges at each stage of the education process, taking into account both country and international experience and best practices?
- What actions should have priority in the short and medium term?

This study is an important contribution to understanding the status and challenges of the education sector in Sri Lanka. Based on analyses of available data and on the review of previous analytical work in Sri Lanka and of international evidence and best practices, it offers an insightful analysis and provides suggestions on how Sri Lanka's education system can be improved to better achieve the country's development goals. We hope the study will promote dialogue and debate with all our partners, not only policy makers but also civil society organizations, academic institutions, development practitioners, and the media.

Jamie Saavedra Chanduvi
Senior Director, Education Global Practice
The World Bank Group

Idah Z. Pswarayi-Riddihough
Country Director for Sri Lanka and the Maldives
The World Bank Group

Acknowledgments

Sri Lanka Education Sector Assessment: Achievements, Challenges, and Policy Options is a comprehensive assessment of Sri Lanka's education sector covering the stages from early childhood education through higher education. The study was prepared by a team led by Halil Dundar, under the general direction of Amit Dar, director of strategy and operations, human development; Keiko Miwa, practice manager, South Asia Region, Education Global Practice; Idah Z. Pswarayi-Riddihough, country director for Sri Lanka and the Maldives; and Francoise Clottes, former country director for Sri Lanka and the Maldives. The core team consisted of Benoît Millot, Michelle Riboud, Mari Shojo, Harsha Aturupane, Sangeeta Goyal, and Dhushyanth Raju.

The book draws on background papers prepared by Reehana Raza (skills development) and Dhushyanth Raju and Ritika Dsouza (private tutoring as well as public school teacher management in Sri Lanka). The peer reviewers for the report were Cem Mete and Juan Manuel Moreno. The team also benefited from advice, inputs, and comments from a number of individuals at critical points in the report's preparation, notably Chitral Amarasiri, Roshini Ebenezer, David Locke Newhouse, Yevgeniya Savchenko, Shalika Subasinghe, and Hassan Zaman.

Many individuals from the Prime Minister's Office, the Ministry of Finance, the Ministry of National Policies and Economic Affairs, the Ministry of Women and Child Affairs, the Ministry of Education, the Ministry of Higher Education and Highways, and the Ministry of Skills Development and Vocational Training participated in and provided extremely useful insights at consultations and dissemination events.

None of the people mentioned above bear any responsibility for the analyses and findings of this report. The authors alone assume full responsibility for its conclusions.

Anne Grant and Kalpana Kaul assisted with the editing of the report. The report would have not been possible without the able assistance of Sandra Alborta, Anita Fernando, Kerima Thilakasena, Elfreda Vincent, and Alejandro Welch. The team also gratefully acknowledges financial support from the Australian Trust Fund for the Sri Lanka Education Sector Development Framework and Program. Finally, we also thank Susan Graham and Jewel McFadden from World Bank Publications, who coordinated the editing, design, production, and printing of this book.

About the Authors

Halil Dundar is the practice manager for the Education Global Practice, Central and Southern Africa (16 countries), at the World Bank. Previously, he was a lead education specialist in the Education Global Practice, leading the Bank's operational and analytical work on tertiary education in Pakistan and skills development in Sri Lanka, as well as the Bank's analytical work on education quality in South Asia. He also managed the Bank's education lending operations and analytical work in Albania, Azerbaijan, Ethiopia, and Nigeria. Before joining the Bank, he worked as a research associate in the Office of Planning and Analysis at the University of Minnesota and subsequently held the position of assistant professor of education policy at the Middle East Technical University in Ankara, Turkey, and served as a policy adviser to the Turkish Ministry of Education. He has published numerous journal articles and book chapters on education finance and productivity issues. He was a lead author of *Student Learning in South Asia* (2014) and *Building the Skills for Economic Growth and Competitiveness in Sri Lanka* (2014). He holds a PhD in education from the University of Minnesota—Twin Cities, with a concentration in the economics of higher education.

Benoît Millot is a former lead education economist at the World Bank, where he specialized in education finance and higher education issues in several regions, having led the Bank's operational and analytical work on tertiary education. He holds a PhD in the economics of education from the University of Burgundy, France, and was a visiting scholar at Stanford International Development Education Center (SIDEC). Before joining the Bank, he was a senior researcher at the Institute for Research on Economics of Education in Dijon.

Michelle Riboud is an economist who started her professional career working in academia, serving at the University of Orléans, France, a Spanish research institute, and the Institut d'Etudes Politiques in Paris. In late 1988, she joined the World Bank where she held senior and lead economist positions, first in Latin America and the Caribbean, and then in Europe and Central Asia. In her last assignment, she was responsible for analytical work and a lending portfolio for education in Afghanistan, Bangladesh, Bhutan, India, Nepal, Pakistan, and Sri Lanka. Since retiring, she has been a consultant for various units of the

World Bank. She has conducted research and published on human capital theory, household economics, labor markets, and social protection issues in both OECD and developing countries. She holds a PhD in economics from the University of Paris I and a PhD in economics from the University of Chicago.

Mari Shojo is an education specialist at the World Bank, where she works on lending and analytical activities in South Asian countries. In recent years, she has focused on primary and secondary education, early childhood development, and higher education in Sri Lanka and the Maldives. Before joining the World Bank, she worked with the Japan International Cooperation Agency (JICA) and universities on education decentralization, school-based management, teacher development, human development, and higher education in Africa and the Middle East. She holds a MA in economics and a PhD in international education policy from Kobe University, Japan.

Harsha Aturupane is a lead education specialist at the World Bank. He is the program leader for human development for Sri Lanka and the Maldives. He currently leads the Bank's operational work on higher education and school education in Sri Lanka and the Maldives and on higher education in Afghanistan. He has a PhD and MPhil in economics from the University of Cambridge, a BA in economics, and a diploma in economic development from the University of Colombo.

Sangeeta Goyal is a senior economist at the World Bank. She has worked extensively in the education sector in India, Nepal, Bangladesh, Sri Lanka, and Bhutan. She obtained her PhD in economics from Columbia University, focusing on the role of income inequality on social outcomes. She has published many articles on the determinants of learning outcomes, decentralization and education, and the labor market outcomes of vocational training and college graduates. Prior to joining the World Bank, she was a visiting professor at the School of International and Public Affairs at Columbia University.

Dhushyanth Raju is a lead economist in the Office of the Chief Economist, South Asia Region, of the World Bank. He currently provides policy advice to client countries and conducts economic research on human development in South Asia. He holds a PhD in economics from Cornell University.

Abbreviations

ADB	Asian Development Bank
ARWU	Academic Ranking of World Universities
ASEAN	Association of Southeast Asian Nations
ATI	Advanced Technological Institute
BPO	business processing outsourcing
COTE	College of Teacher Education
DTET	Department of Technical Education and Training
ECD	early childhood development
ECE	early childhood education
ECEQAS	Early Childhood Education Quality Assessment Survey
EDP	external degree program
EQI	education quality input
ESA	education sector assessment
ESL	English as a Second Language
ETI	external training institute
GCE A-level	General Certificate of Education, Advanced Level
GCE O-level	General Certificate of Education, Ordinary Level
GDP	gross domestic product
GER	gross enrollment rate
GNI	gross national income
HE	higher education
HEI	higher education institution
HETC	Higher Education for the Twenty-First Century
HIC	high-income country
HIES	Household Income and Expenditure Survey
ICT	information and communications technology
ILO	International Labour Organization
IMSCC	Inter-Ministerial Sector Coordination Committee
IQAU	Internal Quality Assurance Unit
ISA	in-service advisor

ISC	Industry Skills Council, Australia
ISCED	International Standard Classification of Education
ISSC	Industrial Sector Skills Council
IT	information technology
KPI	key performance indicator
LFPR	labor force participation rate
LIC	low-income country
LKR	Sri Lankan rupees
LLECE	Latin American Laboratory for Assessment of the Quality of Education
LMIC	lower-middle-income country
M&E	monitoring and evaluation
MHEH	Ministry of Higher Education and Highways
MIC	middle-income country
MOE	Ministry of Education
MOHE	Ministry of Higher Education
MOOC	massive open online course
MSDVT	Ministry of Skills Development and Vocational Training
MWCA	Ministry of Women and Child Affairs
NAITA	National Apprentice and Industrial Training Authority
NCOE	National College of Education
NER	net enrollment rate
NEREC	National Education Research and Evaluation Center
NGO	nongovernmental organization
NHRDC	National Human Resources Development Council
NHREPSL	National Human Resources and Employment Policy for Sri Lanka
NIE	National Institute of Education
NPECC	National Policy on Early Childhood Care and Education
NVQ	National Vocational Qualification
NYSC	National Youth Services Council
OBE	outcome-based education
OECD	Organisation for Economic Co-operation and Development
OJT	on-the-job training
PASEC	Programme d'Analyse des Systèmes Educatifs de la CONFEMEN (Programme for the Analysis of Education Systems of CONFEMEN)
PC	provincial council
PhD	doctor of philosophy
PIRLS	Progress in International Reading Literacy Study

PISA	Programme for International Student Assessment
PISAfD	Programme for International Student Assessment for Development
PPP	public-private partnership
PSDC	Penang Skills Development Centre, Malaysia
PSI	Programme for School Improvement
QA	quality assurance
QAAC	Quality Assurance and Accreditation Council
QIG	Quality and Innovation Grant
QS	Quacquarelli Symonds
SABER	Systems Approach for Better Education Results
SACMEQ	Southern and Eastern Africa Consortium for Monitoring Educational Quality
SDC	staff development center
SEBRAE	Serviço Brasileiro de Apoio às Micro e Pequenas Empresas (Brazilian Micro and Small Enterprises' Support Service)
SENAI	Serviço Nacional de Aprendizagem Industrial (National Industrial Apprenticeship Service, Brazil)
SENAR	Serviço Nacional de Aprendizagem Rural (National Rural Apprenticeship Service, Brazil)
SENAT	Serviço Nacional de Aprendizagem do Transporte (National Transport Apprenticeship Service, Brazil)
SLIATE	Sri Lanka Institute of Advanced Technological Education
SLQF	Sri Lanka Qualifications Framework
SSDP	Skills Sector Development Program
SSEP	Skills Sector Enhancement Program
STEM	science, technology, engineering, and mathematics
STEP	Skills Toward Employment and Productivity
STR	student-teacher ratio
THE	Times Higher Education
TIMSS	Trends in International Mathematics and Science Study
TVEC	Tertiary and Vocational Education Commission
TVET	technical and vocational education and training
UGC	University Grants Commission
UIS	UNESCO Institute for Statistics
UMIC	upper-middle-income country
UNESCO	United Nations Educational, Scientific and Cultural Organization
UNIVOTEC	University of Vocational Technology
VTA	Vocational Training Authority of Sri Lanka
WIPO	World Intellectual Property Organization

Overview

The education system of every country plays a pivotal role in promoting economic growth and shared prosperity. Although Sri Lanka has long outperformed comparable developing countries at the primary and secondary school levels, it still faces major problems in the education sector that undermine the country's inclusive growth goal and ambition to become a competitive middle-income country.

The main objective of this report is to assess the status of the education sector from early childhood development (ECD) to higher education, analyze the most critical constraints on performance, and identify priorities and policy options to address them. This overview briefly summarizes the main findings and presents related strategic priorities and policy actions.

Introduction

Sri Lanka is, in many respects, a development success story. The country's solid economic growth for over a decade has helped to reduce poverty and promoted shared prosperity. In 2010–13, with an average annual growth rate of 7.5 percent, Sri Lanka's was the fastest-growing economy in South Asia. Gross domestic product (GDP) growth continued in 2014, reaching 7.4 percent, driven mainly by services, manufacturing, and construction. In 2016, the country's per capita GDP is expected to reach US$4,000. Measured by per capita consumption and using the national poverty line, Sri Lanka's poverty rate dropped from 22.7 percent in 2002 to 6.7 percent in 2012/13 (World Bank 2016).

Human development indicators are impressive by regional and lower-middle-income standards: Sri Lanka outperformed nearby country comparators on most of the Millennium Development Goals (MDGs), especially those related to education and health. About 96 percent of its citizens have completed primary school, 87 percent have finished secondary school, and there is gender parity in school completion at primary and secondary levels. Maternal and infant mortality rates are now very low, and life expectancy, currently 74 years, has been above that of its regional peers for over a decade.

Sustaining inclusive economic growth is at the heart of the government's development plan. Sri Lanka's goal is to become a competitive middle-income country grounded in a knowledge-based economy. The government aims at achieving an annual growth rate of at least 8 percent in the future and intends to bridge the economic development gap that separates Sri Lanka from Southeast Asian countries such as Malaysia and Thailand; it intends to increase the share of its manufacturing, services, and agricultural, and fisheries products in global markets and promote the creation of an additional million jobs.

Recognizing that Sri Lanka will succeed in these aspirations only if its labor force is highly educated and skilled, the government has made education a priority. It is aware that:

- Although Sri Lankans spend more time in the education system than neighbors in South Asia, employers are questioning the system's quality and its relevance.
- Major skills shortages and mismatches undermine productivity and thus growth.
- Disparities in learning outcomes in primary and secondary education and in access to both technical and vocational education and training (TVET) and higher education undermine the government's inclusive growth objectives.

To help identifying barriers to effective education and designing appropriate reforms, this study attempts to answer the following questions:

- *How is Sri Lanka's education system performing, especially with respect to participation rates, learning outcomes, and labor market outcomes?*
- *How can the country address constraints and respond to challenges at each stage of the education process, taking into account both country and international experience and best practices?*
- *What policy actions should have priority in the short and medium term?*

In seeking answers to these questions, the study carried out a comprehensive assessment of the sector, from ECD to higher education. This assessment uses available data and draws from previous analytical work in Sri Lanka, South Asia, and beyond.

Performance of the Education Sector: A Mixed Success

Sri Lanka made excellent progress in expanding access to education in its early phases of economic development, but now faces several constraints while trying to respond to the needs of a rapidly changing economy (Aturupane et al. 2014). The main constraints are: (a) the limited education and training opportunities offered to youth at the end of compulsory schooling and inequities created by these limitations; and (b) the quality of education and training offerings, which do not meet international standards and are not flexible enough to adapt to the needs of a changing labor market.

Schooling and Training Opportunities

Sri Lanka has provided high and equitable access to primary and secondary education for several decades (World Bank 2011). The net enrollment rate (NER) is 99 percent in primary education and 84 percent in junior secondary, and there is gender parity in both (figures O.1). In senior secondary education, NER is 70 percent, which is relatively high for middle-income countries. On average, Sri Lankan students attend school for about 10 years, compared to six years in South Asia. This coverage success is the result of sustained government commitment: education is provided for free, and also backed by free textbooks and uniforms, scholarships, and adequate numbers of schools and teachers.

Beyond secondary education, however, opportunities are limited for nearly half of youth cohorts. Out of a General Certificate of Education Ordinary-Level (GCE O-level) cohort of about 450,000 students, only about 20 percent will attend a higher education institution (HEI), and another 33 percent will attend TVET programs, leaving about 47 percent of them with no options other than exiting the education and training sector, entering the labor market, or going abroad for further studies.

As a result, the comparative advance that Sri Lanka had and still maintains at the secondary school level, relative to comparator countries, totally erodes (and even reverses) at the tertiary education level (figure O.2). At this level, Sri Lanka has clearly fallen behind over time (figure O.3). In 1960, the proportion of Sri Lankans aged 15 or over with secondary education was comparable to that of Malaysia and higher than that of the Republic of Korea, and the proportion of the population with tertiary education was similar to that in those countries. Fifty years later, in 2010, Sri Lanka's tertiary education completion rate was substantially lower than that of Malaysia and Korea, both countries which have been investing heavily in TVET and higher education for at least three decades.

Figure O.1 Sri Lanka's Access to Education, by Level

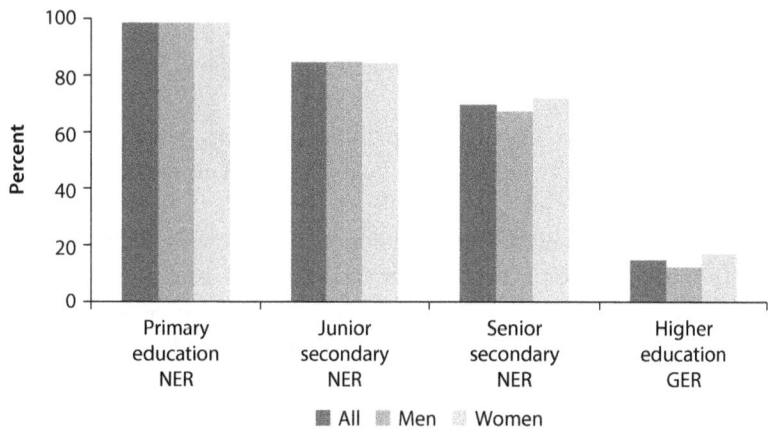

Source: EdStats.
Note: GER = gross enrollment rate; and NER = net enrollment rate.

Figure O.2 Enrollment, Secondary and Higher Education, Sri Lanka and Selected Countries

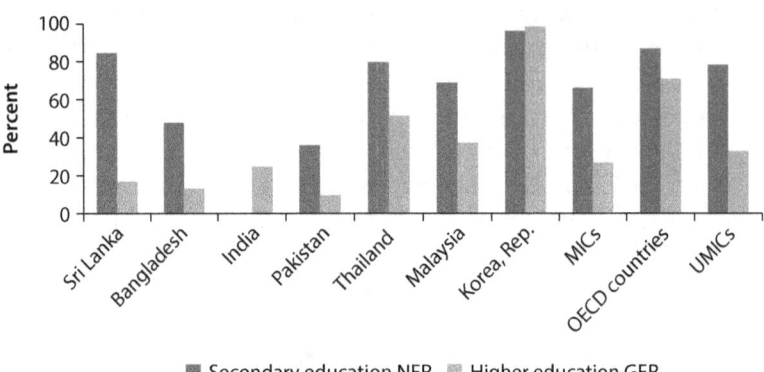

Source: EdStats.
Note: GER = gross enrollment rate; MICs = middle-income countries; NER = net enrollment rate; OECD = Organisation of Economic Co-operation and Development; and UMICs = upper-middle-income countries.

Figure O.3 Educational Attainment in Sri Lanka, Malaysia, and the Republic of Korea

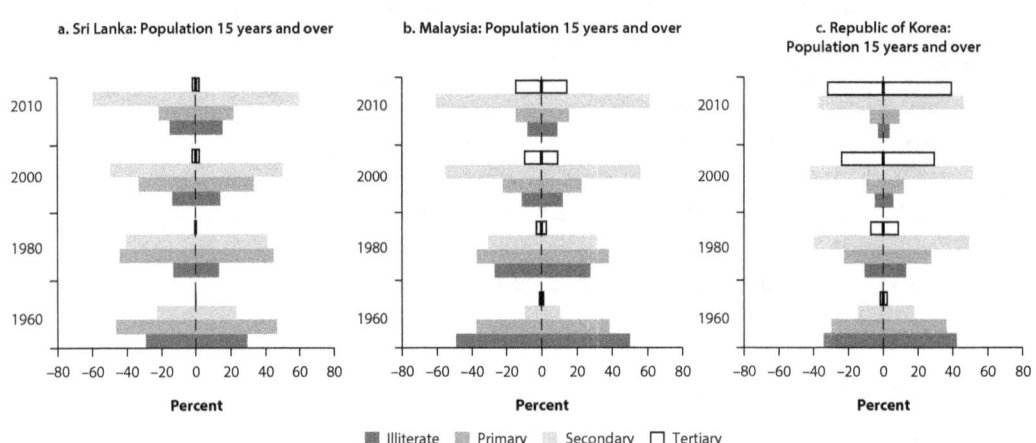

Sources: Riboud, Savchenko, and Tan 2007; and Barro and Lee 2012.

Similarly, there is low participation in TVET programs which primarily target students with GCE O-level and A-level qualifications. This largely contributes to the lack of workers with job-specific skills.

The limited access to higher levels of education has entailed inequities. While participation in education across gender and economic groups is highly equitable at primary and junior secondary levels, it is much less so at senior secondary and higher education levels. Wealthier students are more likely than those from poorer families to pursue their education at levels where participation is constrained: senior secondary NERs range from 64 percent for the poorest to 78 percent for the richest. Similarly, in higher education, the gross enrollment rate (GER) for the poorest quintile is 10 percent and 26 percent for the richest.

Furthermore, there are indications that the gap between the richest and the poorest has been widening over time (figure O.4).

Education Quality
In the early stages of education, learning achievement in Sri Lanka seems relatively good. For example, a 2009 national assessment of grade 4 students conducted by the National Education Research and Evaluation Center (NEREC) found that a large proportion of grade 4 students were able to master the essential learning competencies expected by the national curriculum. The mean achievement score in mathematics was 77 percent in Sinhala-medium schools and 62 percent in Tamil-medium schools (NEREC 2009). A review of learning outcomes in South Asia also found that Sri Lanka is the only country in the region where average achievement does not appear to have fallen over time. The 2013 national assessment also indicated that there are no huge differences in achievement by subject and type of school at this level of education (figure O.5).[1]

Figure O.4 Enrollment Rates, Ratio of Richest to Poorest Quintile, 2006–12

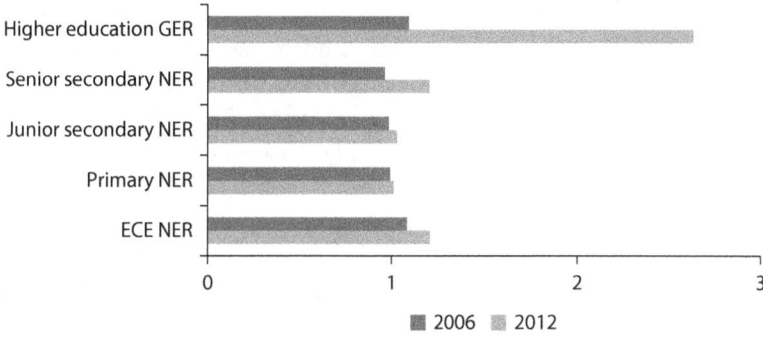

Source: HIES data, 2006/07 and 2012/13.
Note: ECE = early childhood education; GER = gross enrollment rate; and NER = net enrollment ratio.

Figure O.5 Mean Scores in National Assessment for Grade 4, 2013

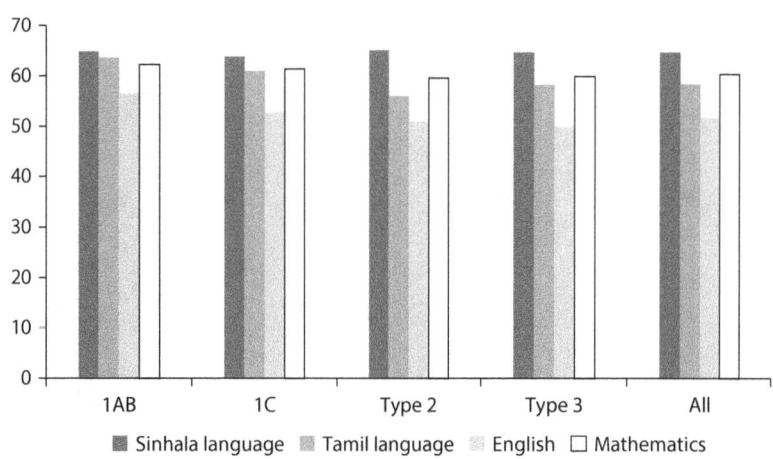

Source: NEREC 2014.

At higher grades, such as grade 8, however, there are concerns about the ability of students to master the curriculum, and growing disparities (figure O.6). Although there is some evidence that test scores—and thus, quality—have been rising over time, the mean scores of grade 8 students in 2012 were still just 51 percent for mathematics, 42 percent for science, and 40 percent for English, indicating that the general education system fails to produce skills that are in high demand in a competitive economy. Disparities by school type have also widened significantly. Furthermore, national averages mask serious disparities in learning outcomes by regional and socioeconomic variations. Students in remote locations—especially in plantations and less-developed provinces—and students from poor socioeconomic backgrounds have far lower learning levels than the comparator groups.

The lack of data allowing a comparison with international standards adds to the difficulty of properly assessing all dimensions of education quality in Sri Lanka, and its improvements over time. Sri Lanka has never participated in international assessments, such as the Programme for International Student Assessment (PISA), Trends in International Mathematics and Science Study (TIMSS), and Progress in International Literacy Study (PIRLS). This prevents benchmarking against international standards and makes it more difficult to identify where issues stand and what their causes are.

The concern about insufficient quality extends to higher levels of education. In both TVET and higher education, not only is access limited, but existing programs' quality and relevance are questionable. Relatively few students are enrolled in programs defined as national priorities, and many graduates remain idle for an extended period between graduation and their first job. Moreover, more than 50 percent of employers, when interviewed, question the quality and relevance of

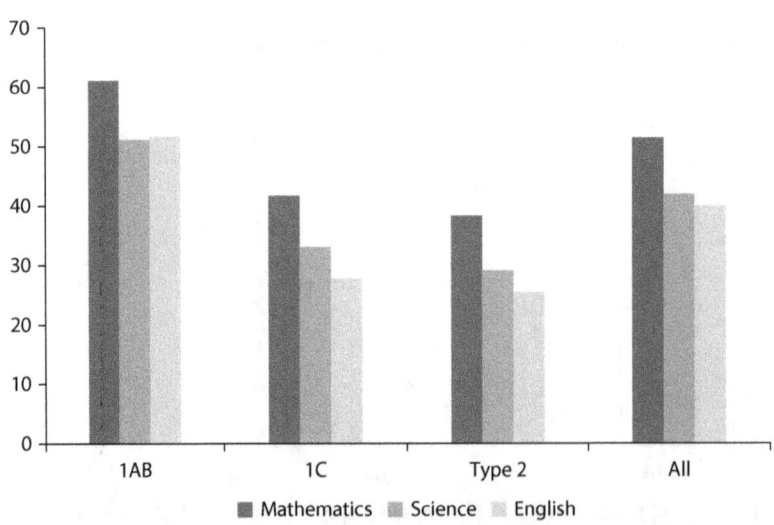

Figure O.6 Mean Scores in National Assessment for Grade 8, 2012

Source: NEREC 2013.

general education, TVET, and universities with regard to conveying up-to-date knowledge or providing relevant skills (figure O.7). Asked about barriers to their growth, Sri Lankan firms put the quality and supply of skilled technicians third after taxes and regulation and financing (Dutz and O'Connell 2013).

Critical Issues by Level of Education

Early Childhood Development: A Missed Opportunity

Increasingly, it is recognized that participation in quality early child development programs leads to greater cognitive development, better readiness for primary school, lower repetition and dropout rates in the early grades, increased capacity for learning in school, and greater lifelong earning potential.[2] Availability of these programs can thus bring substantial benefits in terms of greater quality of primary education and higher learning achievements.

Sri Lanka, however, only has an emerging ECD sector. Considering preschool interventions focused on children aged 3–5, Sri Lanka has low coverage: only 50 percent of children can access preschool (figure O.8). Access is also highly inequitable. Preschool is mostly provided by private and nongovernmental organizations (NGOs) due to lack of public investment, which means there are considerable access disparities by both socioeconomic status and location. In 2012, only 39 percent of children aged 3–5 years from the bottom quintile attended ECD centers/preschools, as against about 56 percent from the top quintile (figure O.9). In urban areas, attendance was around 59 percent versus 50 percent in rural areas. This unequal participation implies that children from poor homes are often permanently disadvantaged in terms of life chances.

Figure O.7 Employer Perception of General Education, TVET, and University, 2013

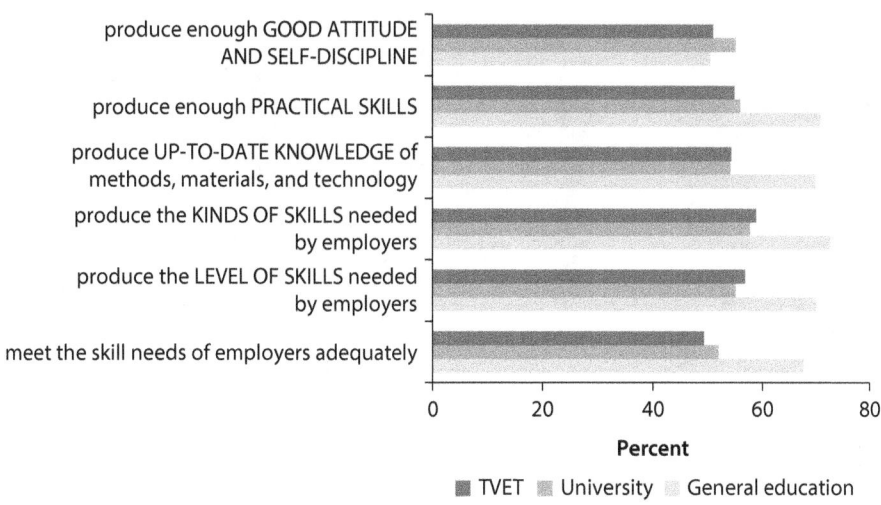

Source: Dundar et al. 2014.
Note: TVET = technical and vocational education and training.

Figure O.8 Preschool Enrollment, an International Perspective

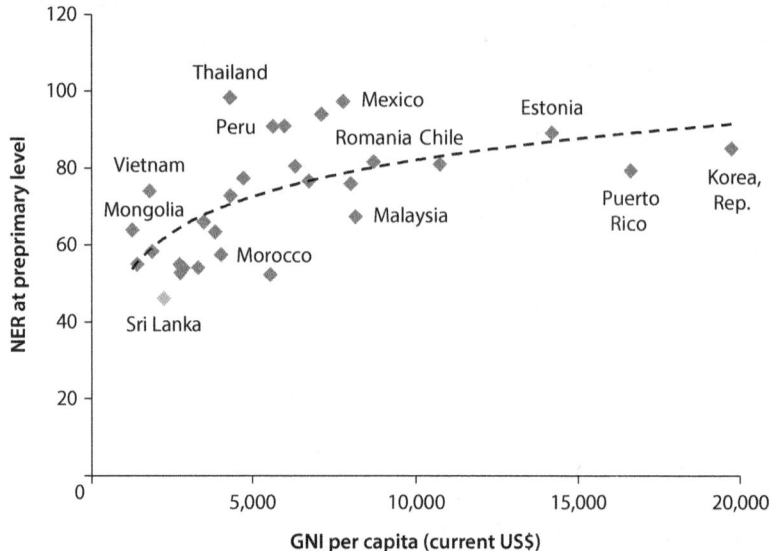

Source: World Bank Education Statistics Data, 2012/13 or nearest year available.
Note: GNI = gross national income; and NER = net enrollment rate.

Figure O.9 Inequality in Access to Preschool by Economic Group, 2012

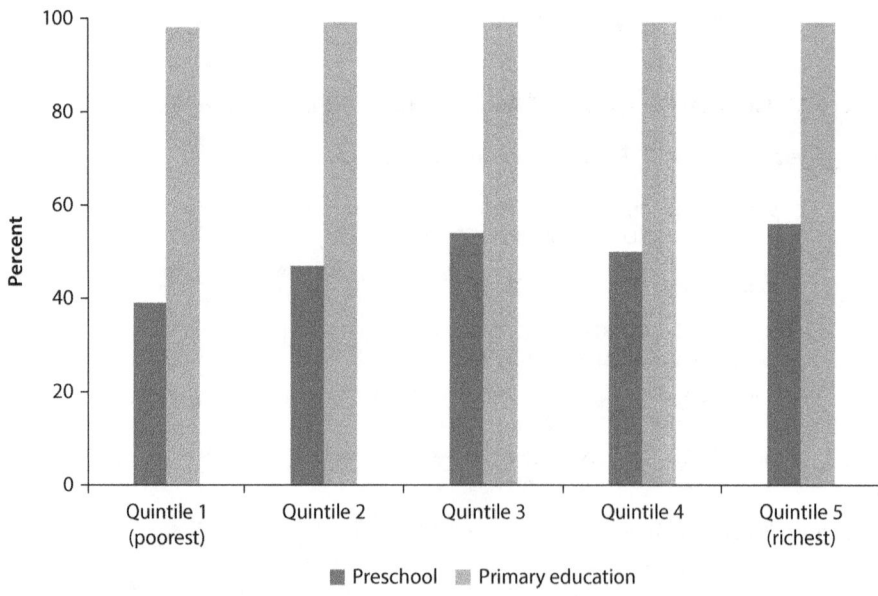

Source: World Bank 2014.

The regulatory structure is still unevenly developed; there is no formal curriculum and early learning standards; a significant percentage of centers lack adequate resources for teaching and learning; and fewer than half the teachers meet the basic qualification requirements. Even though the government's education policy views ECD as a priority, the potential benefits of investment in ECD cannot be maximized unless such problems as low coverage, inequitable access, and the poor quality of services are properly addressed.

Primary and Secondary Education: The Quality Challenge

As discussed in the previous section, Sri Lanka has made impressive progress in getting children into primary and secondary school and having them complete up to 10 years of schooling. The main issue the country faces is now to bring learning achievements of Sri Lankan students to par with those of upper-middle- and high-income countries.

Examining each of the critical factors that, based on international experience, are known to affect the quality of education, this study focuses on the following issues: (a) the types of education offerings available to students; (b) the quality of teachers; (c) the capacity to monitor student learning; and (d) the governance and accountability framework.

Types of Education Offerings

The organizational structure of the school system is both inequitable and detrimental for the future of the country. Education streams offered in small towns and rural areas are limited, reducing the opportunities offered to children in those areas to access science and mathematics streams and learn foreign languages. As a result, besides being inequitable, the distribution of high school graduates is highly skewed toward the arts and humanities, fields that are not in high demand in the labor market.

Teacher Quality

Qualified and motivated teachers are key to imparting good education. In Sri Lanka, the efficiency of the teacher management process is undermined by recruitment rules related to minimum qualifications and subject-specific vacancies that are sometimes relaxed or subject to political influence, leading to an imbalanced deployment of teachers (with surplus of subject teachers in urban areas, and shortages in rural) and an acute deficiency of teachers in mathematics, science and English.

This acute shortage of teachers with adequate knowledge in mathematics, and science affects students scores in those subjects. The National Institute of Education (NIE) assessed the mathematics knowledge of teachers in schools where students scored less than 30 percent on the GCE O-level mathematics test. From the 170 teachers who participated in the study, 36 percent of teachers from the Western province and 51 percent of those from the other provinces scored no more than 5 marks out of 10 (NIE 2008).

Teachers also lack incentives to perform well because promotion is based on length of service rather than on effective teaching and because the pay level is low relative to other countries. In addition, the pay scale is compressed. As a consequence, teachers often seek opportunities outside school (e.g., private tutoring). Finally, absenteeism is a significant problem in terms of teacher accountability, especially in difficult areas. It results in disparities in learning outcomes and completion rates, especially in rural areas and poor provinces.

Monitoring Student Learning

Delivery of quality education requires effective student assessment to provide the information stakeholders need to make policy decisions to improve learning outcomes. Sri Lanka has a fairly well-established assessment system (comprising classroom assessment, public examinations, and large-scale, national surveys), but there is a need to improve the enabling environment—the alignment between different systems and technical aspects, especially for classroom and large-scale assessments.

- *Classroom assessment:* Classroom assessment can be used to diagnose student learning problems, provide feedback to students, and inform parents about their child's learning. Sri Lanka has the foundation in place, but classroom assessment needs to be fully integrated into teaching practice.
- *Examinations*. Sri Lanka has a long history of public examinations. The objectives and content of national examinations (GCE O-level and A-level) are carefully chosen, and textbooks and teaching are aligned with examinations. With the new curriculum reform in place, there is a need for the Department of Examinations and the NIE to maintain that alignment.
- *Large-scale assessments*. National assessments were introduced in 2003 in Sri Lanka and several rounds have been conducted since then. While they permit monitoring learning achievements over time, data limitations do not allow a deeper analysis of determinants of learning that could disentangle the impact of schools and teachers from that of social background. Limited dissemination of results and the nonparticipation of Sri Lanka in international assessments also limit the use of assessment results for policy formulation.

Governance and Accountability

The basic institutional foundation to deliver public education services exists in Sri Lanka, with responsibilities shared between the central government and provincial councils. Nevertheless, the incentive system is feeble. As mentioned above, the promotion system based on seniority and the low and compressed salary structure do not provide incentives for better performance to public employees. At the school level, the government is relying on two tools to improve accountability: an inspectorate system based on the United Kingdom's and Scottish models, and a school-based management program to empower schools and local communities. An initial evaluation suggests that the latter program has had a positive impact on learning outcomes and could be strengthened and implemented more extensively in the future.

Technical and Vocational Education and Training: The Quality and Relevance Issue

The complexity of competing in the global economy requires not only advanced skills but also a workforce that can adjust to shifts in demand (World Bank 2012). Pegged at 68 out of 142 countries evaluated in the 2012/13 Global Competitiveness Index, Sri Lanka compares favorably with the rest of South Asia but trails behind East Asian countries. If the country is to transition from being factor-driven to being efficiency-driven, its workers need the ability to operate the latest equipment and technology, computer knowledge and fluency in foreign languages to communicate with international clients.

The drive for industrial growth is severely deterred by the shortage of technically skilled labor—a scarcity worsened by the migration of many skilled individuals who seek employment overseas and higher earnings. In addition to shortages, recent analysis reveals serious skills mismatches in the labor market. Both could depress the country's growth and competitiveness as a middle-income economy. Although the government has in recent years embarked on reforms in skills development, several factors still contribute to skills constraints in Sri Lanka:

- The complexity of Sri Lanka's skills development system demands more effective coordination, management, and monitoring. The TVET sector is fragmented and uncoordinated, which undermines sector performance and thus the potential to meet the skills needs of the economy. To realize government skills development policies, an interministerial committee, working in tandem with the different units within agencies like the Ministry of Skills Development and Vocational Training (MSDVT), would necessitate both a monitoring and coordinating unit within MSDVT and a revision of the structure, mandates, and functions of the many agencies. The recent setting up of the Inter-ministerial Sector Coordination Committee (IMSCC), has been a first step toward addressing this issue.

- A rigid and supply-driven TVET system with minimal involvement of the private sector undermines the efficiency and effectiveness of the skills supply. A heavily supply-driven TVET system does not take into account either the skills demanded by employers or the needs of the informal sector. In Sri Lanka, employers are still only minimally associated with the activities of public institutions, which compounds the problem.

- There is a shortage of qualified teaching staff, especially staff with industrial experience. There needs to be a better balance between academic credentials and professional experience for instructors in vocational training centers and teachers in technical colleges. In addition, unattractive salaries and inadequate professional development undermine teacher motivation and make retention difficult.

- Many centers could benefit from substantial upgrading of equipment. TVET graduates are often not workplace-ready when they finish their courses.

Vocational centers in particular often lack equipment that would allow trainees to practice what they are being taught. Employers are reluctant to recruit graduates who have no hands-on experience and prefer to hire trainable youth with a good general education whose technical skills can be built in-house.

- Over the past decade Sri Lanka has been proactive in designing a national qualification framework (National Vocational Qualification [NVQ]), but this framework has not been fully implemented, and the design needs to be better actualized if it is to build up the quality and relevance of both public and private training programs and facilitate transfers between training and education streams. Moreover, the image of the NVQ has to be enhanced so that employers recognize the benefit of NVQ qualifications.

- There is a lack of both institutional autonomy and accountability for performance. Public training providers are financed primarily by the national budget, and allocations are provided irrespective of performance. Consequently, public institutions do not have incentives to revamp obsolete training courses, and curricula, and bring the private sector into their decision making.

- The planning process does not regularly ascertain national and regional skills needs based on labor market information. There is no timely and accurate information about current demand for skills and available training opportunities, nor reliable analysis of skills gaps. Moreover, no regular studies track competencies achieved, and it is not possible to evaluate the performance of TVET institutions directly.

Higher Education: Access and Quality Questions

Sri Lanka has a well-established system of higher education, but its expansion is facing major challenges (World Bank 2009). Access to higher education has been increased, but areas of economic and social importance remain underrepresented. The skills of academic staff for student-centered learning are being upgraded, but the pool of faculty staff is still insufficient; learning opportunities have been significantly increased, but the availability of such courses—for example, English and Information and Communications Technology (ICT) is still limited. The country is also working to build research capacity at universities through PhD programs and competitive research grants, but research activities and outputs remain at a low scale.

Participation in higher education in Sri Lanka is exceptionally low for a middle-income country. The country's higher-education enrollment is about half the average for middle-income countries, and well below comparator countries Indonesia, Korea, Malaysia, and Thailand (figure O.10). The higher education GER is 17 percent, compared with an average of 27 percent for middle-income countries and 33 percent for upper-middle-income countries. Though the

Figure O.10 Tertiary Education Outcomes, an International Perspective, 2012–13

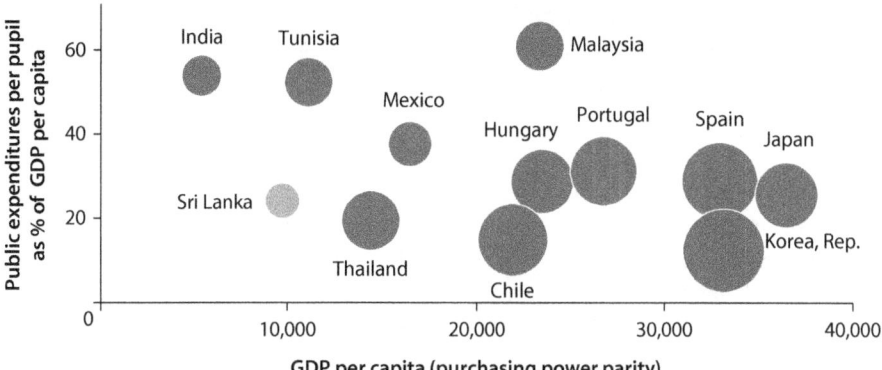

Source: World Bank Education Statistics Data, 2012/13 or nearest year available.
Note: Bubble size corresponds to the gross enrollment rate in tertiary education.

expansion of primary and secondary education is producing unprecedented demand for university education, given the current public university capacity, only a small proportion of those qualifying can be admitted. Moreover, public university capacity to meet growing student demand is inadequate, especially in science- and technology-fields.

The quality and relevance of tertiary teaching and learning are minimal. A significant share of higher education graduates currently fail to meet the requirements of private employers, in particular related to good communication, soft skills, and ICT skills. Moreover, 50 percent of tertiary students are enrolled in external degree programs (EDPs) that offer little academic support and are often not leading to high employment prospects.

Private provision of higher education is limited. Until a few years ago, private sector participation in higher education was restricted; and because of ambiguous and inconsistent regulations, how this sector's participation is to be governed is unclear. Evidence from other countries shows that it is important to set clear, objective, and streamlined criteria and processes for establishing and regulating HEIs, which would include incentives for private providers to invest and independent mechanisms to ensure the quality of the outcomes of both private and public higher education.

The links between industry and academia are minimal. To advance as a middle-income country, Sri Lanka needs to acquire and use technologies of ever-higher complexity, quality, and productivity, and also to generate a continuous stream of improvements and innovations. The government must promote collaboration between universities, research institutes, and companies to establish synergy for networking on R&D. This could be achieved through research partnerships, entrepreneurship initiatives for university students and staff, technology commercialization centers, and technology broker programs.

Crosscutting Issues

Financing Education: Adequacy and Equity

Compared to other countries at similar levels of development, Sri Lanka spends a smaller percentage of its income on education. Among low- and middle-income countries, it has the lowest spending on public education as a percentage of its GDP (Sri Lanka: 2 percent; low- and middle-income country average: 4.5 percent). Moreover, for several years public investment in education has actually declined in real terms (figure O.11). Even as a share of total government spending, public education is among the lowest (Sri Lanka: 10.2 percent; low- and middle-income country average: 17.3 percent) (figure O.12). Public investment mainly goes to general and higher education; TVET, important for the labor market, only gets about 5 percent; and ECE, which has a major impact on subsequent education levels and life chances, receives almost no public resources.

Spending on general education, which gets the highest share of education spending, is inequitably allocated. About 95 percent of schools in Sri Lanka are in the provinces and are attended mostly by poor rural children, but public investment in provincial education is only about 65 percent of total general education spending. The 35 percent spent by the central government goes mainly to national schools, which only account for about 5 percent of schools and are typically attended by affluent urban children. Insufficient accountability and monitoring mechanisms further interfere with the efficient and effective use of education resources.

Figure O.11 Education Spending, 2007–12

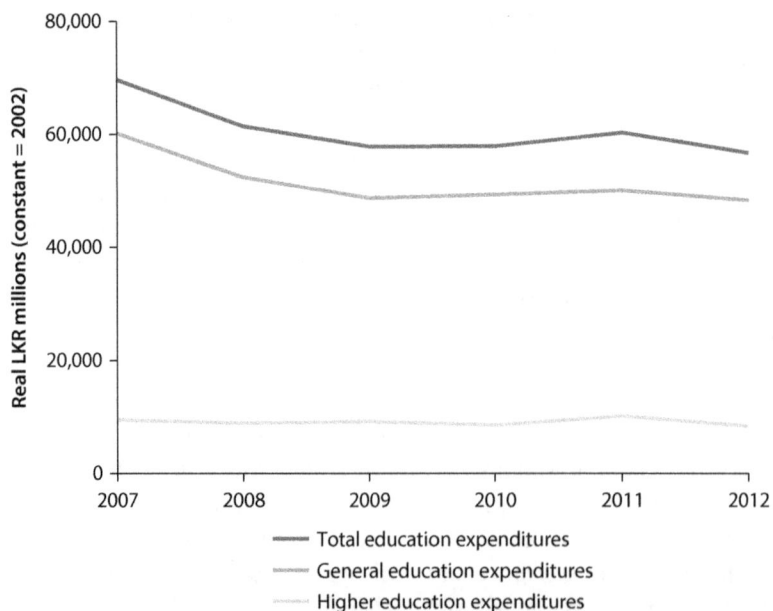

Source: Budget estimates, Ministry of Finance and Planning.

Figure O.12 Spending on Public Education, an International Perspective

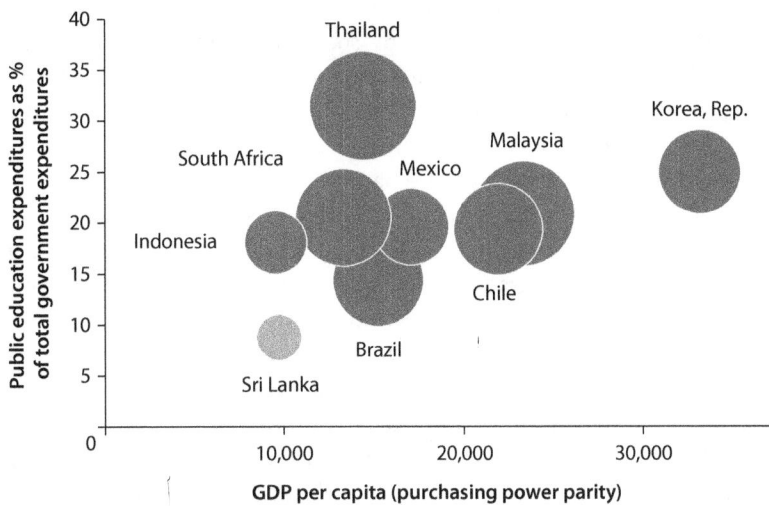

Source: World Bank Education Statistics Data, 2012/13 or nearest year available.
Note: Bubble size corresponds to public spending as a share of GDP.

The unfinished agenda of access, equity, and quality could be achieved through a more efficient use of current resources and by raising public investment by modest amounts. Over the medium term, the government plans to raise its spending on education from 1.7 to 6 percent of GDP. With more modest increases, public spending could be made more effective and achieve better outcomes.

Effective financing might be based on a combination of central government redistribution, local authorities allocating resources according to student needs, and monitoring spending. Sri Lanka has already made significant progress in applying needs-based formula funding: poorer provinces that have worse education outcomes receive more funds than wealthier provinces for primary and secondary education. This is due to a budget formula that promotes balanced regional development. A transparent fund flow and giving a larger role to parents and communities could improve further accountability in the use of resources.

Expanding the resource base by leveraging public resources with increased private funds could lead to sustained financing at higher levels for education and training. In South Asia, public-private partnerships (PPPs) have proved useful in providing educational opportunities, improving access, and presenting choices and competition in education. Although Sri Lanka has only a few PPP initiatives in TVET, more and better-designed PPPs could help it to achieve its objective of quality education for all, especially in TVET and higher education.

Strategic Priorities and Policy Actions

Sri Lanka has enjoyed high school attainment and enrollment rates for several decades. Nevertheless, the education and training system faces three major challenges in terms of performance that affect the country's long-term inclusive growth and competitiveness goals: (a) education quality—measured by learning outcomes—is insufficient, though it has been steadily improving from a low base; (b) there are significant learning gaps by socioeconomic background and location; and (c) in spite of rapidly rising access to general education, ECD, upper secondary and higher education, and TVET have not received much attention, resulting in low participation rates at those levels compared with other middle-income countries. These challenges are barriers to achieving the country's goal of building a competitive workforce that responds to skills demand.

To attain inclusive growth and become globally competitive, Sri Lanka needs to embark on integrated reforms across all levels of education that address both short-term skills shortages and long-term productivity. The government recognizes the ramifications of an inadequately prepared workforce and views its education problems as a national issue. It has proposed an ambitious agenda to raise the qualifications of the population through reforms at all stages of education. The new Government Manifesto, released in 2015, proposes to raise public investment in education from 1.7 to 6 percent of the GDP in the next five years in order to accelerate education development to reach better outcomes.[3] This requires a sequenced plan that first introduces strategic development initiatives and then supports them with additional financing.

Policies for financing education can affect outcomes in terms of both quality and equity. International evidence suggests that strategic deployment of resources for education is more important than the magnitude of funding. Sri Lanka aims to tackle both. Increased resources could support improvement in the teaching and learning environment and fuel the expansion of both TVET and higher education, provided that the allocated funds are used efficiently. However, in a scenario that lacks budgetary transparency and accountability, as well as strong monitoring mechanisms, there is little evidence that additional resources will raise the quality of learning or that more teachers or higher teacher salaries will improve quality.

Resources directed to tools that have shown promise could be used to achieve the government's education policy objectives. These include: (a) performance-related pay and promotion for teachers; (b) a funding formula based on a range of incentives to boost efficiency and equity; (c) PPPs that condition funding on results; and (d) the use of vouchers for students to finance TVET or higher education.

Some initiatives have already been incorporated into the new government's education reform program, but much remains to be done. The following is a rundown of strategic priorities and policy actions by level of education.

Early Childhood Development

By investing little in ECD, Sri Lanka is forgoing the substantial benefits that this investment could provide. The detrimental effects of poor development in early childhood can be particularly severe for poor children. Access to ECD services for children aged 3–5 years needs to be considerably expanded. Here are three priorities:

Priority 1: Enhance access to ECD programs, especially for children from poor households. Equitable access to ECD can be attained through a combination of targeted public investment in ECD for poor regions and disadvantaged populations (e.g., plantation sector) and promoting an enabling environment for nonstate providers. The government should also raise parental awareness about the potential benefits of ECD; set up governance mechanisms for both public and private institutions; and enable nonstate providers to establish centers through PPPs.

Priority 2: Improve the quality of inputs, processes, and outcomes. Key actions include: (a) preparing high-quality curricula and development standards for child outcomes; (b) establishing minimum standards for ECD centers, (c) providing centers enough support to achieve minimum quality standards; and (d) ensuring that teachers receive adequate preservice and in-service professional development training

Priority 3: Tighten sector coordination and governance. Key actions include: (a) clarifying the regulatory structure and, in particular, the responsibilities of central and provincial authorities for implementing ECD programs; (b) putting in place a quality assurance framework; and (c) reinforcing monitoring and evaluation (M&E) to provide regular, comprehensive, and reliable data on ECD.

Given the modest costs of these interventions, raising coverage from the current 50 percent to, let us say, 80 percent would only represent about 0.0004 percent of GDP, a low-cost investment with potentially high returns.

Primary and Secondary Education

Access no longer being an issue, the main objective should be to raise the quality of primary and secondary education. This implies the following five priorities:

Priority 1: Expand and broaden education offerings. Sri Lanka will need to actively expand the range of education offerings across all school types and to widen options for youth. Particular attention should be paid to enable access to science and technology, and to learning foreign languages in secondary schools. This should be accompanied by measures to address teacher shortage issues in new subject areas.

Priority 2: Improve the effectiveness of primary and secondary teachers. Teachers are a central determinant of educational quality. The evidence is robust: what matters more for student learning than teachers' degrees or seniority is how much domain knowledge teachers have, their motivational levels, and teaching ability. Sri Lanka has several policy options to enhance teacher effectiveness: (a) ensure that recruitment rules and requirements are strictly followed. Following recruitment, probation should be used to screen out ineffective teachers or impart remedial training to them. (b) Teacher deployment issue should be addressed, if necessary with an incentive package (possibly transportation subsidies or residential schools, and hardship allowances), especially in remote areas. (c) Teachers should be motivated through regular pay scale revisions and linking promotion to performance. (d) Teacher absence, not only from schools but also from classrooms, should be addressed through regular inspections with credible penalties and rewards, and effective leadership and monitoring by school principals.

Priority 3: Enhanced assessment systems to monitor and induce progress in learning outcomes. Sri Lanka needs to make full use of the various instruments: classroom assessments jointly with examinations to monitor students' progress and tailor any necessary corrective measures; large-scale assessments to demonstrate the performance of the education system as a whole and build in regular feedback to students and parents. Though Sri Lanka regularly conducts systematic large-scale learning assessments, there is scope for improving the technical quality of the assessment instruments, conduct deeper data analyses, and improve the use of assessment results in choosing education policy options. National learning outcomes would also need to be benchmarked against regional and international standards to identify specific areas that need attention and create a political imperative for school quality reform. Participating in international assessments should be considered.

Priority 4: Implement the quality assurance system systematically. Such a system has two broad components that are complementary and mutually reinforcing. First is a quality assurance and school monitoring effort conducted by education officials from outside the school. Second is an internal quality assurance system conducted by key school stakeholders. With regard to the latter, the Program for School Improvement (PSI) should be strengthened by a combination of periodic social audits and rigorous periodic evaluations.

Priority 5: Pursue the funding policies that promote equity. Since national schools in Sri Lanka are usually located in big urban centers—such as Colombo, Kandy, Galle, and Kurunegala—their students are typically from more affluent households than those who attend provincial schools, the majority of which are in rural locations. Hence, expanding the provincial share of general education spending would have favorable equity implications. The government has begun to address this issue by increasing the provincial share of general education spending over time, but needs to speed up the pace.

Technical and Vocational Education and Training

The main objective of any TVET strategy should be to produce skilled labor by expanding access to quality and market-relevant training programs. Strategic priorities in TVET are as follows.

Priority 1: Enhance coordination between the different agencies. To deal with the fragmentation of the TVET sector in Sri Lanka, it is critical to achieve closer coordination among all agencies involved in supplying and demanding job-specific skills, with the MSDVT playing a more effective and visible role. The role of the Tertiary and Vocational Education Commission could be expanded to overseeing financing and curriculum development; supervising skills testing, certification, and accreditation; and providing information on institutional quality and effectiveness. Though increased funding is indispensable, both in the aggregate and for particular institutions, it will not bring radical positive changes if management of this currently supply-driven and uncoordinated sector cannot be made more efficient. An empowered interministerial skills development committee that would represent the entire spectrum of public and private providers, employers, and financing agencies and planners could help addressing this issue.

Priority 2: Ensure the adequacy and effectiveness of public spending on TVET by promoting accountability. It is critical to increase the autonomy and accountability of TVET institutions and to design the financing system so as to ensure adequate resources and improved efficiency and accountability. This could be achieved through performance-based allocations for public vocational and technical institutions. Performance indicators could include graduation, retention, or employment rates (outcomes). When funds are allocated without clear reference to their mission, institutions have no incentive to perform with even minimal efficiency, much less be innovative. Nor does using input-based norms, such as the number of trainees enrolled or courses offered, provide enough motivation to improve quality and efficiency.

Priority 3: Strengthen the quality and relevance of TVET programs by actively engaging with employers to ensure that programs meet the needs of employers. Countries with effective TVET systems involve employers effectively in the design and delivery of programs. Key actions would include: (a) ensuring that all industrial sector skills councils (ISSCs) are operational and assessing their incentives for continued business engagement and sustainability; (b) regularly reviewing and updating competency-based curricula with inputs from employers to ensure that the skills students acquire are both relevant and of high quality; (c) expanding opportunities for the professional development of industry experts and instructors in new and emerging skills; (d) addressing the teaching staff shortage through the implementation of performance-linked compensation for TVET instructors; (e) upgrading the quality of equipment and instructional materials for public TVET institutions; and (f) strengthening and expanding quality assurance mechanisms to cover both public and private providers.

Priority 4: Prevent financial constraints from barring access to training. Though stipends and scholarships are already in use, they do not seem large enough to offset the opportunity cost of attending courses or to encourage course registration and completion. Vouchers given directly to trainees could allow them to purchase training from any eligible institution of their choice, public or private.

Vouchers could also stimulate competition among providers, making them more responsive to trainee demand and producing better quality at lower costs.

Priority 5: Improve the use and dissemination of information on demand and supply for skills. There is a need for more active monitoring and evaluation across the sector, in tandem with the private sector. This requires streamlining data collection mechanisms and procedures across MSDVT agencies, and building M&E capacity to monitor centers' and teachers' performance across trades. It also requires periodic analysis of the labor market to identify changes in the demand for skills. A wide dissemination of information about course offerings, performance of centers, and job prospects could help students become more aware of the prospects for investing in TVET and guide their decisions.

Higher Education

The main purpose of Sri Lanka's higher education reform is to enhance access and quality, as well as to ensure the relevance of teaching and research. Despite decade-long efforts, current public university capacity is unable to handle the unprecedented demand for university education after the expansion of primary and secondary education in the country. Public universities have seats for only a small proportion of those who qualify. The following is a rundown of strategic priorities and actions to address the higher education challenges faced by Sri Lanka.

Priority 1: Broaden and expand access to higher education. A major challenge for Sri Lanka's tertiary education system is inadequate capacity for meeting student demand for higher education. Key policy actions could include: (a) increase intake capacity in both university degree programs and short-cycle, job-oriented HEIs, especially in priority programs for economic development; and (b) introduce PPPs in higher education to stimulate the development of accredited private national and international institutions. While, in the short run, the intake capacity of the existing institution should be expanded to take advantage of economies of scale, in the medium term, new degree programs and universities relevant to economic development should be established to meet the country's increasing demand for advanced skills.

The private sector in higher education currently operates under heavy restrictions. Attracting the participation of this sector, both for-profit and nonprofit, is crucial to meet the double challenge of improving access and quality, given capacity and resource constraints. That the private sector can powerfully complement public education and training initiatives can be seen in dynamic Asian economies like Korea, Malaysia, and Thailand. To enable the private sector to engage fully in the development process, Sri Lanka will need to enact laws to actively promote the participation of private education and training institutions, while introducing robust regulation to ensure quality. Though the private sector has not as yet had much involvement in education, except in the delivery of ECD and TVET programs, there is considerable scope for this to change by: (a) easing barriers to entry;

(b) carefully designing PPPs; and (c) ensuring that there are mechanisms for accountability and quality assurance for private institutions.

Priority 2: Improve the quality and relevance of tertiary education. Key policy actions include: (a) addressing the severe academic staff shortage through the implementation of a faculty development program in priority disciplines (e.g., science, technology, engineering and mathematics—STEM) and the recruitment of qualified local and international academic staff; (b) establishing an autonomous Quality Assurance and Accreditation Agency for both public and private HEIs; and (c) reforming the delivery of EDPs. In the medium term, the focus should be to develop a system for the continuous professional development of academic and managerial staff; review curricula to ensure soft skills are integrated in all higher education programs; promote partnerships between universities and industry to stimulate research and development; and roll out a system of internationally benchmarked quality assurance and accreditation programs for all public and private institutions.

Priority 3: Promote efficiency by reforming higher education finance. Key policy actions in the short term could include: (a) costing out the proposed higher education reforms based on alternative scenarios and (b) adopting a competitive finance scheme to promote research and innovation in universities. In the medium term, two critical actions would be to implement a multiyear strategic development plan based on the quality assurance system, and gradually adopt a performance-based funding model linked to national strategic priorities and institutions' specific missions.

Priority 4: Strengthen system management and governance. An immediate key policy action would be to ensure that all managerial and academic appointments at HEIs follow transparent procedures and are merit-based. In the medium term, key reforms could include: (a) strengthening the link between promotion and academic compensation and performance in teaching and research; (b) implementing the Sri Lanka Higher Education Qualification Framework for horizontal and vertical mobility in public and private HEIs; (c) reforming the EDPs to focus on labor-market-oriented programs, and scaling up reliance on new technologies; and (d) promoting mission differentiation among HEIs in line with national needs.

Conclusion

Sri Lanka has the potential to become a high-income economy if it follows a strategic focus on improving its human capital. It now needs an integrated approach that covers the entire education and training system. Investing in ECD and improving the quality of primary and secondary education will help build a solid foundation of skills in literacy, numeracy, science and technology, and languages. As Sri Lanka moves up the development ladder, it needs to balance the priorities of primary, secondary, and postsecondary education to meet increasingly complex education and skills requirements. A comprehensive package of financial investments and policy and governance reforms will make the existing system more efficient, equitable, and effective. A national vision backed by adequate funding, realistic targets, and a clear implementation strategy can help propel this agenda forward. In introducing reforms, it will be important to use a broad consultative process to engage stakeholders, beneficiaries, and the private sector.

Appendix A summarizes challenges, possible strategic directions, and priorities that the government can consider to build a skilled workforce that will promote inclusive growth.

Notes

1. Type 1AB schools span grades 1–13 or 6–13 and offer arts, commerce, and science streams. Type 1C also spans grades 1–13 or 6–13 but does not offer science at GCE A-level. Type 2 schools span grades 1–11, and Type 3 schools are only primary schools.
2. ECD programs include interventions that range from health and nutrition, and water and sanitation, to parental education and preschool education for children aged 3–5. This report focuses on preschool education.
3. Released on July 2015, the government's manifesto, *A New Country in 60 Months: Five Point Plan*, lays out a five-point plan to build Sri Lanka into a competitive economy. "Developing Education" is listed as the fifth point.

References

Aturupane, H., Y. Savchenko, M. Shojo, and K. Larsen. 2014. *Sri Lanka: Investment in Human Capital*. South Asia Human Development Sector Report No. 69, World Bank, Washington, DC.

Barro, R. J., and J.-W. Lee. 2012. *A New Data Set of Educational Attainment in the World, 1950–2010*. http://barrolee.com/papers/Barro_Lee_Human_Capital_Update_2012April.pdf.

Dundar, H., B. Millot, Y. Savchenko, H. Aturupane, and T. A. Piyasiri. 2014. *Building the Skills for Economic Growth and Competitiveness in Sri Lanka*. Directions in Development Series. Washington, DC: World Bank.

Dutz, M. A., and S. D. O'Connell. 2013. "Productivity, Innovation and Growth in Sri Lanka: An Empirical Investigation." World Bank Policy Research Working Paper 6354, World Bank, Washington, DC.

NEREC (National Education Research and Evaluation Centre). 2009. *National Assessment of Achievement of Grade 4 Students in Sri Lanka*. Colombo: NEREC.

———. 2013. *National Assessment of Achievement of Grade 8 Students in Sri Lanka—2012*. Colombo: NEREC.

———. 2014. *National Assessment of Achievement of Grade 4 Students in Sri Lanka—2013*. Colombo: NEREC.

NIE (National Institute of Education). 2008. *A Study on the Subject Knowledge of Mathematics Teachers in Schools that Perform Poorly in O/L Mathematics*. Colombo: NIE.

Riboud, M., Y. Savchenko, and H. Tan. 2007. *The Knowledge Economy and Education and Training in South Asia*. Washington, DC: World Bank.

World Bank. 2009. *The Towers of Learning: Performance, Peril, and Promise of Higher Education in Sri Lanka*. Washington, DC: World Bank.

———. 2011. *Transforming School Education in Sri Lanka: From Cut Stones to Polished Jewels*. Colombo: World Bank.

———. 2014. *Laying the Foundation for Early Childhood Education in Sri Lanka: Investing Early, Investing Smartly, and Investing for All*. Washington, DC: World Bank.

———. 2016. *Sri Lanka: A Systematic Country Diagnostic—Ending Poverty and Promoting Shared Prosperity*. Washington, DC: World Bank.

CHAPTER 1

Why a Comprehensive Assessment of Education Performance in Sri Lanka?

Introduction

Sri Lanka's goal is to sustain fast growth in the medium and long terms and accelerate the structural transformation of the economy. The government intends to gradually bridge its economic development gap with other Southeast Asian countries, such as Malaysia and Thailand, and reach high-middle-income status. While the recent performance of the economy offers some assurance that this goal can be achieved, it does not guarantee it. Reaching this goal requires a structural transformation of the economy, which in turn depends on a credible macroeconomic framework, stable institutions, a flexible and well-functioning labor market, and, critically, a solid base of human capital.

Human capital refers to the knowledge and skills people acquire during their life cycle. It affects economic growth in a variety of ways. Besides its direct impact on productivity and its indirect effects on health and fertility behavior, it facilitates the transmission of knowledge and will accelerate the rate at which Sri Lanka can take advantage of new ideas and new technology. It will also encourage research and expand innovative capacity. More broadly, it will give Sri Lanka the flexibility and adaptability it will need at each stage of the growth process in a competitive, knowledge-based, globalized world.

While some human capital is acquired within the household and in social contexts, a very substantial part is acquired through formal education and training. How well the education and training system performs thus determines whether students emerging from the system have the knowledge and skills to work in an increasingly diversified economy, and to adjust to a world of unpredictable change.

Despite significant progress achieved in recent decades, there are major deficiencies in Sri Lanka's delivery of education and training that affect its goal of inclusive growth. It is aware that:

- Although Sri Lankans spend more time in the education system than neighbors in South Asia, employers are questioning the system's quality and its relevance.
- Major skills shortages and mismatches undermine productivity, and thus growth.
- Disparities in learning outcomes in primary and secondary education and in access to both technical and vocational education and training (TVET) and higher education undermine the government's commitment to alleviating poverty.

The main objective of this Education Sector Assessment (ESA) is to review the status of education in Sri Lanka from early childhood development (ECD) through higher education; analyze the most critical constraints on performance; and identify strategic priorities and policy options to improve it. This assessment can be a critical input into the government's vision for the future. This study therefore asks:

- How is Sri Lanka's education and training system performing? What are its main achievements to date, and what are the main challenges confronting it?
- How can the country address constraints and respond to challenges at each stage of the education process, taking into account both country and international experience and best practices?
- What actions should have priority in the short and medium terms?

While prior studies have already identified policy issues and interventions in some subsectors (see, e.g., World Bank 2005, 2009, 2011, 2014; Dundar et al. 2014), so far there has been no systematic effort to take stock of the collective evidence on where Sri Lanka's education system is now. This report attempts to present a candid, objective, evidence-based assessment of the main challenges for the education sector, taking into account international experience and best practices. This chapter sets out the context, rationale, and framework for the assessment.

The Economy and the Labor Market

Economic Growth

Sri Lanka is a lower-middle-income country that in 2014 had per capita gross domestic product (GDP) of US$3,811—significantly higher than the average for South Asia. It has been among the fastest-growing economies in South and East Asia for more than 10 years. Between 2002 and 2013 it enjoyed healthy 6.3 percent average annual growth; the cessation of armed conflict in 2009 accelerated growth to 7.5 percent between 2010 and 2013; and in 2014 it was 6.7 percent (see table 1.1).

Table 1.1 Social Indicators for Sri Lanka and Comparator Economies

Indicator	Sri Lanka		LMICs		UMICs		South Asia	
	2000	2014[a]	2000	2014[a]	2000	2014[a]	2000	2014[a]
GDP per capita growth (annual %)	5.5	6.7	2.4	4.1	4.8	3.7	2.1	5.5
Improved sanitation facilities (% of population with access)	81.2	95.1	39.5	51.3	66.2	79.3	44.4	44.8
Life expectancy at birth, total (years)	73.8	74.2	66.1	67.0	73.7	74.3	66.7	67.8
Mortality rate, infant (per 1,000 live births)	14.0	8.4	65.7	40.0	31.4	15.2	68.8	41.9
Prevalence of undernourishment (% of population)	29.8	24.6	15.3	14.2	10.7	9.2	16.8	16.3
Survival rate to the last grade of primary education, both sexes (%)	97.8	98.4	67.2	70.2	87.4	89.8	60.9	62.8

Source: World Bank, forthcoming.
Note: LMICs = lower-middle-income countries; and UMICs = upper-middle-income countries.
a. Or closest year.

With growth, Sri Lanka's economy has changed considerably, to the point where it is no longer based on agriculture. The resultant structural changes are reflected in the composition of GDP, which has shifted to manufacturing and services. Between 1975 and 2014, agriculture's share of GDP declined from 30 to 8 percent, industry's share rose from 26 to 30 percent, and the services share grew from 43 to 62 percent. The 8 percent share for agriculture is close to Malaysia's (9 percent) and lower than the averages for South Asia as a whole (18 percent) and other lower-middle-income countries (17 percent); the share of services is similar to the Republic of Korea's (59 percent). However, the industry share is closer to those of South Asian countries (29 percent) and lower-middle-income countries (31 percent) than to Korea (38 percent) or Malaysia (40 percent).

These structural changes have shifted employment from agriculture to industry and services. Between 1971 and 2014, the share of agriculture in employment declined from 51 to 30 percent. The industry share rose from 11 to 26 percent, and the services share from 38 to 43 percent. With growth, unemployment has more than halved, benefiting all gender and age groups. Demand for skilled workers has risen in such sectors as manufacturing, construction, trade, and financial services, which have seen significant growth in jobs.

Poverty

Since the early 2000s economic growth seems to have lifted many out of poverty; the headcount poverty rate declined from about 23 to 6 percent. Nevertheless, living standards remain low for a large share of the population because about one-quarter of Sri Lankans are still among the "near" poor, as defined by living above the official poverty line but below US$2.50 per day in 2005 purchasing power parity terms (World Bank 2016a, 2016b). The government is committed to lowering poverty further and promoting equity-led growth, but success will depend on a more dynamic labor market that produces better-quality jobs, and on having enough skilled workers to fill those jobs.

Labor Market Trends

Since 1990 Sri Lanka's labor force has grown by 2 percent a year, from 6 million in 1990 to 8.5 million in 2014. The working-age population (15–59) is now expected to grow more slowly, from an estimated 13.3 million in 2011 to 13.9 million in 2026, and then to decline gradually. Furthermore, the labor force participation rate (LFPR) declined from 57 to 55 percent between 2000 and 2014, whereas in faster-growing East Asian economies it is now close to 60 percent. With population and labor force growth slowing down, and a tightening of the job market, labor productivity must rise if the government is to achieve its inclusive growth goals. This makes it even more critical for Sri Lankan workers to acquire more skills.

Average unemployment has been low, at just 4.3 percent in 2014, but youth are three times more likely to be unemployed than adults, suggesting difficulties in the school-to-work transition. Another labor market issue is informality. An estimated two-thirds of Sri Lankan workers are employed informally, among them about 87 percent of agricultural and 51 percent of nonagricultural workers (DCS 2011). Combined with the low youth LFPR and high unemployment, it may be that young people are waiting to get formal jobs, though as time goes by they do accept informal jobs (Dundar et al. 2014). Recognizing the dominant role of the informal sector in the economy, the government now envisions skills training for informal workers (SSM 2012).

Sri Lanka's Education in the Global Context

As will be explained in more detail in the following chapter, Sri Lanka has had uniformly high rates of school enrollment for several decades. The net enrollment rate (NER) for primary education is 99 percent, and for junior secondary 84 percent; there is gender parity in both. In senior secondary education, the NER is 70 percent—still relatively high for middle-income countries. The better performance of girls in secondary education (the NER is 72 percent for girls and 67 percent for boys) is common in middle- and high-income countries. On average, Sri Lankan students attend school for about 10 years, compared to 6 years elsewhere in South Asia. This enrollment success results from a long history of public investment in, and provision of, education; not only is education free, but there are also free textbooks and uniforms, scholarships, a good network of schools, and enough teachers for most subjects.

Despite its wide access and high completion rates in general education, learning achievements are modest. For example, though pass rates for the grade 11 ordinary-level General Certificate of Education examinations (GCE O-levels) improved from 50 percent in 2005 to 63 percent in 2013, that is still below the lower-middle-income countries average of 71 percent; and many students who fail the exam drop out of school. Pass rates for the grade 13 advanced level GCE examinations (GCE A-levels) have stagnated, at about 60 percent for the past five years (they reached 62 percent in 2011). Moreover, in both TVET and higher education, the availability, quality, and relevance of current programs are limited.

Figure 1.1 Educational Attainment in Sri Lanka, Malaysia, and the Republic of Korea, 1960–2010

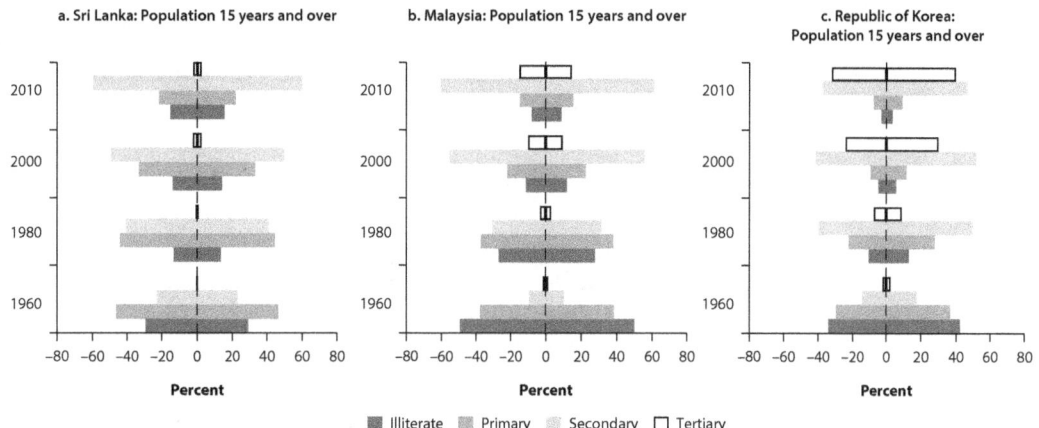

Sources: Riboud, Savchenko, and Tan 2007; and Barro and Lee 2012.

Many graduates are idle for a long time between graduation and their first jobs, and relatively few students are enrolled in programs defined as national priorities.

Although it had long been a leader among developing countries in educational attainment, Sri Lanka has now fallen behind comparator countries with respect to tertiary education. In 1960, the proportion of Sri Lankans aged 15 or over with secondary education was comparable to that of Malaysia and higher than in Korea, and the proportion of the population with tertiary education (2 percent) was similar to that of those countries. Fifty years later, in 2010, Sri Lanka's tertiary education completion rate was substantially lower than that of Malaysia (15 percent) and Korea (40 percent), which have both been investing heavily in TVET and higher education for at least three decades (see figure 1.1). These figures strongly suggest that Sri Lanka has been underinvesting in tertiary education compared with competitive middle- and high-income countries in the region.

A final observation is that national averages mask considerable regional and socioeconomic variations in enrollment and learning outcomes: In recent years, the gap has widened between the quality of education available in more affluent areas and that in many remote locations, especially the plantations. This results in severe inequality in secondary education outcomes. In higher education, the disparities are even wider: the NER for the richest quintile is 17 percent, and for the poorest 7 percent.

The Government's Education Reform Program

Recognizing the risks to the country of an inadequately prepared workforce, the government has proposed an ambitious agenda of policy reforms across the entire education spectrum. The proposed reforms, some of which are spelled out in the new Government Manifesto (Developing Education is the fifth point of the Five-Point Plan), have the following major objectives:

- **Quality:** Increase mandatory schooling from 10 to 13 years, and provide the resources necessary to improve the quality of primary and secondary education.
- **TVET:** Increase access to technical education by upgrading technical schools to colleges of technology; make technical education comprehensive and formal by integrating TVET agencies and departments into the Vocational and Technological Training Agency; and introduce vouchers to attract students to vocational and technical courses.
- **Higher education:** Upgrade public universities; strengthen the nexus between universities and industry to improve student employability and access to jobs; and introduce degree programs that meet the demands of international job markets.
- **Financing:** Increase total public spending for education as a share of GDP from 1.7 to 6 percent over five years.

These objectives demonstrate a definite commitment to improving education and are the basis for constructive discussions. Yet, for several reasons, caution is needed: (1) policymakers have been conditioned to a paradigm of reform in which the prevailing view, as manifested in numerous documents, incorporates such assumptions as that (a) the principal way to increase educational access and equity is to expand the supply of, for example, buildings or teaching staff; and (b) supply-side education policies can solve social problems (e.g., expansion of TVET will reduce youth unemployment and student demand for university education). A thorough assessment of the education system that takes into account international experience and lessons from applied research is essential to clarify the main issues and identify policy options. (2) In formulating new policies and introducing reforms, it will be important to use a broad consultative process to engage stakeholders, beneficiaries, and the private sector.

The Government of Sri Lanka is fully aware that, if the country is to have an educated and highly knowledgeable population with flexible skills, the education and training sector must be reformed. It plans to build on past achievements to address the challenges ahead. This ESA supplements that agenda. After assessing how education is performing in Sri Lanka, it identifies issues, policy priorities, and options that could support the government in formulating its reform program and mapping out proposed short- and medium-term policy priorities and actions.

Approach, Methodology, and Data Sources

Acquiring knowledge and skills is a cumulative life-cycle process that begins in early childhood with ECD and continues through general and tertiary education, TVET, and on-the-job-training (OJT).[1] An efficient skills development system embraces the entire process and provides opportunities for lifelong learning of all types of skills—cognitive, noncognitive (soft or socioemotional), and job-specific. Knowledge and skills can be acquired in a variety of settings and in a variety of ways. The challenge for the government is to better understand the complexities so that it can design policies for meeting demand that are flexible enough to adapt to constantly changing job requirements.

Worker skill sets consist of cognitive, soft (noncognitive), and job-specific skills (box 1.1), which are shaped in different ways. Skills formation proceeds in stages, each building on the previous one (figure 1.2). The most intense phase is during childhood and adolescence. A solid foundation in such basic cognitive skills as literacy and numeracy, typically acquired in primary school, is critical to successful postprimary education, including acquisition of job-specific skills, which are usually acquired through TVET or higher education, apprenticeship, or OJT. Soft skills may be learned at any point, not only within the education and training system but also by interacting with family members, peers, or colleagues.

Skills development crosses institutional boundaries. It can occur in a variety of ways and in a variety of settings, engage a highly diverse clientele, and respond to constantly changing job requirements. The challenge is to better understand its complexities so as to design policies that can meet the growing demand. The Skills Toward Employment and Productivity (STEP) framework illustrates skills

---

Box 1.1 Skill Types

The World Bank Skills Toward Employment and Productivity (STEP) Framework identifies three broad categories of worker skills:

a) *Cognitive skills* are defined as the "ability to understand complex ideas, to adapt effectively to the environment, to learn from experience, to engage in various forms of reasoning, to overcome obstacles by taking thought" (Sanchez-Puerta et al. 2012). The STEP surveys measure the self-reported cognitive skills of numeracy, reading, and writing.

b) *Noncognitive skills* are defined as domains that are not directly associated with intelligence (cognition). They are also referred to as soft skills, personality traits, and behavioral or socioemotional skills. The STEP surveys measure numerous dimensions of noncognitive skills, for example, the Big Five personality traits (extraversion, conscientiousness, openness, emotional stability, and agreeableness), long-term perseverance, decision-making skills, and teamwork and presentation skills.

c) *Technical skills* are defined as specialized skills that are relevant for performing the tasks involved in a specific job. These are the necessary conditions for increasing productivity and fostering economic growth. The STEP surveys use the following measures of technical skills: technology use, computer use, mechanical use, machinery use, English language, ability to work autonomously, and manual labor skills.

Source: Sanchez-Puerta et al. 2012.

Figure 1.2 Skills Formation across the Worker Life Cycle

STEP		Workers' life cycles			
		Preschool age	School age	Youth	Working age
5	Facilitating labor mobility and job matching			Apprenticeships, skills certification, counseling	Intermediation services, labor regulation, social security portability
4	Encouraging entrepreneurship and innovation		Fostering inquiry	Universities, innovation clusters, basic entrepreneurship training, risk management systems	
3	Building job-relevant skills		Basic vocational training, behavioral skills	Vocational training, higher education, apprenticeships, targeted programs	Firm-provided training, recertification, reskilling
2	Ensuring that all students learn		Cognitive skills, socialization, behavioral skills	Second chance education, behavioral skills	
1	Getting children off to the right start	Nutrition, psychological and cognitive stimulation, basic cognitive, and social skills	School health and remedial education		

Source: World Bank 2010.

formation throughout the life cycle and the design of systems to build skills that enhance productivity and growth (figure 1.2).

This ESA focuses on all levels of education and training except firm-based training and re-skilling programs; it applies the STEP framework to selected critical sector issues and topics affecting education in Sri Lanka. This approach is consistent with the Government Manifesto, which proposes to reform all levels of education. The selection of critical issues was based on the team's review of government education reform proposals, previous analytical work, and discussions with government officials.

Data Sources and Limitations
Data Sources

The ESA benefits from numerous documents, both country-specific analyses in Sri Lanka and global and regional analyses of education and skills development. The study benefited heavily from data produced by the Ministry of Skills Development and Vocational Training (MSDVT) and the Ministries of Higher Education, Education, Women and Child Affairs, and Finance and Planning on the characteristics of students and graduates, the number and qualifications of teaching staff, enrollment by field of study, indicators of performance, such as employment placements, and the costs and financing of the system. Additional data sources and key analytical work are as follows:

- *ECD:* The study benefited from *Laying the Foundation for Early Childhood Education in Sri Lanka* (World Bank 2014).
- *School education:* A major source for the study was *Transforming School Education in Sri Lanka: From Cut Stones to Polished Jewels* (World Bank 2011).
- *Skills development:* The report draws heavily on *Building the Skills for Economic Growth and Competitiveness in Sri Lanka* (Dundar et al. 2014). The study also made extensive use of (a) Sri Lanka Labor Force Survey (LFS) data, 1992–2008, to investigate changes in training over time and their effects on earnings and labor market outcomes, and to examine how labor market outcomes vary over time and for different regions and demographic groups; (b) the 2004 and 2010 Enterprise Surveys as sources of data for formal enterprises in Sri Lanka; (c) two national skills measurement surveys (household and employer) carried out as part of a World Bank–financed multicountry study; (d) the Systems Approach for Better Education Results (SABER) Workforce Development Country report, which assessed policies for promoting skills development; and (e) secondary data from the Ministry of Skills Development and associated agencies.
- *Higher education:* The report draws from *The Towers of Learning: Performance, Peril, and Promise of Higher Education in Sri Lanka* (World Bank 2009).
- *Cost and Financing of Education: Investment in Human Capital* (Aturupane et al. 2014) analyzed spending on public education.

- *Student Assessment and Examination:* This aspect of the study relied on the SABER Sri Lanka Student Assessment Country Report and reports produced by the Ministry of Education and the University of Colombo.
- *Regional studies:* The study also benefited from numerous studies examining critical issues in Sri Lanka from ECD through tertiary education; from the recent regional flagship studies *More and Better Jobs in South Asia* (Nayar et al. 2012) and *Addressing Inequality in South Asia* (Rama et al. 2015); and from the regional education quality study *Student Learning in South Asia* (Dundar et al. 2014).

Data Limitations

The ESA was prepared based on an analysis of available data, both secondary and survey data, and on the review of previous analytical work in Sri Lanka and of international evidence and best practices. It was prepared as just-in-time analysis to provide an opportunity for immediate discussion of conclusions with the government. Because of time constraints, it was not possible to gather and analyze new data on some of the issues that were examined. Another limitation relates to the shortage of data on costs and financing of the education system that are central for understanding how efficient the system is and for estimating the potential costs and benefits of providing education and skills for all. Data about private institutions are also scarce.

The remainder of this report is structured in this way: chapter 2 reviews the status of and trends in Sri Lanka's education performance. Chapter 3 reviews the delivery of ECD; chapter 4 reviews primary and secondary education, focusing on such critical issues as teacher effectiveness, supporting and monitoring student learning, management and governance, and cost and financing. Chapter 5 focuses on skills development, and chapter 6 reviews higher education.

Note

1. As described in the World Bank Skills Toward Employment and Productivity (STEP) framework.

References

Aturupane, H., Y. Savchenko, M. Shojo, and K, Larsen. 2014. "Sri Lanka: Investment in Human Capital." South Asia Human Development Unit Discussion Paper Series 69, World Bank, Washington, DC.

Barro, R. J., and J-W. Lee. 2012. *A New Data Set of Educational Attainment in the World, 1950–2010.* http://barrolee.com/papers/Barro_Lee_Human_Capital_Update_2012April.pdf.

DCS (Department of Census and Statistics). 2011. *Sri Lanka Labor Force Survey Annual Report 2011.* Colombo: DCS.

Dundar, H., B. Millot, Y. Savchenko, T.A. Piyasiri, and H. Aturupane. 2014. *Building the Skills for Economic Growth and Competitiveness in Sri Lanka*. Washington, DC: World Bank.

Nayar, R., P. Gottret, P. Mitra, G. Betcherman, Y. M. Lee, I. Santos, M. Dahal, and M. Shrestha. 2012. *More and Better Jobs in South Asia*. Washington, DC: World Bank.

Rama, M., T. Béteille, Y. Li, P. K. Mitra, and J. L. Newman. 2015. *Addressing Inequality in South Asia*. Washington, DC: World Bank.

Riboud, M., Y. Savchenko, and H. Tan. 2007. *The Knowledge Economy and Education and Training in South Asia*. Washington, DC: World Bank.

Sanchez-Puerta, M. L., A. Valerio, G. Pierre, and S. Urzúa. 2012. *STEP Skills Survey Data Analysis Methodology Note*. Draft. Washington, DC: World Bank.

SSM (Secretariat for Senior Ministers). 2012. *The National Human Resources and Employment Policy for Sri Lanka*. Secretariat for Senior Ministers. Colombo: Government of Sri Lanka.

World Bank. 2005. *Treasures of the Education System in Sri Lanka: Restoring Performance, Expanding Opportunities, and Enhancing Prospects*. Washington DC: World Bank.

———. 2009. *The Towers of Learning: Performance, Peril, and Promise of Higher Education in Sri Lanka*. Washington, DC: World Bank.

———. 2010. *Providing Skills for Equity and Growth: Preparing Cambodia's Youth for the Labor Market*. Washington, DC: World Bank.

———. 2011. *Transforming School Education in Sri Lanka: From Cut Stones to Polished Jewels*. Washington, DC: World Bank.

———. 2014. *Laying the Foundation for Early Childhood Education in Sri Lanka: Investing Early, Investing Smartly, and Investing for All*. Washington, DC: World Bank.

———. 2016a. *Poverty and Welfare in Sri Lanka: Recent Progress and Remaining Challenges*. Washington, DC: World Bank.

———. 2016b. *Sri Lanka: A Systematic Country Diagnostic—Ending Poverty and Promoting Shared Prosperity*. Washington, DC: World Bank.

———. Forthcoming. *Sri Lanka Country Partnership Framework*. Washington, DC: World Bank.

CHAPTER 2

Systemwide Performance: Achievements and Challenges

Introduction

Sri Lanka made excellent progress in expanding access to education at its early stages of economic development but now faces several constraints while trying to respond to the needs of a rapidly changing economy. The main constraints are (1) the limited education and training opportunities for youth once compulsory schooling ends; (2) the inequities and inefficiencies that these limitations create; and (3) the low quality and relevance of education and training offerings, which do not meet international standards and are not flexible enough to adjust to the needs of the labor market.

This chapter reviews how Sri Lanka's education system is performing based on a core set of education development indicators and assesses its achievements and challenges based on available evidence.

Overview of the Education and Training System in Sri Lanka

The Sri Lanka education system is complex (figure 2.1). This report covers early childhood education (ECE); general education (primary and secondary); technical and vocational education and training (TVET); and higher education; these are briefly summarized next.

Early childhood development. Early childhood development (ECD) recognizes the different stages of child development from birth until entry in primary school through programs ranging from prenatal health and nutrition, parental education on child-rearing practices to cognitive stimulation through structured school readiness programs. Early childhood education (ECE), a subset of ECD programs, primarily serves children aged 3–5 years and is concerned mainly with school readiness. There are about 17,000 centers in Sri Lanka that enroll a total of 475,000 children aged 3–5. Private businesses manage 60 percent of the centers, nongovernmental organizations (NGOs) 24 percent, and the government 16 percent. There is significant variation by province in the dominant types of

Figure 2.1 The Education and Training System in Sri Lanka

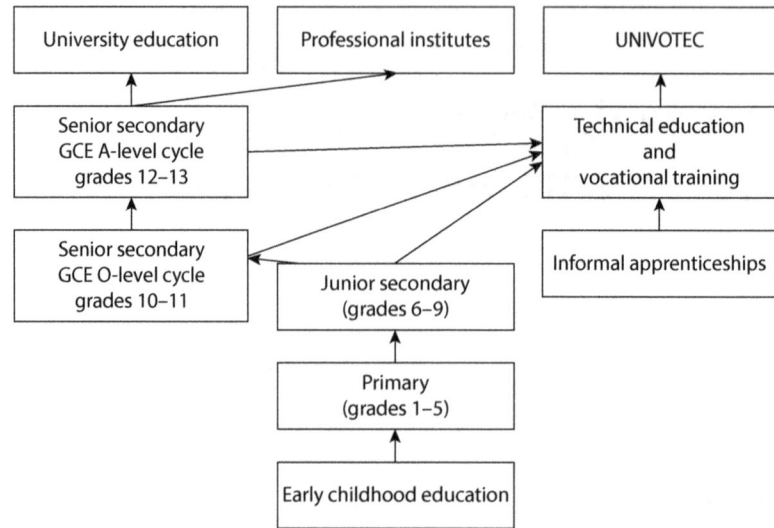

Note: GCE = General Certificate of Education; UNIVOTEC = University of Vocational Technology.

management: In six provinces (Western, Uva, Southern, Sabaragamuwa, Eastern, and Central) more than half the centers are run by private entities; in the other three (North, North Western, and North Central), most are run by government, religious, NGO, and other management types (World Bank 2014a).

General education. General education encompasses primary (grades 1–5), junior secondary (grades 6–9), and senior secondary (grades 10–13). Education is compulsory through grade 11. In 2013 about 4 million students were enrolled in about 10,000 public primary and secondary schools.[1] Private and international schools had about 128,000 students, and another 66,000 were enrolled in state-funded *pirivena* (temple) schools. The system of government schools is widely accessible; private schools account for less than 5 percent of total enrollment. About 4 percent of public schools are managed and financed by the Ministry of Education (MOE), the other 96 percent by local provincial councils (World Bank 2011; MOE 2013). After completing general education, students may enter the labor force, continue on to university, or enroll in TVET. Students in grade 11 take the General Certificate of Education Ordinary Level (GCE O-levels); only about 45 percent pass and qualify to enter grade 12. At grade 13, students must take the General Certificate of Education Advanced Level (GCE A-levels) if they wish to enroll in higher education. Only about 50 percent pass, and of those who do, only 11 percent enroll in universities and advanced technical institutions.

TVET. TVET comprises programs offered by the government, the private sector, and NGOs, mostly targeting school leavers with GCE O-level and A-level qualifications. These institutions offer certificate, diploma, and degree programs. Most TVET students complete vocational training at the certificate level; few get more advanced training. About 150,000 students (43 percent female) are taking TVET courses. In 2011 about 2,300 institutions, operated by public and private institutions and NGOs, were registered with the Tertiary and Vocational Education Commission (TVEC). Several ministries operate training institutions that offer specialized programs. In 2011, 557 public TVET institutions offered 736 accredited courses that covered 23 fields of study that lead to national education diplomas (3- or 4-year courses), diplomas (1 year), and certificates (3–6 months). On average, about 125,000 students a year enroll in registered public TVET institutes (Dundar et al. 2014).

Higher education. Higher education consists of both public and private institutions. There are 15 public universities, including Open University; 8 postgraduate institutes; and 10 affiliated institutes that award bachelor's degrees. Currently, they enroll about 180,000 students. Another 300,000 students are enrolled in a separate external degree program (EDP). Private institutions are mushrooming, often without any official recognition. Estimated enrollment in these institutions is about 120,000. Finally, some 10,000 students are enrolled in universities overseas. The Sri Lanka Institute of Advanced Technological Education (SLIATE) also manages 13 Advanced Technological Institutes (ATIs) that award higher national diplomas and constitute one of the few links between general education and TVET (World Bank 2009; Dundar et al. 2014).

Schooling and Training Opportunities

Education Attainment

Sri Lanka is well-known for fast progress in education attainment. Between 2002 and 2012 the proportion of those who completed O-levels rose from 30 to 35 percent, with higher increases for females than for males and for youth than adults. For example, O-level passers increased by 12 percentage points generally but only 7 percentage points for those aged 25–29. Younger age cohorts are more educated (figure 2.2).

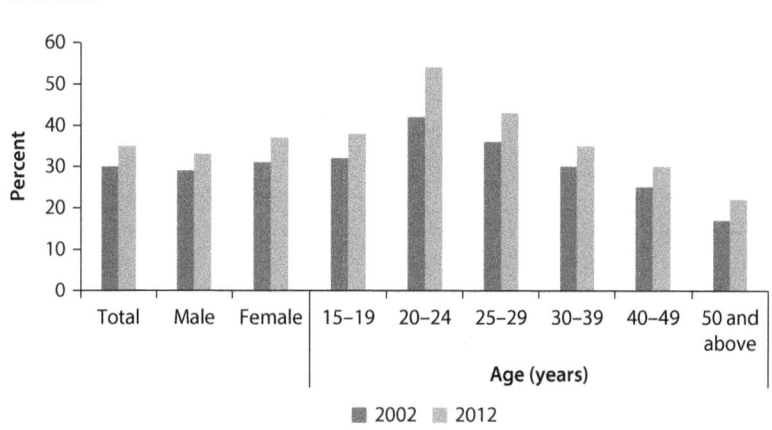

Figure 2.2 Sri Lankans Who Have Passed GCE O-Levels, by Age Group, 2002 and 2012

Source: World Bank 2016b, based on LFS data.
Note: GCE = General Certificate of Education.

Beyond secondary school, however, opportunities to acquire further knowledge and skills are limited for nearly half of youth. Of a cohort of about 450,000 students at GCE O-level, only about 20 percent will move on to higher education institutions (HEIs), and another 33 percent will enter TVET programs, leaving about 47 percent with no option other than exiting the education and training sector, entering the labor market, or going abroad for further studies (see figure 2.3).

Enrollment

As a result of sustained government commitment to education (Aturupane et al. 2014), the gross enrollment rate (GER) and the net enrollment rate (NER) have both gone up steadily over time (figures 2.4 and 2.5). Enrollment in primary and secondary education is impressive by international standards. Universal access to primary education has been achieved: the NER is now 99 percent. The secondary NER has improved from 70 to 84 percent. At preschool and tertiary levels, progress has been more modest, with the NER for preschool rising from 45 to 50 percent and the tertiary GER from 9 to 18 percent.

Although access to preschool has broadened over time, it is still low compared to most middle- and high-income countries (figure 2.6). Throughout the world, preschool investment has been found to consistently bring high cumulative returns to human capital and to be one of the most cost-effective ways to

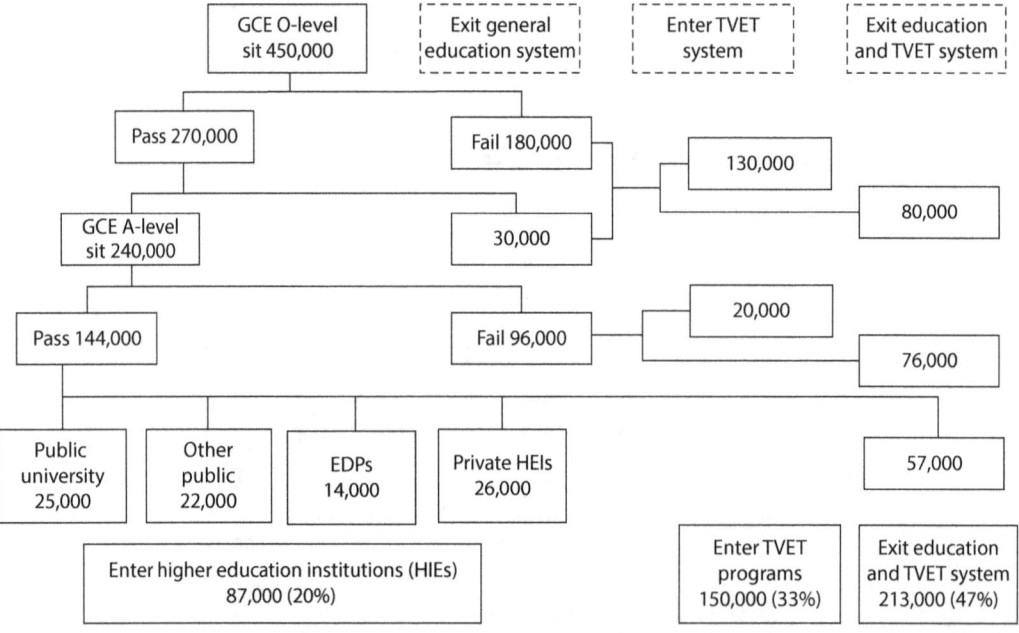

Figure 2.3 Student Flow in the Education and Training System, 2013–14

Note: EDP = external degree program; GCE = General Certificate of Education; HEIs = higher education institution; and TVET = technical and vocational education and training.

Systemwide Performance: Achievements and Challenges 41

Figure 2.4 Gross Enrollment Rates, by Education Level, 2006–12

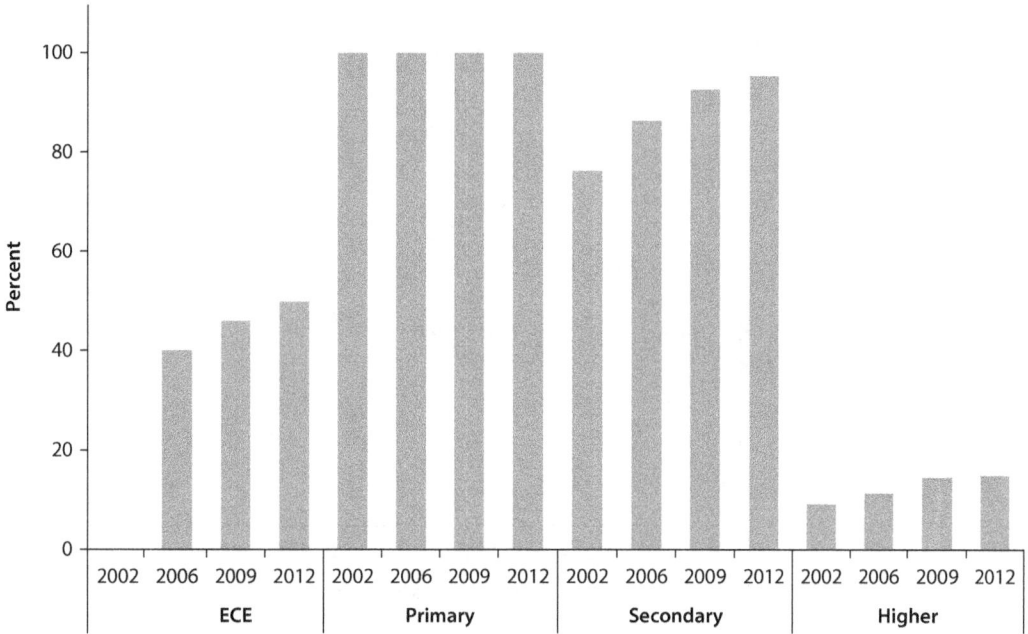

Source: HIES data, 2002, 2006/07, 2009/10, and 2012/13.
Note: ECE = early childhood education.

Figure 2.5 Net Enrollment Rates, by Education Level, 2006–13

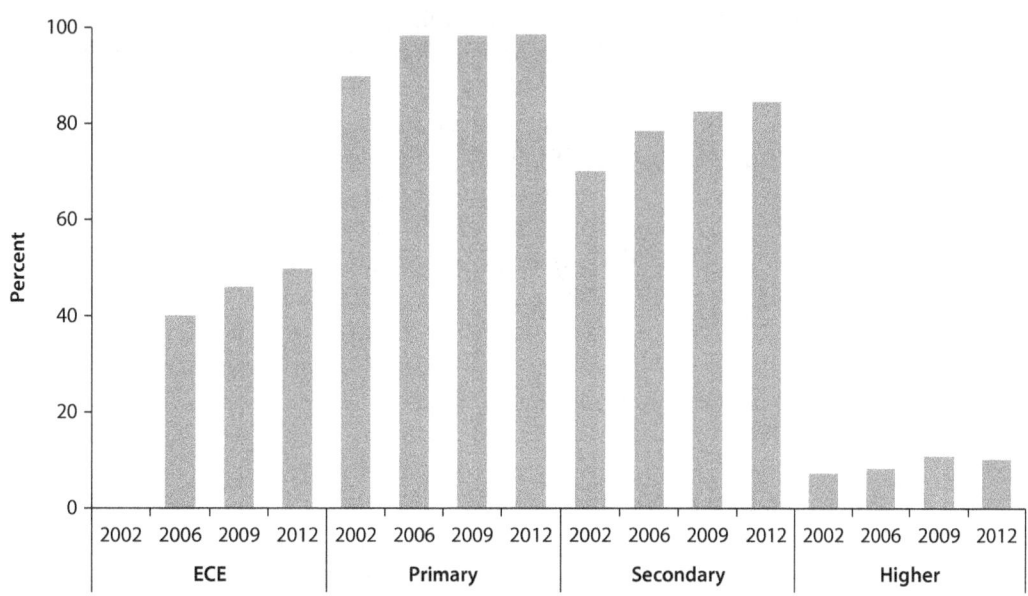

Source: HIES data, 2002, 2006/07, 2009/10, and 2012/13.
Note: ECE = early childhood education.

Figure 2.6 Early Childhood Education Net Enrollment Rate, by GNI per Capita, Middle- and High-Income Countries

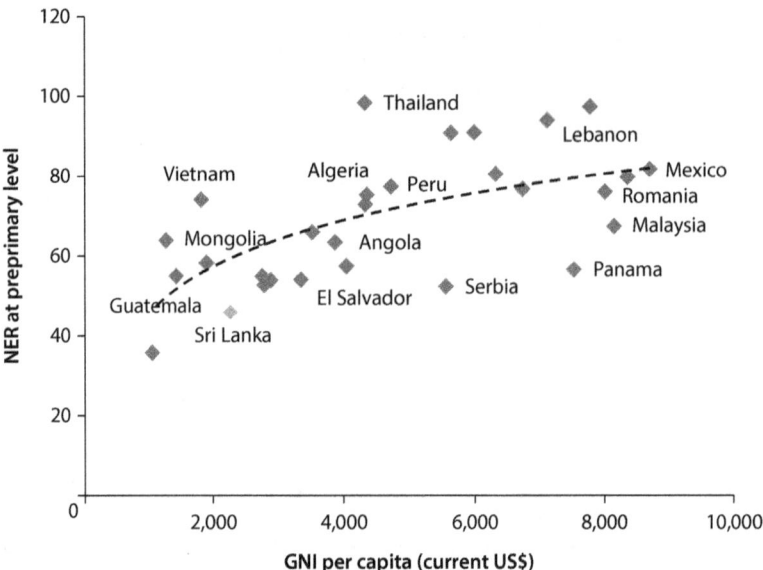

Source: World Bank 2014a, based on EdStats data.
Note: GNI = gross national income; and NER = net enrollment rate.

promote social equity (World Bank 2014b). Since only about half of preschool-aged children in Sri Lanka have access, Sri Lanka is missing an opportunity for high returns, as will be discussed further in chapter 3.

Sri Lanka also trails other middle-income countries in enrollment in higher education. Total enrollment of 20–24-year-olds in Sri Lanka in higher education is about 18 percent, compared to a middle-income country average of about 30 percent (figure 2.7). This is partly because until just a few years ago, private provision of university education was restricted, and there was relatively low public investment in higher education. An additional concern is the decline since 2002 in the proportion of students enrolled in science and engineering. Finally, the formal education system does not do enough to build soft skills like leadership and communication that the labor market values. These factors help explain the concerns of Sri Lankan firms about the difficulty they have in finding the skills they need. This issue will be discussed more in chapters 5 and 6.

Equity in Access to Education

Individual and social circumstances (e.g., gender and socioeconomic status) should not be an obstacle to achieving educational potential. The international literature shows that fair education is one of the most powerful levers to make

Figure 2.7 Enrollment in Secondary and Higher Education, Selected Countries, 2014

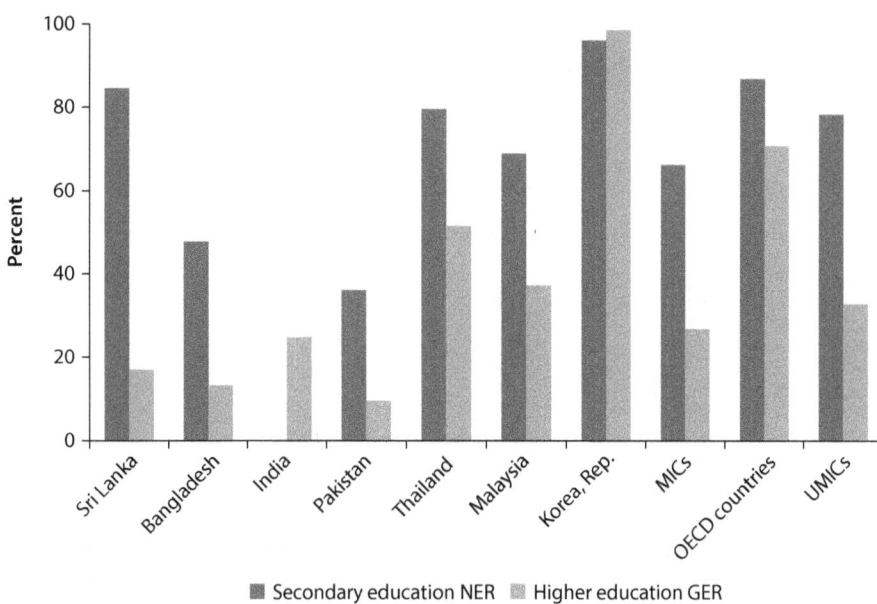

Source: EdStats.
Note: MICs = middle-income countries; OECD = Organisation of Economic Co-operation and Development; and UMICs = upper-middle-income countries.

society more equitable (OECD 2007). Equity in education affects both individual and household behaviors and outcomes.

Sri Lanka has achieved gender parity in enrollment for ECE, primary, and junior secondary students, but not for senior secondary and higher education (figure 2.8). Although the NER for ECE is still low, gender parity has been achieved. Primary education is universal for both boys and girls. There is also no gender difference in junior secondary enrollment, with the NER for boys at 85 percent and for girls 84 percent. Education through grade 11 is compulsory (it was through grade 9 until recently), which supports gender parity in enrollment. At the senior secondary level, the NER for boys is 67 percent, lower than the 72 percent for girls. This is due to a lower retention rate for boys than for girls. In higher education, too, more girls participate than boys: their GER is about 5 percentage points higher. The better performance of girls than boys at these levels is common in middle-income and developed countries.

Access to education by income level is equitable in primary and junior secondary education but less so in ECE, senior secondary, and higher education. Primary and junior secondary NERs are very evenly spread across economic groups, partly because enrollment is compulsory. Variations between income quintiles arise when education is not compulsory (figure 2.9). NERs for ECE range from 45 percent for the poorest quintile to 54 percent for the richest.

Figure 2.8 Enrollment Rates, by Gender

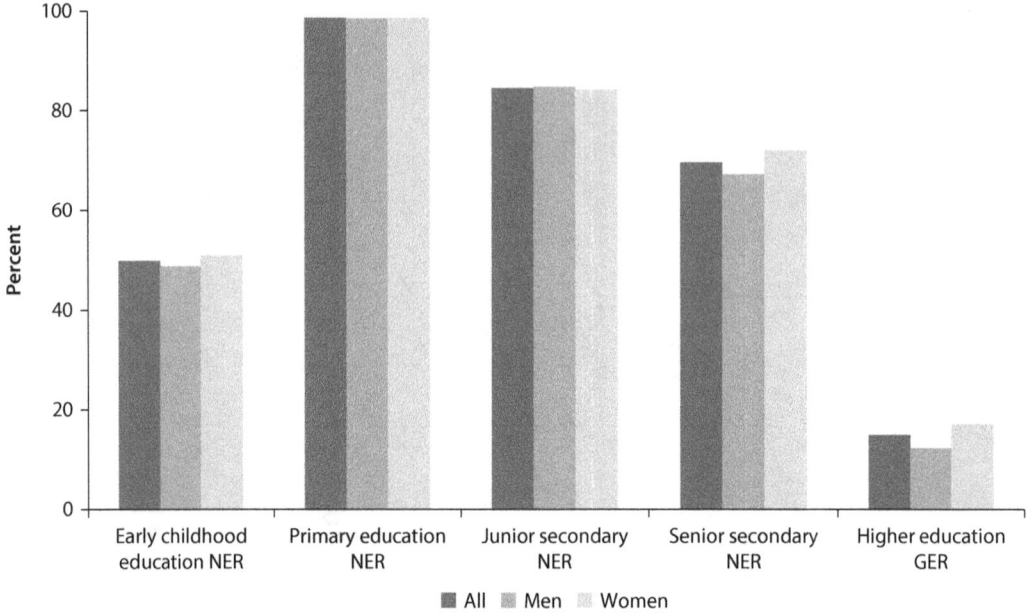

Source: HIES data, 2012/13.
Note: GER = gross enrollment rate; and NER = net enrollment rate.

Figure 2.9 Access to Education, by Income Quintile

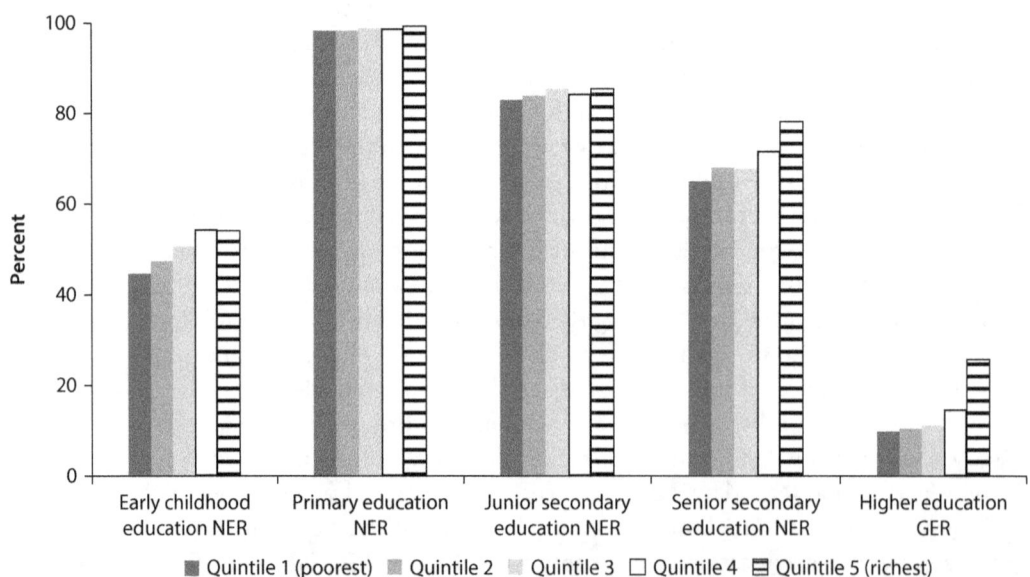

Source: HIES data, 2012/13.
Note: GER = gross enrollment rate; and NER = net enrollment rate.

Senior secondary NERs range from 65 percent for the poorest to 78 percent for the richest. The pattern is similar for higher education, where the GER for the poorest quintile is 10 percent and for the richest 26 percent; this suggests that wealthier students are more likely than those from poorer families to stay in senior secondary and proceed to higher education. Even though education is free up to university, the opportunity cost and the additional direct costs (e.g., transportation, books, and tuition fees) for moving up in the system still keep many families out.

The gap between rich and poor entering senior secondary and higher education is growing (figure 2.10). Between 2006 and 2012 the ratio of the richest to the poorest in higher education enrollment went up steeply, from 1.1 to 2.6, which suggests that equity in access to higher education has deteriorated. The senior secondary ratio rose slightly, from 1 to 1.2. The growing disparity between poor and rich in access to these education levels is a serious problem that could have long-term consequences for the country's poverty reduction goals (World Bank 2016b).

There are also disparities in school participation by location. Compared to those in the urban and rural sectors, plantation enrollment rates are the lowest at all education levels (figure 2.11). Although this sector accounts for only about 4 percent of the total population,[2] it has traditionally trailed rural and urban sectors. Less education makes it more difficult for plantation workers to shift to more productive sectors (World Bank 2016a). There are also notable regional gaps (figure 2.12), with poverty in part associated with unequal access to education (box 2.1).

Figure 2.10 Enrollment, Ratio of Richest to Poorest Quintile

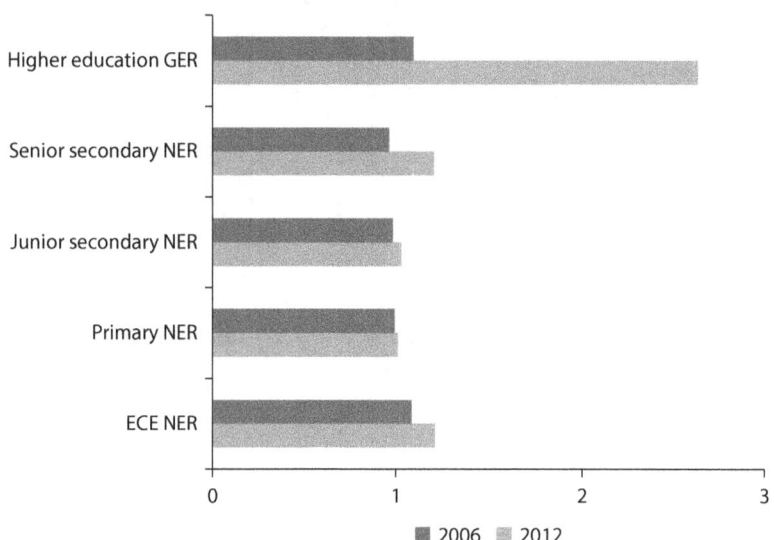

Source: HIES data, 2006/07 and 2012/13.
Note: ECE = early childhood education; GER = gross enrollment rate; and NER = net enrollment rate.

Figure 2.11 Access to Education, by Level and Location, 2012–13

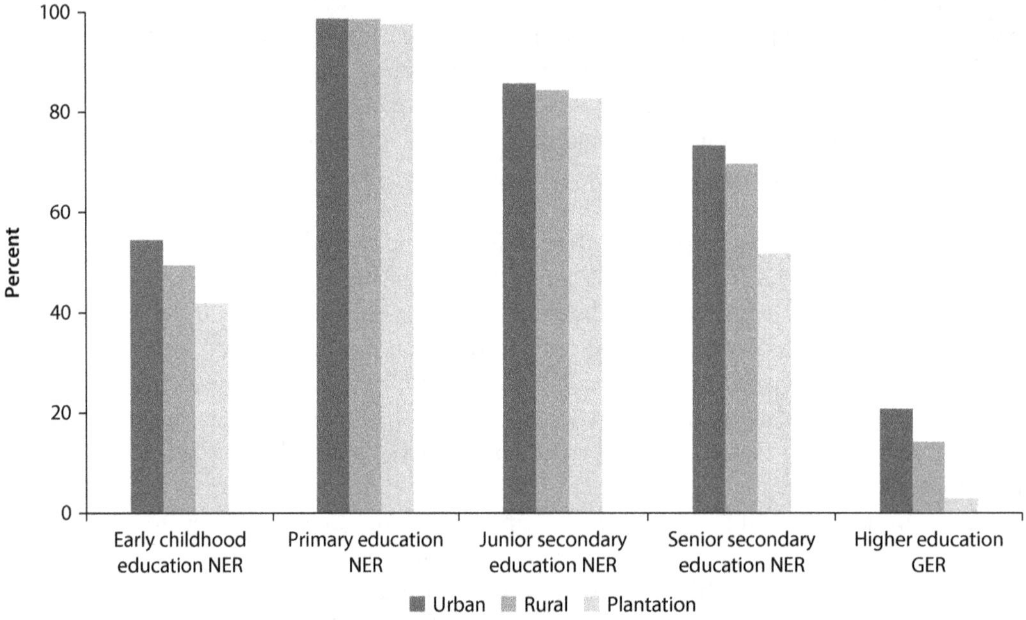

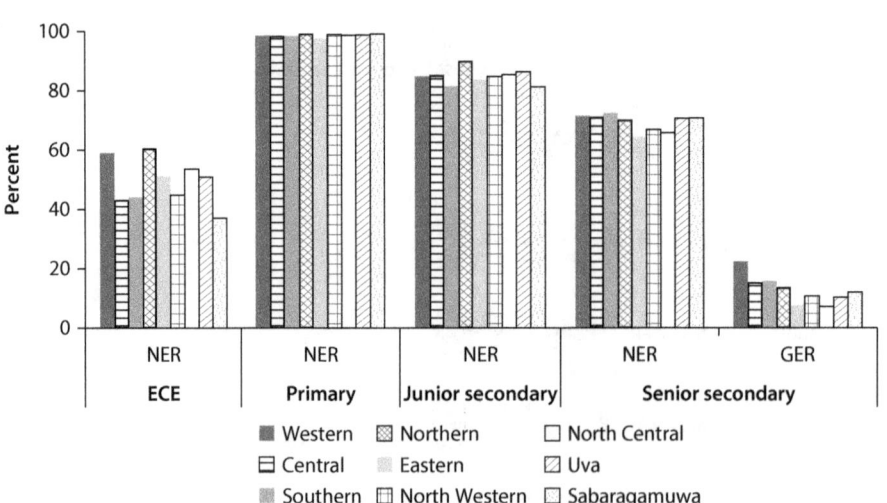

Source: HIES data, 2012/13.
Note: GER = gross enrollment rate; and NER = net enrollment rate.

Figure 2.12 Access to Education, by Level and Province, 2012–13

Source: HIES data, 2012/13.
Note: ECE = early childhood education; GER = gross enrollment rate; and NER = net enrollment rate.

Box 2.1 Characteristics of the Poor in Sri Lanka

The World Bank (2016b) has analyzed progress on poverty reduction and continuing challenges in Sri Lanka.

Based on data from the Household Income and Expenditure Survey (HIES) for various years, the report points out that while Sri Lanka has made significant progress in reducing poverty, living standards are still modest and pockets of severe poverty persist. The main findings and conclusions are:

- The poor and near-poor tend to be rural, young, and unable to access productive earnings opportunities.
- Sri Lanka is the only country in the South Asia region to experience a recent increase in both consumption and income inequality.
- This inequality contributes to unequal access to education and health services (see table B2.1.1).
- Inequality between the poor and the rich in education access and attainment has been rising.
- Additional support for the poor is needed to ensure continued economic growth and close the gap between the poor and the nonpoor.

Table B2.1.1 Profile of the Poor and Nonpoor

Sector	Overall	Bottom 40%	Top 60%	Poor National	US$1.25	US$2.25
Industry						
Agriculture	30.7	41.9	23.0	48.8	47.9	43.2
Industry	23.8	24.9	23.1	23.8	21.4	24.5
Services	45.3	32.8	53.9	27.2	30.7	31.9
Education						
Average years of education						
Head of household	8.2	6.6	9.1	5.5	5.4	6.4
Individuals (age 20 and over)	8.9	7.5	9.7	6.5	6.3	7.3
Health						
Average distance (km)						
Clinic	2.4	2.9	2.1	3.5	3.5	3.0
Dispensary	2.1	2.8	1.6	3.5	3.4	2.9
Hospital	6.6	7.5	6.0	8.2	8.5	7.6
Maternity clinic	5.2	6.0	4.7	6.3	6.1	6.0

Source: World Bank 2016b.

Several factors may be contributing to Sri Lanka's lackluster performance in ensuring equitable access to education. In Sri Lanka household economic status and income have been found to be highly correlated to the amount of schooling. Opportunity costs and direct schooling costs may deter enrollment in higher levels of education. Parents' education is also a major factor in whether children access education. Furthermore, lack of ability to access ECE and higher levels of education is associated with a lower probability of enrollment for poorer students, especially in rural and disadvantaged provinces (World Bank 2014b, forthcoming).

Completion Rates

Over time, male and female completion rates of both primary and secondary education have gone up (figure 2.13).[3] Almost all students (99 percent) complete primary education. In secondary education, school completion rates have also gone up, with rates higher for females than for males. Although senior secondary completion rates did fall from 26 to 22 percent, there was a significant increase for females (from 24 to 36 percent).

Rural and plantation children are less likely than urban children to complete both primary and secondary education. The inequality between urban, rural, and plantation sectors (figure 2.14) is significant. Completion rates for plantation children are much lower than for urban and rural children. While the senior secondary completion rate went up from 30 to 42 percent for urban students, the rise was only from 7 to 10 percent for plantation students.

Another concern is that the gap in completion rates between the richest and the poorest quintiles is widening. Poverty and low completion rates are highly correlated. Completion rates are much lower for the poorest than for the richest quintile, and the gap has been growing (figure 2.15). While between 2006 and 2012 the junior secondary education completion rate went up by 24 percent points for the richest quintile, it went up by only 3 percent points for the poorest quintile.

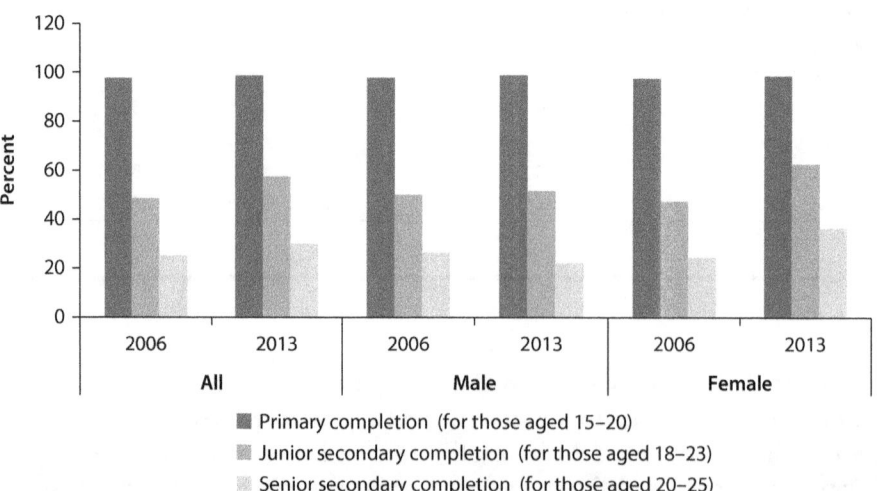

Figure 2.13 Completion Rate, by Gender, 2006 and 2013

■ Primary completion (for those aged 15–20)
■ Junior secondary completion (for those aged 18–23)
■ Senior secondary completion (for those aged 20–25)

Source: HIES data, 2006/07 and 2012/13.

Systemwide Performance: Achievements and Challenges

Figure 2.14 Completion Rate, by Location, 2006 and 2013

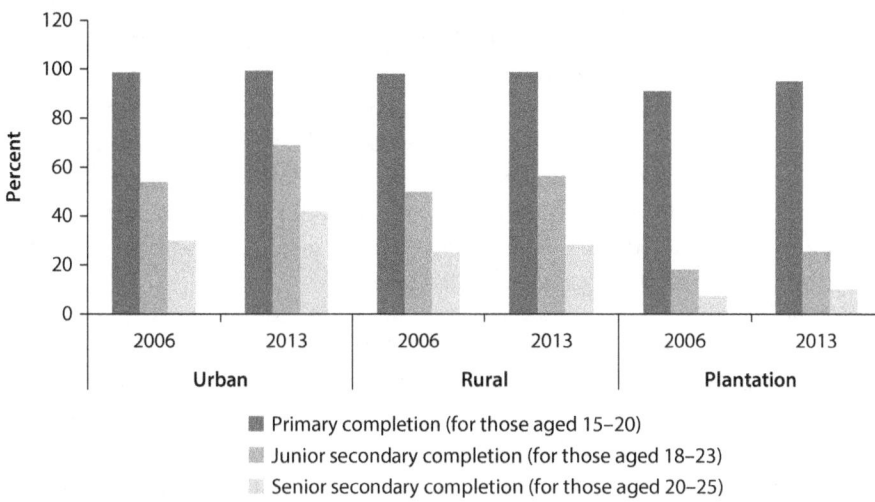

Source: HIES data, 2006/07 and 2012/13.

Figure 2.15 Completion Rates, Poorest and Richest Quintiles, 2006 and 2013

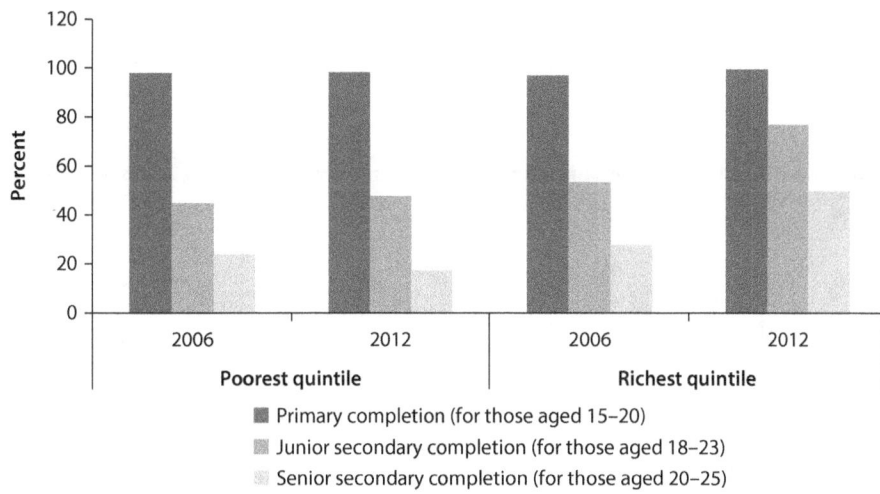

Source: HIES data, 2006/07 and 2012/13.

The Quality and Relevance of Education and Training

Learning Outcomes in Primary and Secondary Education

Despite wide high access and high completion rates, learning achievements are modest. In the lowest grades, Sri Lankan children seem to learn fairly well, which should speak well for educational quality. A 2009 national assessment of grade 4 students conducted by the National Education Research and Evaluation Center (NEREC) found that a relatively large proportion were able to master the essential learning competencies expected. The mean achievement score in mathematics was 77 percent in Sinhala-medium schools and 62 percent in Tamil-medium schools (NEREC 2009). A review of learning outcomes in South Asia also found that Sri Lanka is the only country where average achievement does not seem to have fallen over time: NEREC national assessments of fourth-graders between 2003 and 2009 show appreciable improvement in all subjects. The 2013 assessment also indicated that at this level there are no major differences in achievement by subject or type of school (figure 2.16).[4]

Nevertheless, at higher grades, learning outcomes are weaker, raising concern about the quality of general education, the ability of students to master the curriculum, and growing disparities (figure 2.17). Although there is evidence that scores, and thus quality, have been rising, mean scores of grade 8 students in 2012 were still just 51 percent for mathematics, 42 percent for science, and 40 percent for English; the general education system seems to have little capacity to produce the skills most in demand in a competitive economy. Pass rates are particularly low in science, mathematics, and English—subjects that are essential if graduates are to succeed in the knowledge economy. Disparities by school type have also widened starkly. In GCE O-level examinations taken after grade 10 and in GCE A-level examinations, pass rates have been fairly stable, at about 50–60 percent (figures 2.18 and 2.19).

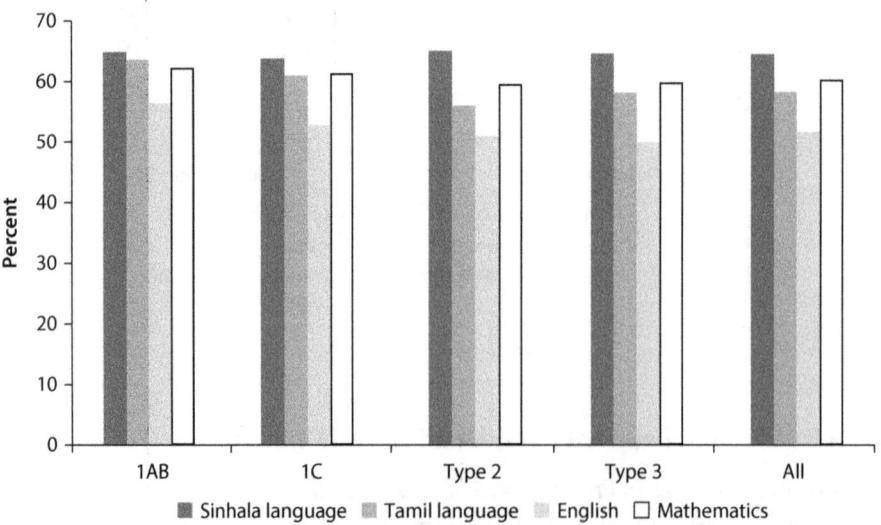

Figure 2.16 Mean Scores, National Assessment for Grade 4, by Subject and School Type, 2013

Source: NEREC 2014.

Figure 2.17 Mean Scores, National Assessment for Grade 8, by Subject and School Type, 2012

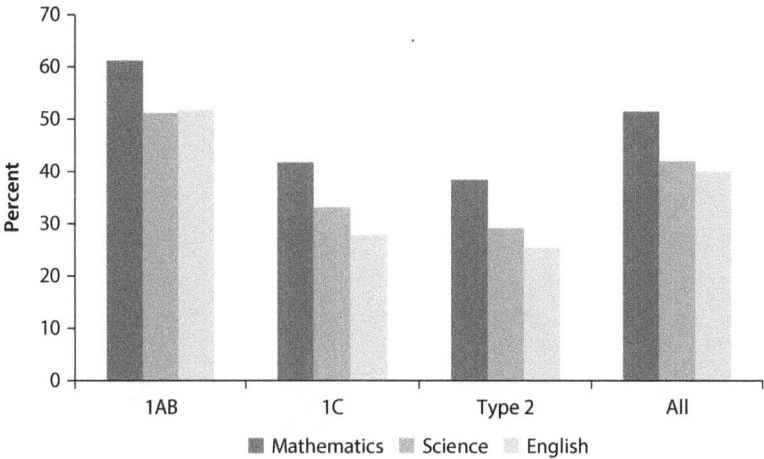

Source: NEREC 2013.

Figure 2.18 Pass Rates, GCE O-Level Examination, 2005–12

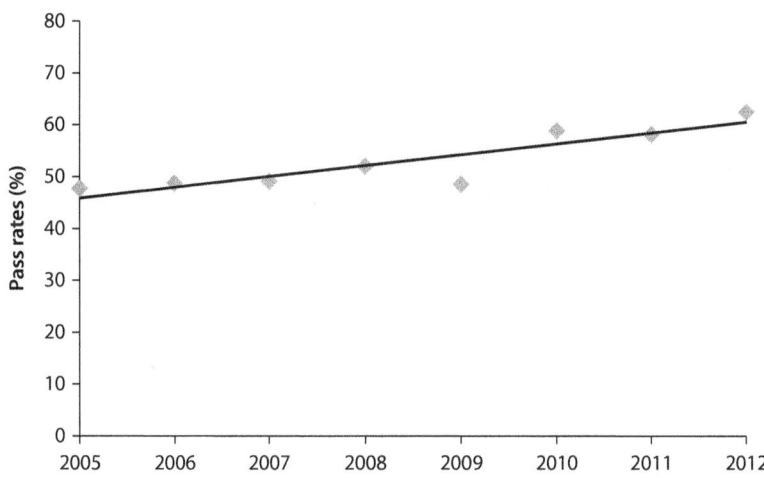

Source: Aturupane et al. 2014, based on MOE data.
Note: The structure of the General Certificate of Education (GCE) O-level examination changed in 2010.

There is significant variation in learning outcomes in secondary education by province, gender, income, and location (figures 2.20 and 2.21). Figure 2.20 shows that students in more developed provinces (e.g., Western and Southern) perform better than those in less-developed provinces (e.g., Eastern and Uva). Figure 2.21 indicates that those in the richest group have the highest test scores and those in

Figure 2.19 Pass Rates, GCE A-Level Examination, 2005–12

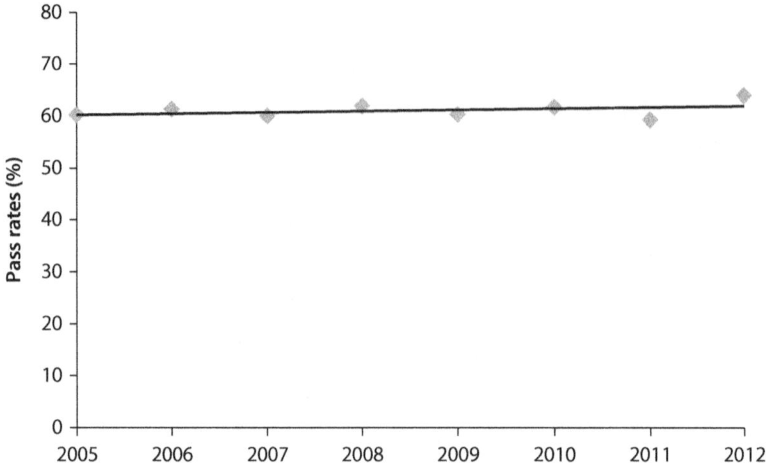

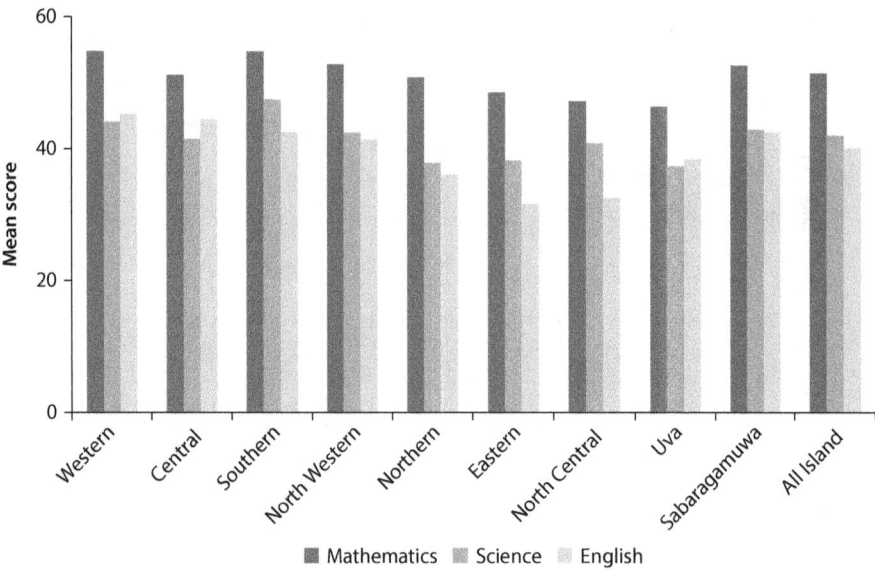

Source: Aturupane et al. 2014, based on MOE data.
Note: The structure of the General Certificate of Education (GCE) A-level examination during this period was constant, so that the performances of students at this level can be compared over time.

Figure 2.20 Grade 8 Learning Outcomes, by Province, 2012

Source: NEREC 2013.

the poorest group have the lowest ones. Urban students perform better than rural ones, and girls score higher than boys. Of course, the disparities are not all related to the schools. Although the large variation in learning is often attributed to flaws in the education system, some students may also come to school with huge disadvantages that prevent them from performing well.

Figure 2.21 Standardized Test Scores, Grade 8, 2012

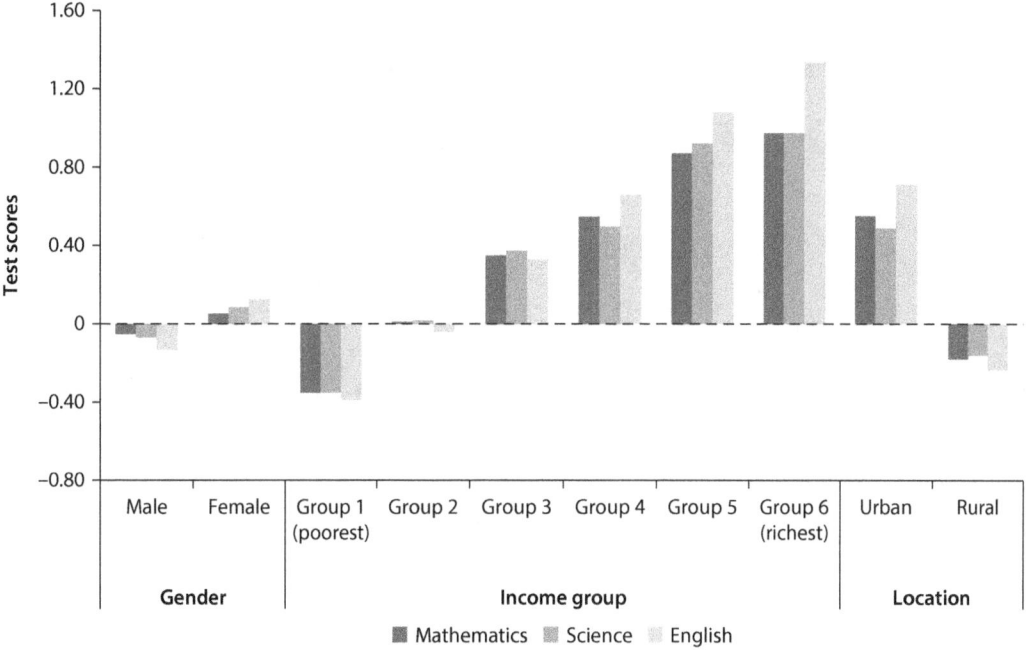

Source: Data from the 2012 National Assessments of Learning Outcomes for Grade 8.
Note: Scores are standardized with respect to the mean. Income Group 1 = Household monthly income below Rs. 10,001; Group 2 = Rs. 10,001–20,000; Group 3 = Rs. 20,001–30,000; Group 4 = Rs. 30,001–40,000; Group 5 = Rs. 40,001–50,000; Group 6 = > Rs. 50,000.

The available evidence suggests that learning outcomes in Sri Lanka do not meet international standards. Sri Lanka has never participated in such international assessments as the Programme for International Student Assessment (PISA), Trends in International Mathematics and Science Study (TIMSS), and Progress in International Reading Literacy Study (PIRLS). However, in 2009 it added a TIMSS module to the National Assessments, which made it possible to benchmark some national learning outcomes against international standards (figure 2.22). The result shows where Sri Lanka stands in terms of mathematics test scores and spending per student in public education as a percentage of gross domestic product (GDP) per capita: Sri Lanka spends much less per pupil, and its learning outcomes trail those of middle- and high-income countries. That must change if Sri Lanka is to become internationally competitive.

Several student- and school-related factors contribute to differences in achievement in Sri Lanka (Aturupane, Glewwe, and Wisniewski 2013; World Bank forthcoming). Consistent with the vast international literature, family background, such as socioeconomic status and parental education, heavily influences student performance. Male students are more likely to have lower scores than female ones. Older siblings do not perform as well as younger siblings, partly because of resource dilution. Students who speak English at home have books

Figure 2.22 Sri Lanka's Learning Outcomes, an International Perspective

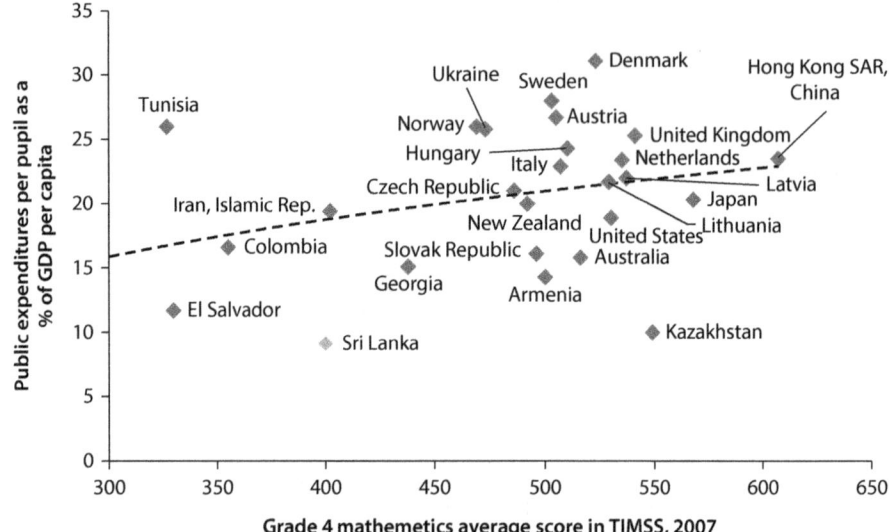

Sources: Mullis, Martin, and Foy 2008. Data for Sri Lanka from NEREC 2008. Expenditure data from EdStats.

available at home, and those who have an undisturbed home environment tend to have higher scores. Private tutoring has a powerfully positive influence on student learning.

School characteristics are also associated with substantial differences in student performance. There is a wide gap in student performance between Type 1AB schools and the other types of schools (see figure 2.23). School location also matters; urban schools tend to have higher scores than rural ones. However, the findings on teacher characteristics have not been consistent. A study based on national assessments of grade 4 found teaching experience to be positively associated with student performance (Aturupane, Glewwe, and Wisniewski 2013), but a study based on national assessments of grade 8 argued that teachers' years of experience in teaching have no significant effect (World Bank forthcoming).

The Quality and Relevance of TVET and Higher Education

Education is increasingly important for preparing students for work and providing the skills the labor market demands. Because Sri Lanka's economy is changing rapidly as it grows, its education system needs to be able to ensure that all students acquire the skills they need to make a smooth transition from education to work.

In both TVET and higher education, the quality and relevance of current programs and the employability of graduates are limited—relatively few students are enrolled in programs defined as national priorities, and it takes a long time for many graduates to find their first job. Moreover, more than 50 percent of employers questioned the quality and relevance of general education, TVET, and universities in terms of conveying up-to-date knowledge or producing the kinds of skills employers need (figure 2.24).

Figure 2.23 Student Performance Measured by the 2012 National Assessment

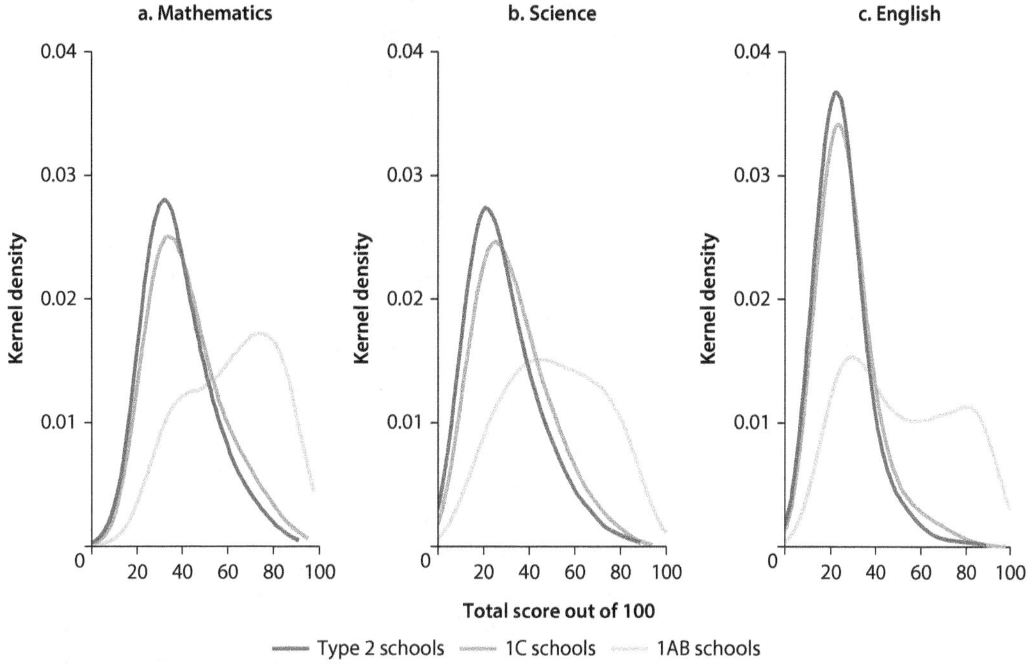

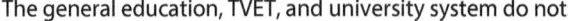

Source: World Bank, forthcoming.

Figure 2.24 Employer Perceptions of General Education, TVET, and University

The general education, TVET, and university system do not:

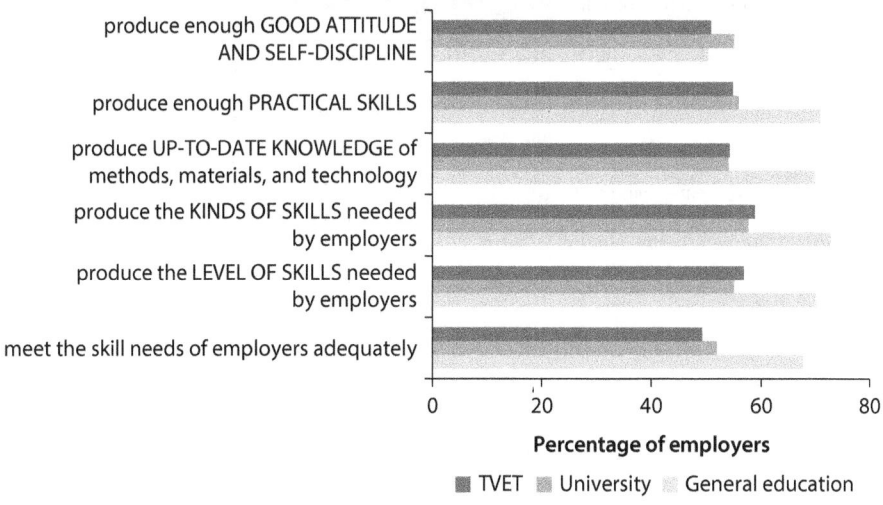

Source: Dundar et al. 2014, based on data from the World Bank STEP Survey.
Note: TVET = technical and vocational education and training.

Employers are concerned about the quality and relevance of Sri Lanka's education and training and whether graduates are actually employable. The Sri Lankan workforce lacks adequate job-specific skills to meet the increasing demand. While many employers believe the education and training system should be producing job-specific skills, they question the extent to which it is actually doing so. For example, 70 percent of employers report that general education does not produce people with up-to-date knowledge of methods, materials, and technology; 70 percent report the same about university, and 54 percent about TVET (figure 2.24). Despite heightened demand for mid-level technicians, only 16 percent of workers have completed TVET, and not many of those acquired job-relevant skills. Many TVET programs are irrelevant to the skills employers need. Similarly, Sri Lanka has very few highly skilled workers; even those who complete higher education may not have the productive skills employers demand. The mismatch between skills supply and demand is reflected in declining returns to education (Dundar et al. 2014; World Bank 2016b).

Although job-specific technical skills are considered important, demand for soft skills is also high. The Skills Toward Employment and Productivity (STEP) survey findings suggest that employers consider job-specific technical skills to be most important for retention of both low-skilled and high-skilled workers (figure 2.25). The second highest skill need identified is literacy in Sinhala or Tamil. Literacy in English is ranked as third, though more for high-skilled than for low-skilled workers. About 14 percent of firms consider leadership skills more

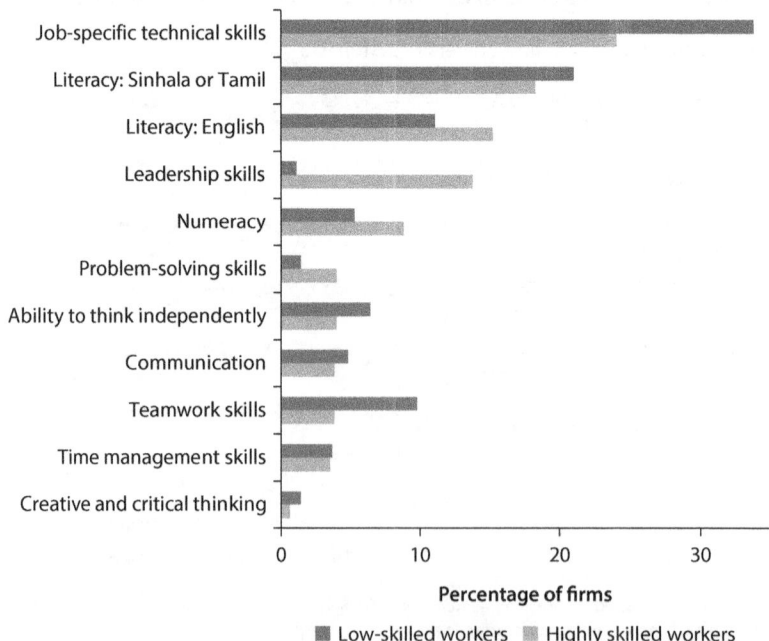

Figure 2.25 Skills Most Important for Retention Decisions

Source: Dundar et al. 2014, based on data from the World Bank STEP Survey.

Figure 2.26 Firms Identifying Lack of Skilled Workforce as a Major Problem

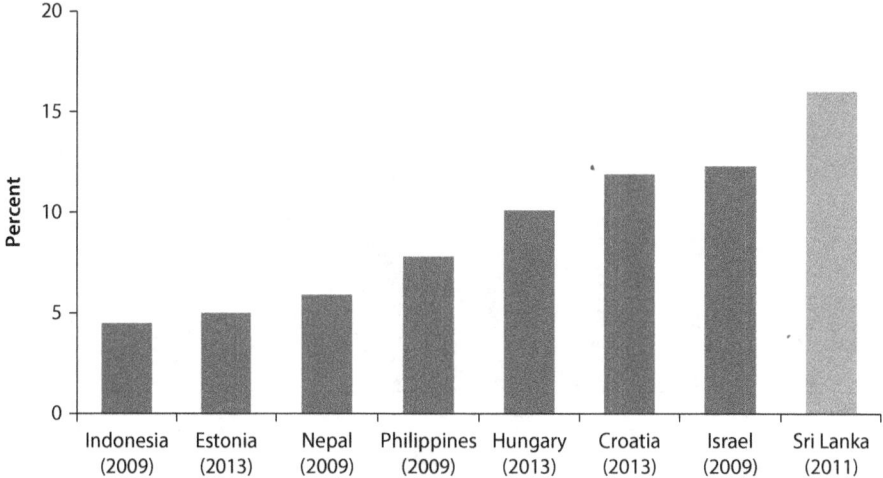

Source: Adapted from Dundar et al. 2014, based on data from the World Bank Enterprise Survey.

important for high-skilled workers, compared to just 1 percent for low-skilled workers. Other soft skills identified as important were problem-solving, communication, teamwork, and creative thinking. The education and training system has not been producing these adequately (Dundar et al. 2014).

The limited skills of its people are putting the brakes on Sri Lanka's growth and competitiveness. While employers increasingly seek workers with solid work and soft skills, the education system is still struggling to ensure that all youth acquire even the most basic skills. Finding it difficult to access the skills they need, many employers question the quality and relevance of education and training. According to the World Bank Enterprise Survey, in Sri Lanka the proportion of firms that identify a shortage of adequate skills as a major or severe constraint is higher than in other middle-income and developing countries (figure 2.26). The drive for industrial growth is especially blocked by the shortage of technically skilled workers—many of whom migrate overseas for jobs.

Labor Market Outcomes

Employment

Sri Lanka has made remarkable progress in bringing down unemployment, but the proportion of women participating in the labor force is relatively low by international standards. Unemployment dropped from 8 percent in 2000 to 4 percent in 2013. The labor force participation rate (LFPR) as a proportion of the total population aged 15–64 was 59 percent in 2013, but there is a significant gender gap: 85 percent of men participate, but only 43 percent of women. The female LFPR in Sri Lanka is below the average for middle-income countries and such countries as Bangladesh, Thailand, Malaysia, and the Republic of Korea (figure 2.27).

Figure 2.27 Labor Force Participation, Selected Countries

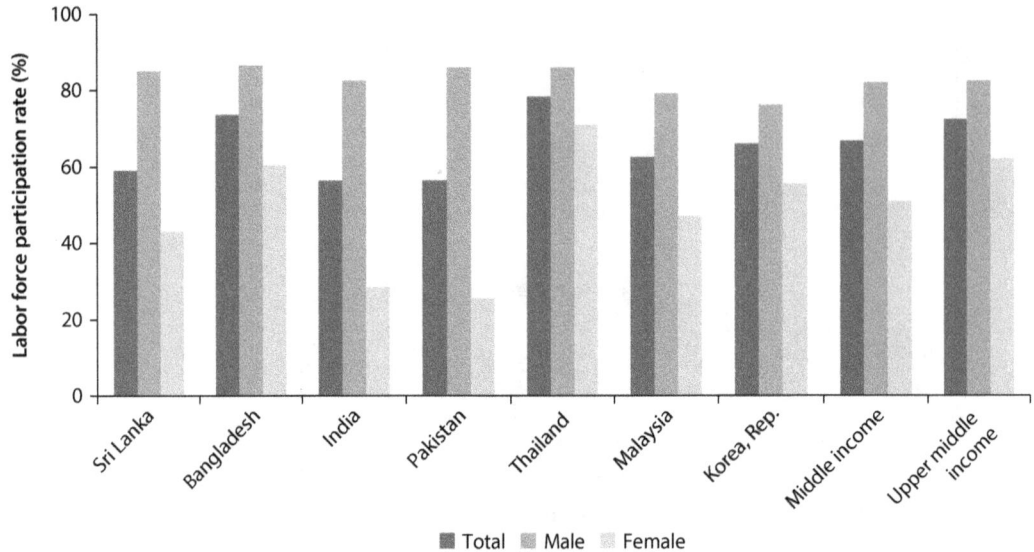

Sources: Data for Sri Lanka: STEP Survey; for other countries: World Development Indicators.

Unemployment may be low, but underemployment is high (table 2.1). In the World Bank STEP survey, of the 59 percent of the respondents who were in the labor force, only 6 percent were unemployed—but of the employed, 18 percent were underemployed and 37 percent self-employed. Average weekly earnings of an employed worker were about LKR 5,100. Only 56 percent of the urban population is in the labor force compared to 61 percent of the rural, but 20 percent of the latter are underemployed. In general, women and rural residents are more likely to be underemployed than other groups.

Though the LFPR for youth is relatively low, youth unemployment is high by international standards (table 2.1). At 47 percent, youth participation in the labor force is lower than adult (64 percent). Youth unemployment is 13 percent—higher than in Malaysia (3 percent) or Korea (9 percent). Given the steady aging of the Sri Lankan population, sustained high growth will require not only raising the productivity of labor but also attracting more entrants into the labor force.

Returns to Education

While earnings increase with education and TVET, the relationship between TVET and labor market outcomes is not clear (table 2.1). Individuals with TVET and apprenticeship training are more likely to participate in the labor market than those without. More than 80 percent of those with bachelor's

Table 2.1 Labor Market Outcomes, by Demographic Characteristics, Education, and Training

		Labor force participation (%)	Unemployment (%)	Underemployment (%)	Self-employment (%)	Weekly earnings, employed (LKR)
Total	Total	59	6	18	37	5,098
Gender	Male	85	3	15	33	5,990
	Female	43	10	22	42	3,729
Location	Urban	56	6	14	37	5,818
	Rural	61	6	21	37	4,622
Adults/Youth	Adults (aged 30–65)	64	4	18	40	4,928
	Youth (aged 15–29)	47	13	17	24	5,749
Education	No education	61	8	26	13	2,891
	Below primary	66	4	14	35	2,936
	Primary (grade 5)	65	3	18	34	3,431
	Lower secondary (grade 9)	58	5	19	43	4,520
	Passed GCE O-levels	52	8	19	47	4,844
	Passed GCE A-levels	61	7	17	28	7,049
	Bachelor's	84	8	18	7	7,322
	Master's +	82	0	29	7	11,269
Training	No TVET	56	6	18	38	4,698
	TVET	73	8	17	34	6,573
	No apprenticeship	56	6	19	38	5,018
	Apprenticeship	75	4	16	35	5,425

Source: Dundar et al. 2014, based on data from the STEP household survey 2012.
Note: This is based on the STEP household survey, which may not be comparable to figures computed using the Labor Force Survey. GCE = General Certificate of Education; and TVET = technical and vocational education and training.

degrees and above participate. Interestingly, unemployment is higher for the uneducated, people with completed GCE O-levels and A-levels, and holders of bachelor's degrees than for other education levels. It is also higher for those who completed TVET than for those who did not. Self-employment peaks at 47 percent for those with no more than GCE O-levels; 93 percent of those with bachelor's degrees and above work in the formal economy (Dundar et al. 2014).

Returns to education have declined over time. The mismatch between skills in demand and workforce education seems to be reflected, at least in part, in declining returns to education. Despite higher educational attainment, the premium for additional years of education has been declining, especially for higher education and GCE A-level graduates (figure 2.28). This may be expected when average education attainment increases without a commensurate increase in demand. However, the decline in the returns to education is also consistent with the finding that the education sector is not providing the skills demanded by the market, since companies report shortages of well-trained workers (World Bank 2016b).

Figure 2.28 Returns on Education, by Level, 2006–12

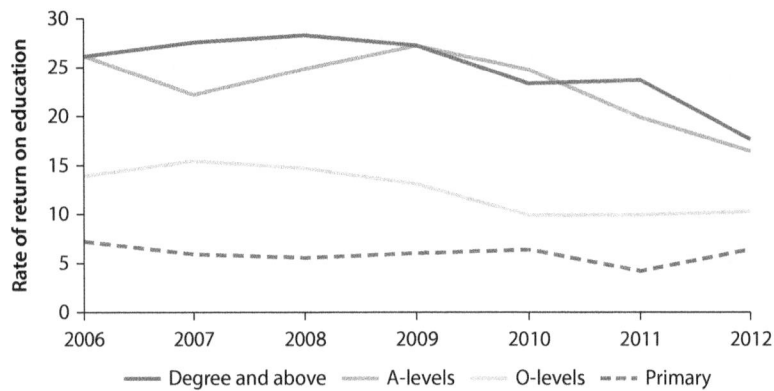

Source: Arunatilake et al. 2015, using Labor Force Surveys excluding Northern and Eastern provinces.

Trends in Sri Lanka's Public Spending on Education

Policies on education finance affect equitable access to quality education services. While a minimum level of resources is necessary to ensure that students have access to a reasonable standard of resources and materials, *how* resources are spent on education is more important than *how much* is spent. Governance affects the quality of service delivery.

General and higher education in Sri Lanka are dominated by public financing and provision. Sri Lanka's Free Education Scheme subsidizes primary to tertiary education for all eligible students. Private schools enroll only about 5 percent of students in general education. The Higher Education (HE) system is largely owned and managed by the state, with state universities having the sole legal right to confer degrees. Only in ECE and in TVET is there a large contribution from nonstate resources.

Compared to other countries at similar levels of development, Sri Lanka spends much less of its income on education. Among low- and middle-income countries, Sri Lanka has the lowest spending on public education as a percentage of its GDP (Sri Lanka: 2 percent; low- and middle-income country average: 4.5 percent). In fact, for several years public investment in education has actually declined in real terms (figure 2.29), making Sri Lanka one of the lowest spenders on public education among middle-income countries (figure 2.30). Even as a share of total government expenditures, the country's spending on public education is among the lowest (Sri Lanka: 10.2 percent; low- and middle-income country average: 17.3 percent).

Spending on public education has largely followed historical trends in Sri Lanka. Per pupil expenditures are low overall, though across provinces they reflect a redistributive pattern. A very small share of public resources is provided in the form of equity funds to schools based on their characteristics. Because of this, education outcomes from grade 8 on, and enrollment in higher levels of education, especially senior secondary and tertiary, are closely and positively correlated with household socioeconomic status.

Figure 2.29 Education Spending, 2007–12

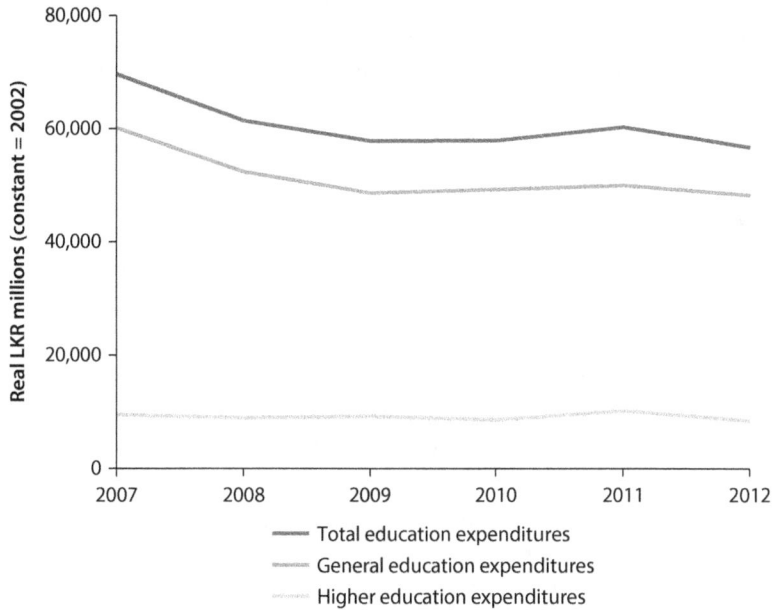

Source: Budget estimates, Ministry of Finance and Planning.

Figure 2.30 Spending on Public Education, an International Perspective

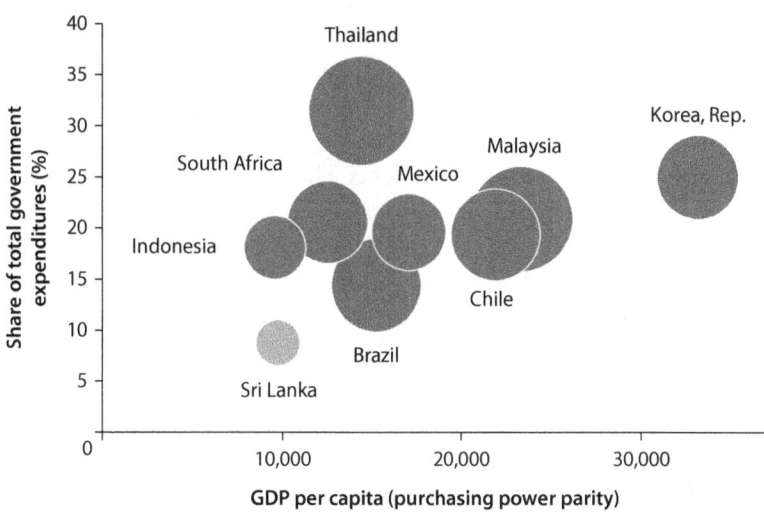

Source: EdStats, 2012/13 or nearest year available.
Note: Bubble size corresponds to public spending as a share of GDP.

Low public spending undermines the effectiveness of Sri Lanka's education system, since government institutions enroll over 95 percent of school and university students. Public investment mainly goes to general and higher education; TVET, which is important for the labor market, gets only about 5 percent. ECD, which is known to have a major impact on subsequent education levels and life chances, receives almost no public resources.

Summary

This chapter reviewed Sri Lanka's educational achievements and challenges. The main findings are as follows:

- *Access to education.* Sri Lanka has made remarkable progress in expanding access to general education (primary and secondary), but access to ECE, TVET, and higher education needs improvement. While there is equitable access to primary and junior secondary education, accessing ECE, senior secondary, and higher education is still not always easy for the poor, those living in the rural and plantation sectors and in less developed provinces, and women. The access gap between poor and rich has been widening.
- *Learning outcomes.* Although learning outcomes in general education have been rising, the results of national examinations and achievement assessments suggest that by international standards, learning levels in Sri Lanka are still low. There are serious disparities in all subjects by province, gender, economic group, and location. The quality and relevance of TVET and higher education programs are also questionable. Empirical studies have found that both student- and school-related factors also influence student learning outcomes.
- *Education and labor market outcomes.* Though the Sri Lankan labor market is characterized by low unemployment, the informal economy is large and underemployment is relatively high. A special concern is the magnitude of youth unemployment, the low LFPR of women, and high underemployment, especially for women and rural residents. Though earnings increase with education and TVET, there is evidence that the premium for additional years of education has been declining over time—perhaps because of the mismatch between the skills in demand and the education of the workforce. Sri Lanka's inclusive growth and competitiveness are jeopardized by the low skills of its population and the mismatch with labor market needs.

Notes

1. There are four types of government schools: Type 1AB (9 percent of the total), Type 1C (19 percent), Type 2 (37 percent), and Type 3 (35 percent). Type 1AB schools have classes for grades 1–13 or 6–13; they offer all three curriculum streams for the GCE A-level courses (arts, commerce, and science). Type 1C also has classes up to grade 13, but only for two streams (arts and commerce). Type 2 schools offer classes only up to grade 11 in preparation for GCE O-level examinations, and Type 3 has classes only up to grades 5 or 8.

2. In 2012/13 the plantation sector accounted for 4.4 percent of the country's population, and the rural sector for 77.3 percent (World Bank 2016a).
3. The definitions used here are as follows. Primary education completion: Proportion of population aged 15–20 who completed primary education. Junior secondary education completion: Proportion of population aged 18–23 who completed junior secondary education. Senior secondary education completion: Proportion of population aged 20–25 who completed senior secondary education.
4. Type 1AB schools span grades 1–13 or 6–13 and offer arts, commerce, and science streams. Type 1C also spans grades 1–13 or 6–13, but only arts and commerce streams at GCE A-level. Type 2 schools span grades 1–11, and Type 3 schools are only primary schools.

References

Arunatilake, N., G. Inchauste, P. Jayawardena, and Y. Savchenko. 2015. "Understanding Labor Markets in Sri Lanka." Background Paper for the Sri Lanka Systematic Country Diagnostic. World Bank, Washington, DC.

Aturupane, H., P. Glewwe, and S. Wisniewski. 2013. "The Impact of School Quality, Socioeconomic Factors, and Child Health on Students' Academic Performance: Evidence from Sri Lankan Primary Schools." *Education Economics* 21 (1): 2–37.

Aturupane, H., Y. Savchenko, M. Shojo, and K. Larsen. 2014. "Sri Lanka: Investment in Human Capital." South Asia Human Development Unit Discussion Paper Series 69, World Bank, Washington, DC.

Dundar, H., B. Millot, Y. Savchenko, T.A. Piyasiri, and H. Aturupane. 2014. *Building the Skills for Economic Growth and Competitiveness in Sri Lanka.* Washington, DC: World Bank.

Dutz, M. A., and S. D. O'Connell. 2013. "Productivity, Innovation and Growth in Sri Lanka: An Empirical Investigation." World Bank Policy Research Working Paper 6354, World Bank, Washington, DC.

MOE (Ministry of Education). 2013. *School Census.* Various Years. Colombo: Ministry of Education.

Mullis, I. V. S., M. O. Martin, and P. Foy. 2008. *TIMSS 2007 International Mathematics Report: Findings from IEA's Trends in International Mathematics and Science Study at the Fourth and Eighth Grades.* Chestnut Hill, MA: TIMSS & PIRLS International Study Center.

NEREC (National Education Research and Evaluation Centre). 2007. *National Assessment of Achievement of Grade 4 Students in Sri Lanka.* Colombo: NEREC.

———. 2008. *National Assessment of Achievement of Grade 8 Students in Sri Lanka.* Colombo: NEREC.

———. 2009. *National Assessment of Achievement of Grade 4 Students in Sri Lanka.* Colombo: NEREC.

———. 2013. *National Assessment of Achievement of Grade 8 Students in Sri Lanka—2012.* Colombo: NEREC.

———. 2014. *National Assessment of Achievement of Grade 4 Students in Sri Lanka—2013.* Colombo: NEREC.

OECD (Organisation for Economic Co-operation and Development). 2007. *No More Failures: Ten Steps to Equity in Education.* Paris: OECD.

World Bank. 2009. *The Towers of Learning: Performance, Peril, and Promise of Higher Education in Sri Lanka*. Washington, DC: World Bank.

———. 2011. *Transforming School Education in Sri Lanka: From Cut Stones to Polished Jewels*. Washington, DC: World Bank.

———. 2014a. *Laying the Foundation for Early Childhood Education in Sri Lanka: Investing Early, Investing Smartly, and Investing for All*. Washington, DC: World Bank.

———. 2014b. *Project Appraisal Document for an Early Childhood Development Project*. Washington, DC: World Bank.

———. 2016a. *Poverty and Welfare in Sri Lanka: Recent Progress and Remaining Challenges*. Washington, DC: World Bank.

———. 2016b. *Sri Lanka: A Systematic Country Diagnostic—Ending Poverty and Promoting Shared Prosperity*. Washington, DC: World Bank.

———. Forthcoming. *Family Background, School Choice and Students' Academic Performance: Evidence from Sri Lanka*. Washington, DC: World Bank.

CHAPTER 3

Early Childhood Development: A Missed Opportunity

Introduction

Among the benefits of early childhood development (ECD) programs are better health and nutritional status, acquisition of socioemotional skills, cognitive development, accumulation of more human capital, and greater productivity in adult years. Attention in a child's early years reduces the negative effects that can result from poor nutrition and reduced cognitive and socioemotional development due to a lack of stimulation and early learning opportunities.

Investment in ECD can enhance both equity and efficiency. The efficiency perspective is obvious: the costs of ECD are generally modest, and the returns high. Providing early learning and development opportunities has been found to improve learning outcomes in terms of basic literacy and numeracy, reduce dropouts, and increase school retention (Nadeau et al. 2011). Interventions in early childhood can have higher returns than interventions in later years because returns accrue over more years, and early gains lay a foundation for greater gains later. Where estimates exist, returns on investment in ECD range from 7 to 16 percent—higher in many contexts than returns on investment in education and job training.

There is substantial evidence that children from poorer households have lower cognitive development than those from richer households (Alderman 2011; Nadeau et al. 2011). Since ECD programs foster school readiness, which makes the transition of children into new learning environments smoother and thus leads to better performance in school and higher employability later in life, they can reduce the gaps in cognitive development between children from different socioeconomic backgrounds and contribute to greater equity. Children who miss out on early opportunities to build a foundation for cognitive, social, and emotional development fall behind and drop out of school earlier.

The range of ECD interventions include combinations of activities for the child, caregivers, and communities. They may include home-based visits involving caregivers and children younger than 2 years and through center-based preschool programs or programs delivered through general schools. These programs may include sub-interventions related to health and nutrition, water and sanitation, parental education on child-rearing practices, cognitive stimulation, and child protection.

Because its ECD sector is just emerging, Sri Lanka is forgoing the substantial benefits that such investment could provide. This chapter examines how ECD programs are run, how they are performing, barriers to the delivery of ECD services, and policy options to address the barriers.

Overview of Early Childhood Development in Sri Lanka

Access to Early Childhood Development

Enrollment in ECD programs in Sri Lanka is not universal (table 3.1). Only 65 percent of 3–4-year-old children are enrolled in center-based preschool programs, although 95 percent of 5-year-olds are enrolled either in an early childhood center or are in school.[1] Thus, 76 percent of 3–5-year-olds are in some form of learning program—preschool or the entry grade in basic education. Precluded from attending primary school, only 50 percent of children aged 3–5 attend a preschool program. Parents are equally likely to send boys and girls to preschool.

Income and location are the key determinants of enrollment, although cultural beliefs related to age also matter (figure 3.1). Only 39 percent of 3–4-year-olds in the poorest quintile are enrolled in a preschool program, compared to 56 percent in the richest quintile. Similarly, the enrollment rate is 59 percent in urban areas but only 50 percent in rural areas and 49 percent on plantations. Across quintiles, ECD enrollment increases with the age of the child: for 5-year-olds there is little difference between enrollment of the poorest and the richest. The dominant norm seems to be to send 5-year-olds to school.

Preschool attendance varies considerably by province. For example, there is a 22 percentage point difference in the ECD net enrollment rate (NER) between Sabaragamuwa and Western provinces. Everywhere in Sri Lanka households headed by women do slightly better than those headed by men in terms of ECD enrollment for their children.

Table 3.1 Enrollment of 3- to 5-Year-Olds in Preschool or School

Age	Total	Preschool	School and other educational activity	Share in preschool/school (%)
3	361,960	162,405	130	45
4	363,564	314,701	99	87
5	362,156	74,170	270,232	95
Total	1,087,680	551,276	270,461	76

Source: Census 2012.

Figure 3.1 Early Childhood Development Net Enrollment Rates Disaggregated, 2012–13

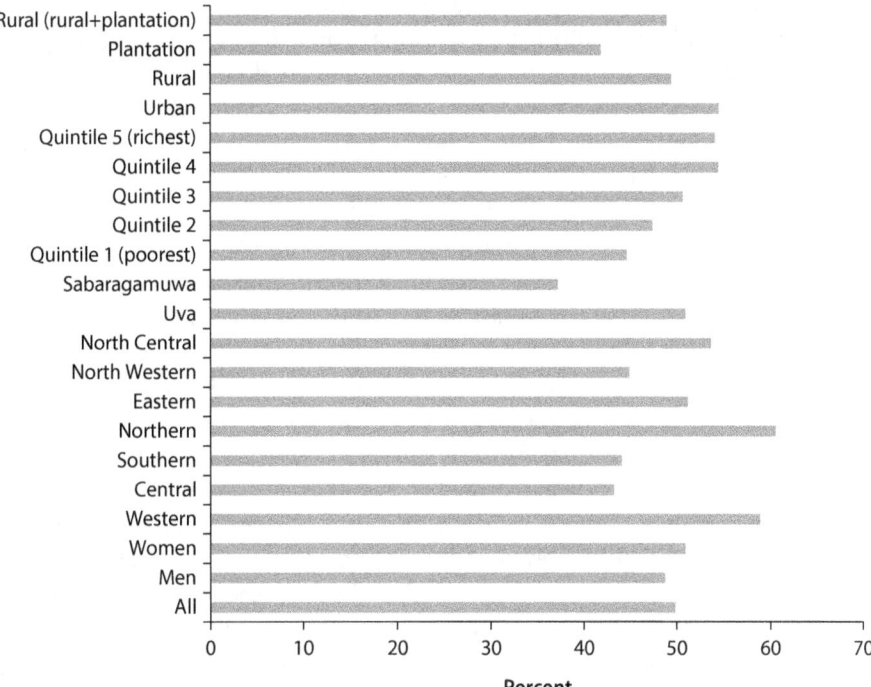

Source: HIES 2012/13 data.

Parental understanding of the need for ECD is not widespread. Anecdotal evidence and interviews with parents suggest that most consider the age of 3 too young for children to be away from home. Moreover, in addition to cultural norms and household wealth, other factors that affect enrollment in preschool may be (a) distance to centers on plantations and in poor areas, (b) belonging to an ethnic or linguistic minority, (c) being poor in otherwise advanced regions, and (d) children's disabilities. On the other hand, parents may want to send children to ECD programs to prepare them for school.

While there is no universally accepted age for early learning programs, ages 2–3 are considered critical in terms of brain development and acquisition of cognitive and socioeconomic skills. That being the case, raising parental awareness of the importance of providing early cognitive stimulation and care will be important for pushing up demand for ECD services.

Regulatory Framework

In recent decades, successive Sri Lankan governments have not only had as an objective broad-based equitable economic growth; they have also been aware that human capital is a major driver of such growth. Consequently, early childhood care and education have been recognized as important for achieving

Sri Lanka's human capital and equity objectives. Various policy and plan documents also situate ECD in an integrated, multisectoral context, factoring in inputs from health and nutrition (including the health and well-being of pregnant and lactating mothers), school education, and children's affairs.

In 2004, the cabinet approved the comprehensive draft National Policy on Early Childhood Care and Education, formulated by the then–Ministry of Child Development and Women's Affairs, but it has never been enacted into law. Nevertheless, since then, the policy (see box 3.1) has structured the country's ECD activities. The National Child Protection Authority, established in 1998, is mandated to formulate child protection laws and coordinate and monitor the prevention of child abuse. The Ministries of Health and Education are responsible for formulating and applying policies related to health, nutrition, and the care and educational development of children in their early years (0–2 years for health; 6 years and older for education).

The policies and provisions for early childhood education (ECE) and health constitute an unevenly developed regulatory structure. Analysis of Sri Lanka's ECD policies and provisions using the World Bank Systems Approach for Better Education Results (SABER) revealed that (a) health, nutrition, social, and child protection policies are relatively advanced; and (b) policies on ECE are at best just emerging. The policies themselves, which cover the entire nation, envisage equity; but ECE financing, quality standards, intersectoral coordination, and data availability are still at an emergent stage (World Bank 2014).

How ECD is to be implemented has not been made clear. The policy proposes that the Ministry of Women and Child Affairs (MWCA) take the lead role with support from the Ministry of Education. In practice, there is neither a consensus nor clarity on this among key players. There is also a lack of clarity about its administration, decentralization, and mechanisms for engaging with the private sector.

Box 3.1 Sri Lanka's National Policy of Early Childhood Care and Education, 2004

- Articulates a holistic and integrated vision for early childhood development (ECD) in Sri Lanka
- Inclusive in its approach to children with special needs
- Provides some clarity on the responsibilities of central, divisional, and local government actors and agencies
- Articulates the relationship between identified stakeholders
- Aims to mobilize resources for ECD
- Promotes the role of parents, caregivers, and the community in child development, and promotes support for their capacity to do so
- Covers home-based ECD activities, day-care facilities, and preschools.

Source: World Bank 2014.

While the 2004 policy acknowledges a role for the private sector, it does not propose any mechanisms for regulation or quality assurance in the oversight of service delivery or child development outcomes.

There is also a lack of coherence about how the center and the provinces are to apply the policy. The 13th Amendment to the Constitution assigns primary responsibility to the provincial councils (PCs), especially for management of preschools. The policy also proposes coordination committees at different levels that, along with the MWCA subnational units, do not align with PC management structures.

Supply of Early Childhood Development Services

In Sri Lanka ECD services are largely provided by nonstate entities (figure 3.2). According to the latest data available, there are 17,023 centers in Sri Lanka with 29,341 teachers catering to between 470,000 and 550,000 children. Nearly 84 percent of these are managed by nongovernmental organizations (NGOs) or other private entities, such as temples and churches, and governments manage the other 16 percent, which are concentrated in the North Central, North Western, and Southern provinces.

The typical center is locally run and enrolls a median of 20 children. Apart from a few urban centers that enroll far more, larger centers typically have about 120 children. The government endorses a ratio of 1 professionally trained teacher per 20 children. In districts for which center data are available, the average child:teacher ratio is 21:1 (not factoring in teacher qualifications). Most centers fall within the prescribed ratio, and almost all those that do not have no more than 30 children.

Figure 3.2 Early Childhood Development Centers, by Ownership Type and Province

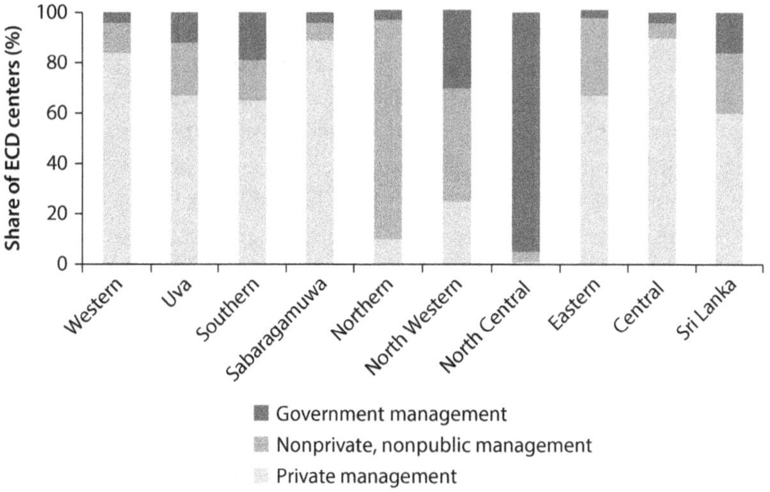

Source: World Bank 2014.

Quality of ECD Services

Sri Lanka must improve ECD quality to ensure that its young children fully benefit. There is substantial evidence that higher-quality preschool programs have a greater and more sustained impact on cognitive outcomes (Yoshikawa et al. 2013)—the effects of low-quality programs are negligible or even detrimental to a child's development (World Bank 2013). Quality can be evaluated by analyzing the quality of inputs, teaching, and outcomes, and by assessing monitoring and quality assurance processes. As will be demonstrated below, there are substantial geographic variations along all these dimensions that are likely to be present even within provinces, with poor households not being able to access high-quality preschool programs.

A significant percentage of ECD centers in Sri Lanka lack adequate resources for teaching and learning, especially materials for children with special needs. Findings from the 2010 National Survey on ECD and the Early Childhood Education Quality Assessment Survey (ECEQAS) 2013 suggest that a large percentage of centers lack such basics as protected drinking water, first-aid boxes, blackboards, toys, and scrap materials.[2] The situation is even worse in facilities for children with special needs. To provide a safe learning environment and stimulate both cognitive and noncognitive development, these basics are crucial.

In many of the ECD centers surveyed, children aged 2 to 7 share the same classrooms, which is unlikely to be optimal for learning. Because the early childhood years are particularly sensitive developmentally, it is important to ensure that young children receive developmentally appropriate educational opportunities. One teacher may not be able to adequately address the different developmental needs of 20 students if there is too much variation in their ages. This aspect of ECD center quality needs to be regulated.

The average child-teacher ratio in Sri Lanka, 21:1, is close to the norm of 20 recommended in the national *Guidelines for Child Development Centers* (MCDWA 2006). Quality interaction with the teacher is particularly important for a young child. The ability of the teacher to devote time and attention to each child affects the quality of learning and teaching. The ideal child-teacher ratio depends on such factors as the age of the child (smaller classes benefit younger children more); whether ECD is provided in mixed-age-group settings; and the behavior expected of children in a particular cultural context (Nadeau et al. 2011). Most developed countries have age-specific standards for child-teacher ratios. For instance, in the United States, some states recommend teacher-student ratios of 1:7 to 1:10, depending on the age of the child and the size of the class (NYC 2014). Although this ratio may not be feasible for Sri Lanka due to resource constraints, efforts should be made to reduce the ratio to ensure that children receive the necessary care and education.

Centers on plantations and in rural areas seem to have fewer resources than those in urban areas. While the three sectors track each other quite closely on infrastructure, the plantation and rural sectors are relatively deficient in terms of classroom learning environment and materials (figures 3.3 and 3.4). Plantations

Early Childhood Development: A Missed Opportunity

Figure 3.3 Quality of Preschool Infrastructure, 2013

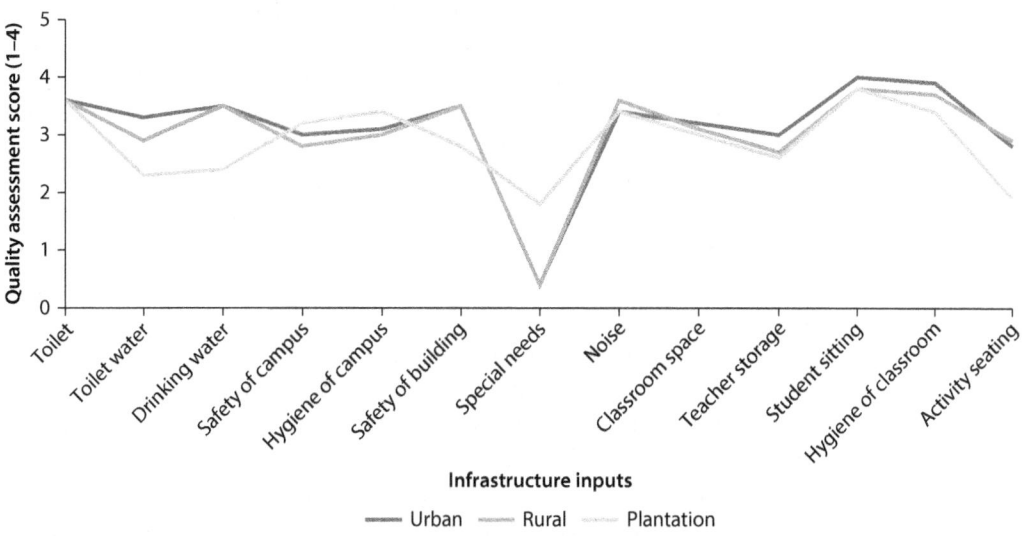

Source: World Bank 2014.

Figure 3.4 The Learning Environment in Sri Lankan Preschools, 2013

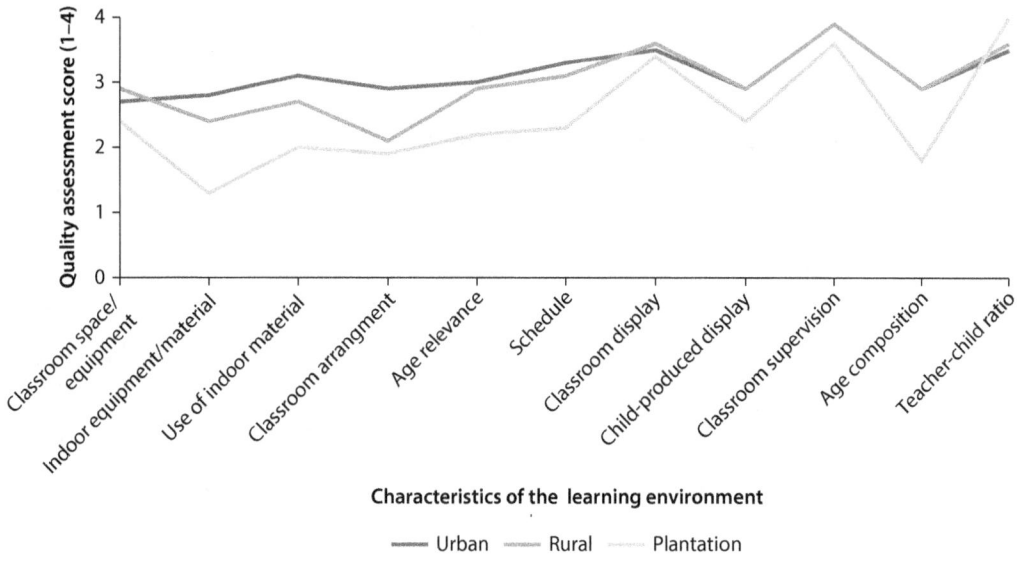

Source: World Bank 2014.

suffer particularly from the poor quality of materials and equipment for indoor use, seating arrangements, and the age composition of students. It is important that classroom seating arrangements take into account age and developmental needs, so that teachers can give each child the necessary attention while ensuring that the needs of other children are also met.

Sri Lanka Education Sector Assessment • http://dx.doi.org/10.1596/978-1-4648-1052-7

Teacher Quality

The quality of early childhood teachers in Sri Lanka is inadequate. Well-qualified educators are the cornerstone of any high-quality ECD system. In Sri Lanka, fewer than half the teachers meet the basic requirements to qualify as ECD professionals—national guidelines require A-level qualifications and at least one year of training in ECD (MCDWA 2006). Only about 43 percent have General Certificate of Education Advanced Level (GCE A-level) qualifications, and only 39 percent have the full year of professional training. Moreover, there is significant variation by province: over half the teachers in Sabaragamuwa meet both qualifications, but fewer than 30 percent in the Northern Province are qualified on either count (see figure 3.5).

Sri Lanka's system for professional development of ECD teachers is also in desperate need of improvement. A professional development system requires a comprehensive system for both preservice training and in-service development and support for ECD education professionals (NAEYC 2014). At present, some 35 ECD training programs are registered with the Children's Secretariat or the Tertiary Vocational Education Commission (TVEC), among them those of a few public entities, such as the Open University, the National Institute of Education (NIE), and the Eastern University, and programs conducted by the MWCA and PCs. However, there is no national authority charged with regulating ECD preservice training and professional development in Sri Lanka.

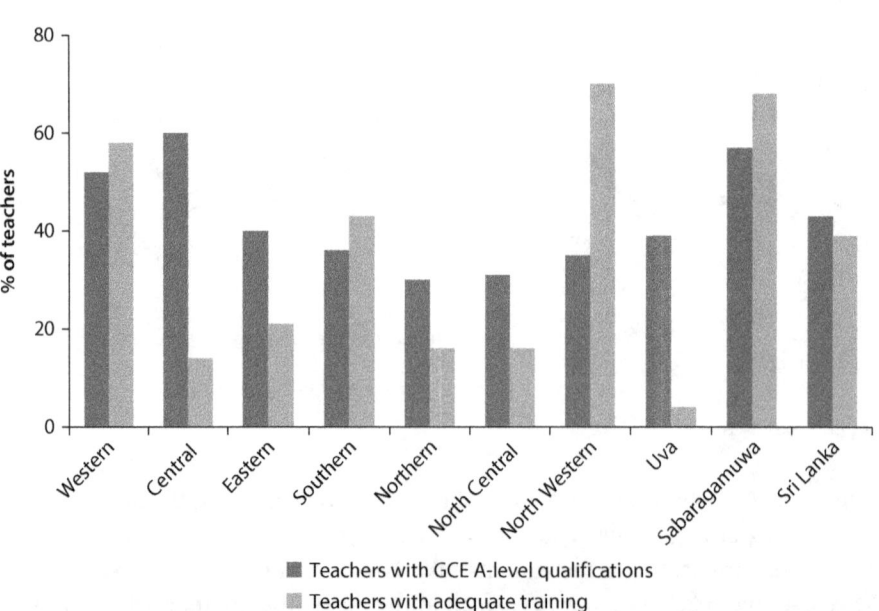

Figure 3.5 Teacher Qualifications, by Province, 2002

Source: World Bank 2014.

The ECE Curriculum

Sri Lanka has not yet adopted a formal curriculum or established early learning standards. Some countries use a common curriculum to maintain quality. Others have chosen to allow an open curriculum to balance the need to adapt to children's different development patterns while ensuring quality. Box 3.2 presents common features of an open curriculum approach. Although Sri Lanka's *Guidelines for Child Development Centers* contain some features of the open approach, they do not set out clear pedagogical guidelines for developmentally appropriate practices. Setting learning standards is an important component of the open approach. It is important for Sri Lanka to set standards for children at each stage: for 3-year olds, 4-year-olds, and 5-year-olds.

Teaching and Learning Processes and Outcomes

ECD centers in Sri Lanka perform well on some teaching and learning processes but are far from satisfactory in developing cognitive skills and catering to students with special needs. The activities of children and teachers related to the personal care, hygiene, and habit formation of the children are satisfactory, but their approaches to facilitating learning by children with special needs and to activities and use of materials to build cognitive skills are inadequate (World Bank 2014).

Sri Lankan children fall below global developmental averages, particularly in analytical thinking and emotional control. Analytical thinking can be viewed as advanced learning that enables individuals to perform complex tasks well. Demonstrating self-control in early years, in particular, has been shown to be important for later learning and success in life (Heckman and Kautz 2012). According to the ECEQAS, Sri Lankan 5-year-olds performed better on simple questions (pattern recognition) than on those that involved sequential thinking, sentence making, and comparisons. They also scored low on patience, emotional

---

Box 3.2 Features of the Open Approach to Early Childhood Education Curricula

UNESCO has identified the following features of an open approach to ECE curricula:

- A statement of principles or values to guide early childhood centers
- A summary of program standards that parents can expect in an early childhood center, e.g., child/staff ratios, teacher qualifications, indoor and outdoor learning environments
- Orientation about content and outputs: an outline of the center's broad goals and the attitudes, dispositions, skills, and knowledge children can be expected to attain at different ages
- Pedagogical guidelines outlining the processes through which children achieve the expected outcomes; they may also propose how educators should support children in their learning.

Source: UNESCO 2004.

adjustment, and emotional expression. As there is no comparison group, it is difficult to say whether ECD services have reduced the negative effects that would have resulted without them.

Quality Assurance

Quality assurance (QA) in ECD programs in Sri Lanka in practice is limited to tracking the minimum quality standards for ECD centers set out in the MWCA guidelines, and the standards are largely used to assess eligibility for center registration. PCs are usually the registration authority for ECD centers, though the urban council, primary development authority, and other entities may also register them (figure 3.6). PCs vary substantially in their registration criteria and processes. Of the 10,000 ECDs for which registration data are available, a quarter are not registered by any entity, usually because they cannot meet the standards, such as those for qualified teachers and such ancillary infrastructure as a playground or boundary wall.

The Cost and Financing of ECD

Sri Lanka spends little on ECD. Through the MWCA it currently allocates US$5.5 million—0.0001 percent of gross domestic product (GDP) and 0.0004 percent of total spending on public education. Although primary through tertiary education is state-funded and therefore free, preschool education is largely funded by NGOs, the private sector, households, and to some extent local governments. While recognition of its importance has been growing, that recognition has not been matched by increased investment in the sector. Sri Lanka has one of the lowest ratios of public spending on ECD in the

Figure 3.6 Registered Early Childhood Development Centers, by District

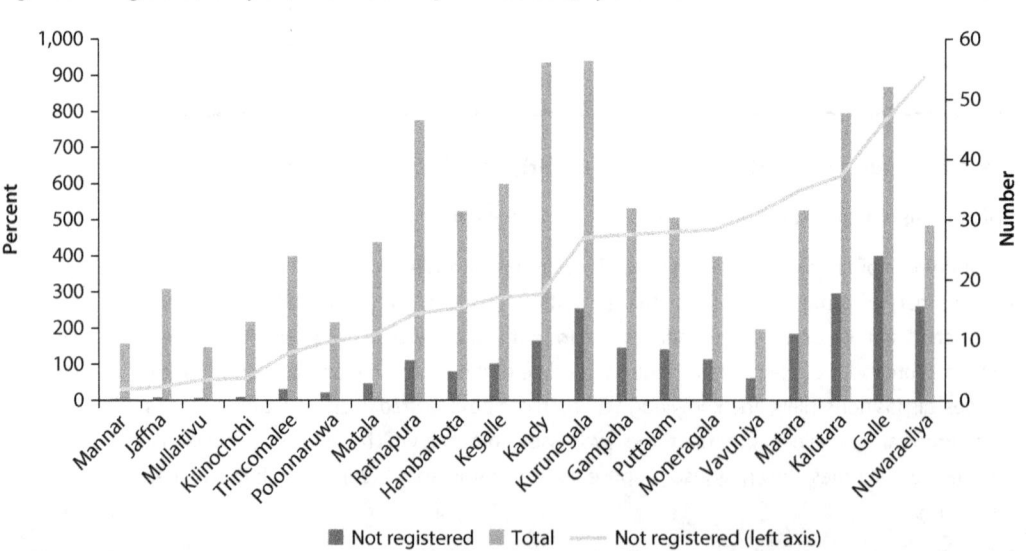

Source: MWCA National Survey 2010.

world—not only lower than its South Asian neighbors but lower even than many very poor Sub-Saharan African countries.

Private spending accounts for most of what is spent on ECD in Sri Lanka. Even poor households typically pay fees of LKR 500–1,000 per child per month on ECD (the cost is much higher for elite private preschools). Those fees are used for rent and teacher salaries, learning materials, and other necessary expenditures. MWCA support is limited to ad hoc nutrition programs, teaching-learning packages distributed in small numbers annually, and some training or recognition of teacher training courses. PCs have very small budgets that must cover thousands of provincial centers, largely to provide specific items like water filters. There is little to spare for enhancing ECD center quality.

Lack of public investment is particularly problematic for areas that are unserved or underserved by ECD services and for the quality of ECD services generally, public and private. Rural and plantation children are the most deprived. Since households in these areas are also likely to be poorer, a private market in ECD services, while effective, will exclude those who most need the services. Lack of access to developmental resources, however, depresses the quality of private ECD because the centers are dependent on household and community contributions to cover both capital and recurrent expenditures.

Raising ECD enrollment from 50 percent of 3- and 4-year-olds to 80 percent would require that the services cover another 250,000 children. Because public capacity is limited, enabling private provision may be the most cost-effective and feasible strategy for expansion. Beyond land, the main costs of establishing a center are for the building, play area, furniture, and equipment. Table 3.2 estimates what it would cost to build enough centers to raise the enrollment rate to 80 percent. This brief analysis focuses only on center-based preschools; there is evidence that these have a positive effect on children from disadvantaged families when alternative options are of low quality or nonexistent (Elango et al. 2015).

Even if ECD enrollment shot up to 80 percent in a single year, the share of GDP required for the additional services would be just 0.0004 percent. To benefit from economies of scale (and using the example of successful centers), the midpoint of 50–60 children can be used as the benchmark for typical center capacity. The costs of the building and ancillary material have been computed using conservative estimates based on current prices to meet minimum center

Table 3.2 Estimated Public Financing Required to Reach 80 Percent Early Childhood Development Enrollment

Number of children to be enrolled	Average center size (assumption)	Number of centers needed	Cost of building (LKR)	Cost of furniture, play area, and equipment (LKR)	Total per center (LKR)	Estimated total cost	
254,000	50–60	4,233	400,000	200,000	600,000	LKR 2.6 billion	(US$19 million)
254,000	30–40	6,350	300,000	200,000	500,000	LKR 3.17 billion	(US$ 24.5 million)

Source: World Bank Staff estimates.

quality standards. These estimates can be considered a lower bound in terms of assumptions used to derive the estimates; centers may be smaller or larger, may include day-care sections, and may need subsidies for teacher training.

Lessons from International Experience

A great deal of international experience is now available that can offer Sri Lanka lessons about outcomes targeted, target beneficiaries and criteria, location and types of services offered, intensity of intervention and delivery mode, program reach and scale, and funding sources and financial allocation mechanisms.

Intensive Small-Scale Programs for At-Risk Children

The HighScope Perry Preschool Project in the United States targeted low-income 3- and 4-year-olds. Children participated in a half-day program for one to two years, taught by certified teachers who also made weekly 90-minute home visits with mother and child. Participating children performed better on cognitive and language tests at age 7; on school achievement tests at ages 9, 10, and 14; and on literacy tests at ages 19 and 27. As adults, those who had participated in the programs also had higher median incomes and were more likely to be employed as adults (Belfield et al. 2006).

The Carolina Abecedarian Program in the United States assigned infants from high-risk, low-income families to very intensive childhood interventions, including full-time day care (8 hours), with an educational curriculum from infancy to the point of school entry. Children in the program were less likely to repeat grades and were almost four times as likely to have earned college degrees (Campbell et al. 2012).

Adaptable Large-Scale Programs

Head Start and Early Head Start in the United States are comprehensive, large-scale programs for children aged 3–5 that incorporate early childhood education, development, health, and nutrition services. Local programs could opt for home- or center-based delivery or a combination of both. Although how the program is implemented can vary considerably over time and sites, all versions must meet specific performance standards, and the federal government assesses compliance every three years. Several studies have found positive, long-lasting effects of Head Start for participating children, as documented by test scores, high school completion rates, and college attendance (Deming 2009).

Comprehensive Program

The ECD Program in the Philippines was designed to be both intensive and comprehensive. Its overarching goal is to improve the survival and developmental potential of children, particularly the most vulnerable and disadvantaged, by (a) minimizing risks to the health of very young children; (b) contributing to the knowledge of parents and the community about child development and encouraging their active involvement in the program; (c) advocating for child-friendly policies and legislation; (d) improving the abilities and attitudes of providers of child-related services; and (e) mobilizing resources and establishing viable financing mechanisms for ECD projects.

Positive results were documented on children's cognitive, motor, language, and social development skills and their short-term nutritional status. Children in treatment areas also showed substantial improvement in all seven domains of child development compared to children in control areas. The study also documented that the duration of participation increased program impact, with more impact found for participation longer than 12 months. Finally, the impact was larger for children under age 4 (Armecin et al. 2006).

Community-Based Program
The Uganda Nutrition and Early Childhood Program provided community-based grants for food security and ECD programs, organized parish child health fairs every six months, and supported community activities to promote growth. Positive effects included improved nutritional status of children younger than 1, better child-care practices, and, with respect to cognitive outcomes, greater facility with numbers. However, the program design was neither intensive nor comprehensive, which may have limited its impact (Alderman 2007).

Mixed Home-Based and Center-Based Program
The Turkish Early Enrichment Project offered an optimal combination of ECD through preschool centers and home-based interventions to promote the development of socioeconomically disadvantaged children from low-income neighborhoods in Istanbul. Mothers attended group meetings where they were trained in promoting child language development and problem-solving skills. Ten years later, children participating were 30 percent more likely to be in school and had higher grades and more self-confidence.

Parenting Program
The Jamaica Program on Early Development provided nutritional supplements or psychological stimulation or both to a group of stunted children aged 9 to 24 months. The psychological stimulation consisted of one-hour weekly home visits by a health worker to improve mother-child interaction using play techniques, homemade toys, and a semistructured curriculum. Two years after the program ended, follow-up surveys showed large positive effects on child development, especially for children who had received both interventions (Powell et al. 2004).

Area-Based Program
Chile's Know Your Child Program targeted rural and indigenous mothers below the poverty line in areas that lack ECD centers. Services included early stimulation of the child, parent education and support, nutrition services, social protection, preschool education, early intervention services for children with developmental delays or disabilities, and community activities.

The program had positive effects on the language development of children between 2 and 5 years old. Participating children also had higher cognitive scores in first grade (Vegas and Santibanez 2010).

Conclusion and Policy Options

The adverse effects of poor development in early childhood are long-lasting, with negative effects on health, productivity, and general well-being when children reach adulthood. For poor children, the detrimental effects can be particularly severe. Experience around the world has shown that ECD programs can improve child outcomes and reduce achievement gaps between population groups. They also build school readiness and lay the foundation for greater acquisition of human capital and higher returns to education and training.

The preschool sector emerging in Sri Lanka is largely private. Though official policy recognizes that ECE and proper development of children in the early years matter for lifelong productivity, health, and well-being, the supply and quality of ECD services in Sri Lanka have been dependent on nonstate resources and incentives; the state's role has mainly been regulatory, and even that has lacked clarity. As a result of minimal public provision and oversight, there is considerable geographic variation in the quantity and quality of ECD services, reflecting the economic status of those affected.

In order to expand access to quality ECD services, there are a number of key policy actions to be completed within the next 1–2 years, and others within 5 years. What needs to be done is to (a) clarify the regulatory structure, especially administration, at the center, provincial, and other levels of government; (b) gain a consensus among affected departments and structure effective mechanisms for their coordination; (c) raise public spending on ECD to bring in more children from poor households, bring existing ECD centers up to minimum quality standards, and expand access through public-private partnerships (PPPs) in areas with few centers; (d) draw up plans for the professional development of instructional staff; (e) define and monitor quality standards for ECD centers, including standards for child developmental outcomes; (f) establish a framework for engaging with the nonstate sector; and (g) regularly complete data on ECD provision in Sri Lanka (see table 3.3).

Table 3.3 How to Achieve Early Childhood Development Program Goals

Common ECD program features	Sri Lankan ECD context	Interventions
Outcomes targeted	Cognitive, socioemotional, behavioral, health (limited)	Parenting skills
Target beneficiaries	3–5-year-old children	Parents of 0–5 year olds, community
Targeting criteria	Children in ECD centers	Center and home-based intervention
Location of services	Center-based (non-home)	

table continues next page

Table 3.3 How to Achieve Early Childhood Development Program Goals *(continued)*

Common ECD program features	Sri Lankan ECD context	Interventions
Types of services offered	Educational, nutrition (limited)	School readiness, health
Intensity of intervention	4–5 hours a day, 5 days a week	
Delivery mode	Small or large group (20–120 children)	
Program reach	National (but not universal)	Universal
Funding sources	Largely private, limited public, domestic and international donors	Public, public-private partnerships, donor funds
Financing mechanism	Government budget line, household and community resources	Matching funds, vouchers, grants, conditional cash transfers, means-targeted support, earmarked budget/tax revenues, in-kind support through land/capital subsidies
Regulatory framework	National Policy (2004), National Child Protection Act (1998)	Interministerial coordination with clarity on responsibilities, quality assurance framework, evidence-based guidance for policy, investment, and interventions and financial allocations

Source: Adapted from Vegas and Santibanez 2010.

Unless more resources are directed to ECD, access, equity, and quality are unlikely to improve fast enough to have effects beyond the marginal. In addition to expanding access, public resources could be channeled to entities that assess the quality of ECD services, such as curriculum development agencies, teacher professional development systems, and quality assurance mechanisms. Eventually, public finance might be enhanced to a level that is adequate and sustainable in the long run.

Notes

1. However, in Sri Lanka the starting age for grade 1 is officially 6.
2. ECEQAS, the Early Childhood Education Quality Assessment Survey, was conducted in 2013 as part of the study for World Bank 2014.

References

Alderman, H. 2007. "Improving Nutrition through Community Growth Promotion: Longitudinal Study of the Nutrition and Early Childhood Development Program in Uganda." *World Development* 35 (8): 1376–89.

———. 2011. *No Small Matter: The Impact of Poverty, Shocks, and Human Capital Investments on Early Childhood Development.* Washington, DC: World Bank.

Armecin, G., J.R. Behrman, P. Duazo, S. Ghuman, S. Gultiano, E.M. King, and N. Lee. 2006. "Early Childhood Development through an Integrated Program: Evidence from the Philippines." World Bank Policy Research Working Paper 3922, World Bank, Washington, DC.

Belfield, C. R., M. Nores, W. S. Barnett, and L. Schweinhart. 2006. "The High/Scope Perry Preschool Program: Cost-Benefit Analysis Using Data from the Age-40 Follow-Up." *Journal of Human Resources* 41 (1): 162–90.

Campbell, F. A., E. P. Pungello, M. Burchinal, K. Kainz, Y. Pan, B. H. Wasik, and C. T. Ramey. 2012. "Adult Outcomes as a Function of an Early Childhood Educational Program: An Abecedarian Project Follow-Up." *Developmental Psychology* 48 (4): 1033–43.

Deming, D. 2009. "Early Childhood Intervention and Life-Cycle Skill Development: Evidence from Head Start." *American Economic Journal: Applied Economics* 1 (3): 111–34.

Elango, S., J. L. Garcia, J. J. Heckman, and A. Hojman. 2015. "Early Childhood Education." NBER Research Working Paper 21766, National Bureau of Economic Research, Cambridge, MA.

Heckman, J. J., and T. Kautz. 2012. "Hard Evidence on Soft Skills." *Labor Economics* 19 (4): 451–64.

MCDWA (Ministry of Child Development and Women's Affairs). 2006. *Guidelines for Child Development Centers*. Colombo: MCDWA.

NAEYC (National Association for the Education of Young Children). 2014. *What Is Professional Development in Early Childhood Education?* Washington, DC: NAEYC.

Nadeau, S., N. Kataoka, A. Valerio, A. J. Neumann, and L. L. Elder. 2011. *Investing in Young Children: An Early Childhood Development Guide for Policy Dialogue and Project Preparation*. Washington, DC: World Bank.

NYC (New York State Council on Children and Families). 2014. *Comparison of Early Childhood Program Standards*. Albany: NYC.

Powell, C., H. Baker-Henningham, S. Walker, J. Gernay, and S. Grantham-McGregor. 2004. "Feasibility of Integrating Early Stimulation into Primary Care for Undernourished Jamaican Children: Cluster Randomized Control Trial." *British Journal of Medicine* 329: 89.

UNESCO (United Nations Educational, Scientific, and Cultural Organization). 2004. "Curriculum in Early Childhood Care and Education." Policy Brief 26, UNESCO, Paris.

Vegas, E., and L. Santibanez. 2010. *The Promise of Early Childhood Development in Latin America and the Caribbean*. Washington, DC: World Bank.

World Bank. 2013. *What Matters Most for Early Childhood Development: A Framework Paper*. Washington, DC: World Bank.

———. 2014. *Laying the Foundation for Early Childhood Education in Sri Lanka: Investing Early, Investing Smartly, and Investing for All*. Washington, DC: World Bank.

Yoshikawa, H., C. Weiland, J. Brooks-Gunn, M. R. Burchinal, L. M. Espinosa, W. T. Gomley, J. Ludwig, K. A. Magnuson, D. Phillips, and M. J. Zaslow. 2013. *Investing in Our Future: The Evidence Base on Preschool Education*. Ann Arbor, MI: Society for Research in Early Child Development and Foundation for Child Development.

CHAPTER 4

Primary and Secondary Education: The Quality Challenge

Introduction

As discussed in chapter 2, Sri Lanka has made impressive progress in getting children into primary and secondary school and having them complete up to 10 years of schooling. Universal access to primary education has been achieved, and the net enrollment rate (NER) for secondary education—84 percent in 2014—is higher than in Thailand (79 percent) or Malaysia (69 percent), and also higher than the middle-income country average (66 percent). Almost all students complete primary school, and close to 60 percent complete junior secondary. The gains in expanding access now need to be accompanied by commensurate improvements in the quality of education and learning.

In primary and secondary education, the main objective should clearly be to bring the knowledge and skills of Sri Lankan students to par with those of upper-middle- and high-income countries. As discussed in chapter 3, increasing access to and the quality of early childhood education (ECE) will help, but international experience suggests that other critical factors also affect the quality of primary and secondary education, among them (a) the quality of teachers; (b) capacity to monitor quality improvements; (c) governance and accountability; and (d) the cost and financing of schooling.

This chapter looks at each of these critical factors, identifying weaknesses and proposing policy options to address them. It first describes the different types of school and curriculum streams offered to Sri Lankan students and identifies the shortcomings of the current system. It then reviews the management and performance of Sri Lanka's public school teachers; the aim is to delineate critical issues and propose options for addressing them, informed by rigorous international evaluations of interventions to improve teacher effectiveness. The fourth section discusses the current status of Sri Lanka's assessment system and areas for improvement, presenting practices and options from other countries. The fifth section examines how to improve governance and accountability.

The sixth section looks at the cost and financing of schooling, with a special focus on equity. The chapter concludes by summarizing the findings.

Education Offerings

Sri Lanka has four types of government schools that cover different grades and offer different curriculum streams (table 4.1): (a) Type 1AB schools (9 percent of the total), which either cover the full primary and secondary cycle (grades 1–13) or secondary education alone (grades 6–13) and offer all three curriculum streams for the General Certificate of Education Advanced Level (GCE A-level) courses (arts, commerce, and science); (b) Type 1C schools (19 percent of the total), which also span grades 1–13 or 6–13 but offer only GCE A-level arts and commerce; (c) Type 2 schools (37 percent of the total), which only go up to grade 11 and prepare students for General Certificate of Education Ordinary Level (GCE O-level) examinations; and (d) Type 3 schools (35 percent of the total), which go up only to grade 5 or 8. Most 1AB schools are in cities and towns; Types 1C and 2 are mainly in semi-urban and rural areas; and Type 3 are mostly in rural areas.[1]

As might be expected, there are substantial differences in learning outcomes associated with school characteristics. For instance, the mean score in mathematics, as measured by the 2012 National Assessment for grade 8, is 61 for Type 1AB schools, 41 for Type 1C, and 38 for Type 2. In science, the mean score is 51 for Type 1AB, 33 for Type 1C, and 29 for Type 2 schools. Schools in urban areas tend to have higher scores than those in rural areas (see chapter 2).

This organizational structure clearly limits the opportunities offered to children. Those living in rural areas are learning less as early as grade 8. Although this may be partly explained by differences in social background, some may also be due to lower school quality. Furthermore, these children have to move to semi-urban or urban areas to complete senior secondary education and then access higher education. Even for children living in urban areas, there are limits to their choices. Type AB schools, which enroll less than 40 percent of students, are the only ones offering all education streams, including the science stream. Type 1C schools, which enroll another 25 percent, only offer arts and commerce streams; their students cannot aspire to become scientists, doctors, or engineers. Programs where children can study subjects in English are only offered in about 30 percent of senior secondary schools.

Table 4.1 Government Schools, Enrollment, and Teachers, by School Type, 2013

	Number of schools	Number of students	Number of teachers
Type 1AB	868	1,521,983	69,837
Type 1C	1,910	1,141,383	64,492
Type 2	3,730	862,983	64,162
Type 3	3,504	510,808	28,492
Total	10,012	4,037,157	226,983

Source: MOE 2013.

The result of this limitation in offerings is a distribution of high school graduates highly skewed toward the arts, humanities, and social sciences. This largely determines what will be, later on, the distribution of students in higher education by fields of study. As chapter 6 discusses in detail, this has implications for the labor market outcomes of graduates and for Sri Lanka's growth potential. As growth and technological change challenge the structures of economies, labor markets worldwide increasingly value individuals with scientific and mathematical backgrounds and with language abilities that facilitate effective communication and access to the global community. Students with those skills will be preferred for jobs that pay more, enhancing their well-being.

The Government of Sri Lanka recognizes that this organizational structure is not only inequitable; it is detrimental for the future of the country. It is seeking to expand senior secondary education opportunities for rural students. About 1,000 senior secondary schools throughout the country are being upgraded to offer all three GCE A-level streams. Currently, all have the necessary facilities and equipment. In all 1,000 schools, a new technology stream will also be introduced to prepare students for technical and vocational training programs; 250 schools are already offering it. Building up the bilingual education program introduced in recent years, in particular through better teaching materials and more qualified teachers, would also widen the options for students. A major problem, however, is the shortage of teachers willing to work in remote areas. Still, these efforts need to be pursued vigorously because expanding and diversifying opportunities in senior secondary education are critical to improving the performance of the education sector.

In parallel with these efforts to expand opportunities in senior secondary education, Sri Lanka is fine-tuning and upgrading the primary and secondary school curricula. Previous studies have identified a number of areas for improvement, mainly related to the timing and balance of curriculum content; assessment and evaluation strategies; use of technology; teacher instruction manual activities: mismatch between curriculum objectives and the centrally controlled examination system; and better horizontal and vertical integration of the curriculum. In response, the National Institute of Education (NIE) has begun to draft a new curriculum based on the conclusions of these studies.

The objective is to better reflect modern international trends in curriculum practice; effectively disseminate curriculum goals, values, and aims to stakeholders; orient the education system more closely to the world of work; and support schools as the curriculum is upgraded. Major programs already under way are dealing with curriculum rationalization; teacher capacity development programs; research; and building the capacity of NIE.

One aspect that needs particular attention is the ability to enable both cognitive learning and the acquisition of soft, or noncognitive, skills (see box 1.1 for types of these skills). In a modern economy, curriculum is increasingly called upon to forge skills and competencies that support students' personal development. It has been found that success in life and the labor market largely depends on the acquisition of both cognitive and noncognitive skills. As economies develop and diversify, demand for higher-level, especially noncognitive, skills rises. Currently, the curriculum in Sri Lanka is thought to be overloaded but also too narrowly focused on cognitive skills and not enough on noncognitive skills. Schools can build those skills in a variety of ways. For instance, problem-solving skills, a reasoned approach to issues, and creativity can be instilled partly through subjects that are already part of the curriculum. Arranging classrooms so that students can engage in group work can enhance the collaboration and cooperation necessary for teamwork. Child-centered pedagogy that encourages active learning can also help to promote such soft skills as enterprise and initiative.

In updating the curriculum, it would be useful to benchmark it to a few strategically selected, high-performing international education systems, with performance defined in terms of both learning outcomes and soft skills. Changes could be rolled out across the grades and supported by teacher development programs, education resources, and examinations.

Public School Teacher Management in Sri Lanka

Teacher Effectiveness

Any assessment of school system performance would necessarily have to examine the effectiveness of the frontline service delivery agents: teachers, who have been found to be a major determinant of school quality and an important influence on student outcomes, both academic and nonacademic (Hanushek and Rivkin 2006).

A good teacher is someone able to generate growth in student achievement. It is therefore customary to measure teacher effectiveness in terms of value added to student test scores. Teacher effectiveness has been found to vary widely within school districts, and even within schools; it influences the longer-term outcomes of students, as studies for the United States document. A 1-standard-deviation increase in teacher effectiveness (i.e., going from an average teacher to one at the 84th percentile) corresponds to a 0.1- to 0.2-standard-deviation increase in average student test scores over one school year for public primary and secondary school students (see, e.g., Rockoff 2004; Rivkin, Hanushek, and Kain 2005; Aaronson, Barrow, and Sander 2007; Kane, Rockoff, and Staiger 2008; Chetty, Friedman, and Rockoff 2013). There is also evidence that effectiveness persists over time. Over five- and ten-year periods, teacher effectiveness in early years has been significantly correlated with teacher effectiveness in later years (McCaffrey et al. 2009; Goldhaber and Hansen 2013). Having a relatively more effective teacher even for only one school year is positively associated with such outcomes in adulthood as the likelihood of a student going to college, the quality of the college the student attends, and annual earnings (Chetty, Friedman, and Rockoff 2014).

Public School Teachers in Sri Lanka

There is no major difference between provincial and national schools in such teacher characteristics as gender, age, and years of service. As discussed in chapter 2, about 4 percent of public schools are national schools, managed and

Table 4.2 Descriptive Statistics for Public School Teachers

Characteristic	Provincial (1)	National (2)	All (3)
Gender			
Female	0.728	0.708	0.725
Male	0.272	0.292	0.275
Age (completed years)	44	42	44
Years of service (completed years)	16	16	16
Academic qualification			
GCE O/L	0.037	0.023	0.035
GCE A/L	0.502	0.472	0.498
Bachelors	0.442	0.480	0.448
Masters or higher	0.019	0.025	0.020
Professional qualification			
None	0.140	0.103	0.134
Trained teacher certificate—distance-based	0.203	0.061	0.181
Trained teacher certificate—classroom-based	0.214	0.169	0.207
Postgraduate diploma in education	0.266	0.329	0.276
NCOE diploma in teaching	0.150	0.306	0.175
Bachelors in education or higher	0.026	0.032	0.027
N	37,277	194,683	231,960

Source: 2014 school census data from the Ministry of Education.
Note: A/L = advanced level; GCE = General Certificate in Education; NCOE = National Colleges of Education; and O/L = ordinary level.

financed by the Ministry of Education (MOE); the other 96 percent are provincial schools, managed and financed by provincial councils. Table 4.2 reports basic descriptive statistics. There are over 230,000 teachers in the system—84 percent in provincial schools and 16 percent in national ones. Of the total, among both provincial and national teachers, 73 percent are female, aged 44 years on average, and have taught in public schools an average of 16 years. These characteristics are similar between provincial and national school teachers.

In terms of academic qualifications, the vast majority have either a GCE A-level (50 percent) or a bachelor's degree (45 percent). National school teachers tend to be somewhat more academically qualified than provincial ones. They also tend to be more professionally qualified: 62 percent of national school teachers have a postgraduate diploma in education or a diploma in teaching, compared to 40 percent of provincial school teachers. The differences in average academic and professional qualifications are probably due in large part to differences in the requirements to teach in provincial and in national schools.

Teacher Management and Performance in Sri Lanka
Responsibility for Teacher Management

The MOE is responsible for setting service rules for public education employees—principals, teachers, teacher educators, and education administrators.

It is also responsible for executing all aspects of human resource management for national schools. Primary responsibility for general human resource management for provincial schools lies with the provincial departments of education and their zonal and divisional offices.

In 1995, the MOE introduced a single five-tier structure for public school teaching service. Teachers previously in different categories and salary structures were all subsumed within the new structure, which also streamlined eligibility criteria for entry and promotion (Pillay et al. 2015).

The roles and responsibilities of zonal and divisional education officials are not well defined and sufficiently enabled, which may complicate effective human resource management for provincial schools (World Bank 2011). There have been points associated with political cycles when the recruitment, deployment, and promotion of public education employees are thought to have been subject to political influence (Aturupane 2009; IPS 2014; Pillay et al. 2015), which may have benefited less-deserving teachers. Irregularities may also create uncertainty and a sense of unfairness, potentially dampening the interest of higher-caliber prospects in public school teaching, as well as the efforts of incumbent teachers.

Recruitment

Prospects may enter public school teaching through either the provincial councils or the MOE. Recruitment for both is generally based on subject-specific job vacancies. Provincial councils' public service commissions recruit applicants from across the country who have at least a bachelor's degree. Although recruitment is based on academic qualifications, if there are more applicants than vacancies, applicants are subject to a screening test and interview (Pillay et al. 2015). The MOE recruits candidates with GCE A-level qualifications to become trainee teachers; they then undergo a three-year diploma in teaching program at a National College of Education (NCOE). Holders of this diploma can be assigned to national or provincial schools anywhere in the country (Balasooriya 2012; Little, Aturupane, and Shojo 2013). All teachers are on probation for three years and are then made permanent (Pillay et al. 2015).

There have been points when rules related to minimum academic qualifications and subject-specific vacancies were relaxed, which may have undermined the efficiency and effectiveness of teacher recruitment (Pillay et al. 2015). For example, provincial councils at times have recruited individuals with GCE A-level qualifications rather than university degrees to fill critical vacancies in certain subjects or in disadvantaged locations. As a political concession, public sector jobs were also dispensed to university degree holders during periods when the private labor market was weak. At those times, teacher recruitment was based on total vacancies rather than on their subject breakdown, leading to overrecruitment in certain subjects (e.g., arts and social science subjects) and underrecruitment in others (e.g., science, math, English, and computer literacy) (Aturupane 2009; Balasooriya 2012; Pillay et al. 2015).

Deployment

Based on 2014 school census data, public schools generally have adequate numbers of teachers (see figure 4.1), with an average school-level student-teacher ratio of 14:1. The 95th percentile of the distribution is 29:1, which is within the range considered acceptable internationally. However, a sizable number of schools do not have the right mix of teachers. Rural schools (which here include plantation schools) find it especially difficult to attract and retain teachers of English, science, and mathematics (World Bank 2011; Balasooriya 2012). Because of their relative undersupply in the teaching force and better alternative earnings options, teachers of these subjects have significant market power and can secure positions in desirable schools (Balasooriya 2012).

New teachers are required to serve in rural schools for a fixed term, after which they can apply to transfer to other schools. Typically, teachers seek transfers to urban schools or schools near their original residence (Pillay et al. 2015). Deployment rules and practices induce responses from teachers that undermine

Figure 4.1 Densities of School Student-Teacher Ratios

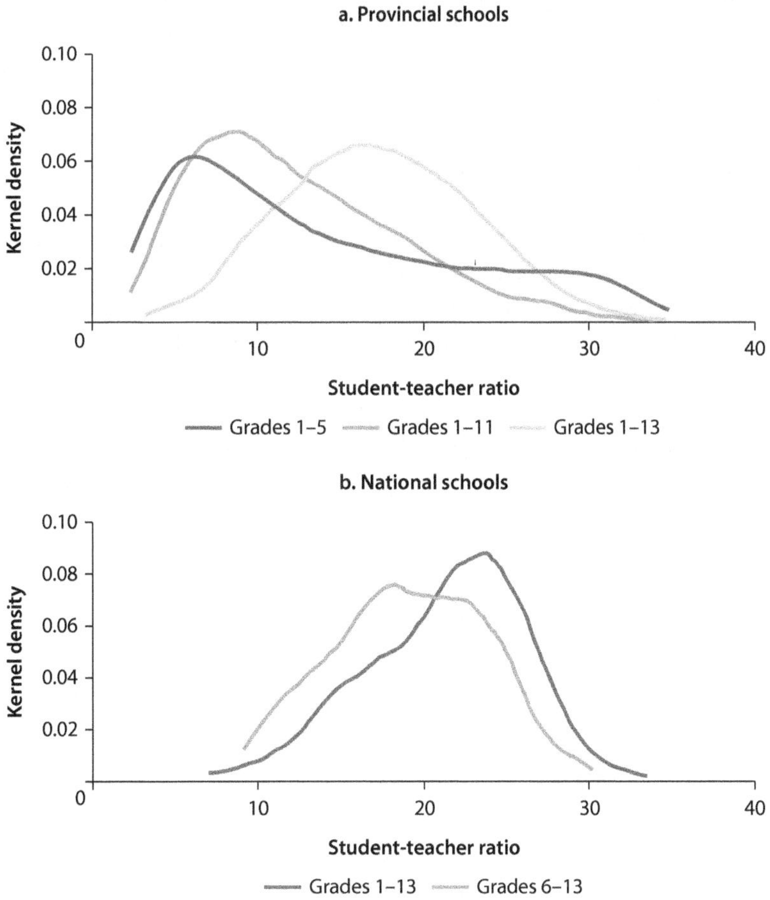

a. Provincial schools

b. National schools

Source: 2014 school census data from the Ministry of Education.

effective teaching and learning in rural schools. New teachers may not have gained minimum teaching proficiency (Wehella and Balasooriya 2014). U.S. studies have found that gains to teacher effectiveness from experience tend to be highest in the early years of teaching (Harris and Sass 2011; Papay and Kraft 2015); thus, the departure of teachers from rural schools after a few years and their replacement with new teachers can have a deleterious effect on student learning. Whether newly recruited or not, teachers assigned to rural schools expend considerable time and effort visiting education administrative offices to push through their transfer applications (IPS 2014). Those who are unsuccessful can become demoralized, with negative effects on their job motivation and effort (Balasooriya 2012).

Training
Preservice Training. Applicants recruited by the MOE with GCE A-level qualifications are usually assigned to schools after they earn NCOE diplomas in teaching, although a small number, those whose GCE A-level z-scores are on average higher than the recruited pool at large, enroll in a bachelor's in education program offered by the University of Colombo. Both the diploma and bachelor's programs cover subject knowledge, pedagogy, and supervised practical teaching experience; but in the diploma program, the entire third year is spent practice teaching in schools (Pillay et al. 2015).

In-Service Training. Incumbent teachers who have not undergone preservice training must obtain training during service. There are two main options: (a) Universities offer a postgraduate diploma in education program via full- or part-time classroom education, and the Open University of Sri Lanka offers the same program via distance education. (b) Teacher training colleges offer a two-year certificate of teacher training program. The NIE offers the postgraduate diploma in education and certificate of teacher training programs through part-time classroom and distance education modes (Pillay et al. 2015).[2]

Table 4.3 reports the distribution of teacher professional qualifications, calculated using 2014 school census data. The patterns are consistent with the eligibility requirements for the various training options: 95 percent of teachers with GCE O-level qualifications have a trained teacher certificate, as do 64 percent of teachers with GCE A-level qualifications; and 30 percent of teachers with GCE A-level qualifications have a diploma in teaching. The majority of teachers with at least a bachelor's degree have a postgraduate diploma in education, but 26 percent of those with a bachelor's degree and 13 percent of those with a master's degree or higher have no pedagogical training. These tend to have become teachers within the last 10 years (figure 4.2).

The effectiveness of training can be undermined by both demand- and supply-side issues. On the demand side, the incentive structure is such that teachers may take training to gain credentials for the purpose of entry or advancement rather than to become more effective teachers—which then feeds back to hollow out training programs. Teachers also face tension between satisfying requirements to

Primary and Secondary Education: The Quality Challenge

Table 4.3 Distribution of Professional and Academic Qualifications of Teachers

	Academic qualification			
Professional qualification	GCE O/L (1)	GCE A/L (2)	Bachelor's (3)	Master's or higher (4)
None	0.024	0.031	0.259	0.127
Trained teacher certificate	0.949	0.644	0.070	0.043
Postgraduate diploma in education	0.011	0.021	0.572	0.530
NCOE diploma in teaching	0.015	0.302	0.051	0.032
Bachelor's in education or higher	0.001	0.002	0.048	0.268
N	8,043	115,404	103,175	4,226

Source: 2014 school census data from the Ministry of Education.
Note: A/L = advanced level; GCE = General Certificate in Education; NCOE = National Colleges of Education; and O/L = ordinary level.

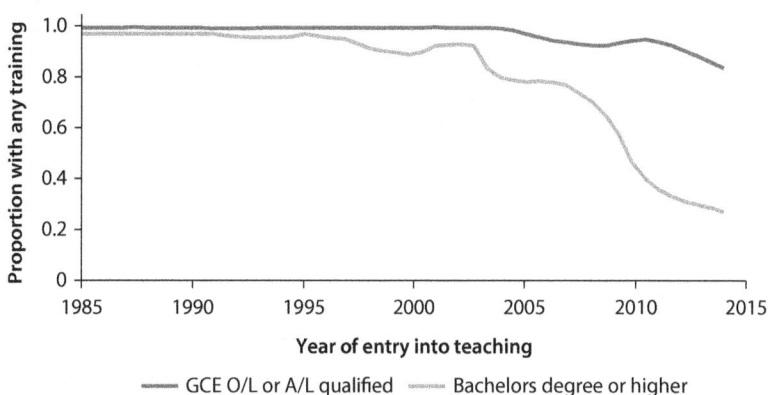

Figure 4.2 Teachers with Any Training and Year of Entry into Teaching, by Academic Qualification

perform their school duties and attending training, which requires authorization for extended leave from school. Though training through part-time classroom or distance education modes helps to relieve this tension, teacher attention and absorption may be impaired by having to perform teaching and other duties alongside training (IPS 2014). Indeed, a U.S. study found that contemporaneous in-service training is at times negatively associated with teacher effectiveness, presumably because training takes teachers away from the classroom or makes teaching additionally burdensome (Harris and Sass 2011).

On the supply side: (a) On average, trainer proficiency and performance are poor. (b) The pressure to expand the amount of training to meet the needs of large numbers of teachers has degraded training quality. (c) The quality of training in part-time classroom and distance education modes is especially low because trainers in these modes are even poorer, and excess enrollment also has negative effects (World Bank 2011; Little, Aturupane, and Shojo 2013; IPS 2014; Pillay et al. 2015).

Career Advancement

Promotion can help to induce effective teaching and school leadership because it confers job status, authority, and autonomy as well as a jump in pay. Leveraging promotion to this end would reward effective teachers by moving them up to senior teacher and principal positions and reward effective principals by promoting them to education administrative positions.

In line with practice across government service, promotion is, however, based on service length in Sri Lanka (along with professional qualifications and satisfactory performance in basic professional bar exams) (MOE 2014). While some U.S. studies have found that teaching experience, from early to late career, is positively associated with teacher effectiveness (see, e.g., Harris and Sass 2011; Wiswall 2013; Papay and Kraft 2015), others suggest that teaching experience seems to explain only a small fraction of the variation in teacher effectiveness (Goldhaber and Hansen 2013; Jackson, Rockoff, and Staiger 2014).

Accountability

Although, in principle, promotion, school inspections, teacher performance appraisal, and dismissal can encourage better teacher performance, they are not designed or executed to that end in Sri Lanka. Promotion is linked to seniority rather than effective teaching and school leadership (World Bank 2011). School inspections, performed by zonal and divisional education officials, are undermined by a lack of adequate time and funds for officials to visit schools, particularly schools distant from education administrative offices (IPS 2014). Every year, school principals appraise teacher performance, using standardized forms and following written guidelines provided by the MOE and provincial departments of education, but for the vast majority of teachers the exercise is considered perfunctory. Teachers mainly cease to teach because of retirement; dismissals are exceedingly rare. For example, at most a handful of teachers were dismissed in 2013 and 2014, and the grounds were not directly related to teaching performance.

There is little evidence from Sri Lanka that monitoring and accountability policies and practices related to teacher and student behavior and outcomes are effective. However, Aturupane, Glewwe, and colleagues (2014) evaluated the Program for School Improvement (PSI), an intervention to enhance school autonomy and parental engagement with schools, the intent being to give teachers and principals incentives to be more effective. Randomizing the assignment of the intervention across sample schools, the study found short-term positive effects on the test scores of grade 4 students. But the channels through which the effects materialized did not appear to run through teachers—the study found no effects on various measures of teacher management by principals or teacher behavior.[3]

Compensation

Low pay diminishes job satisfaction and attractiveness. As a result, it can discourage higher-caliber prospects and more effective incumbent teachers, who might have better alternative earnings opportunities, from joining or staying in teaching;

undermine the motivation and effort of those who decide to join or stay; and encourage teachers to take up side jobs, such as private tutoring, or seek rents to supplement pay.

The basic pay scale for public school teachers fits within the country's basic pay scale for public sector employees: a single salary structure, based on service grade and years of service. In addition to basic pay, there are such standard cash benefits as a flat-rate cost of living adjustment allowance and, occasionally, a percentage special allowance, as in 2011, when a special allowance of 5 percent of basic pay was introduced (Ministry of Public Administration and Home Affairs 2010). There is no pay incentive linked to teacher effectiveness. Both basic pay and allowances are revised periodically by government-appointed pay commissions.

Public school teachers seem to be paid less in Sri Lanka than in other countries in South and Southeast Asia. Average pay is equal to national per capita income, while in other South Asian countries teacher salaries are two to three times national per capita income (Aturupane, Savchenko et al. 2014; Dundar et al. 2014).

The pay scale also seems to be compressed relative to other countries (World Bank 2011), dampening any potential incentive effect of promotion on teacher performance derived from higher pay. Candidates with GCE A-level qualifications enter service at the lowest grade in the teacher pay scale. Moving from this grade to the highest can take about two decades, and still results in less than a doubling of pay, even accounting for expected future revisions in pay scales based on past revisions (MOE 2014).

Subject Deficiencies

One symptom of poor teacher management in Sri Lanka is acute and chronic shortages of teachers of specific secondary school subjects. Studies have found that a significant number of schools have teachers of English, mathematics, and science who are underproficient or have no one at all to teach these subjects (Pillay et al. 2015).

The reasons are manifold. Deployment is highly unbalanced; there are surpluses of subject teachers in urban schools and shortages in rural and plantation schools. In some cases teachers of Tamil and Sinhala have been reassigned to teach English, math, and science. Education officials and teachers report that training programs are not sufficiently effective for teachers to become proficient in subject knowledge and teaching practice, perhaps partly because there are not enough trainers who themselves are sufficiently proficient in the needed subjects. Though the content of training programs assumes that both teachers and trainers have gained subject proficiency through schooling and university education, the results of school-leaving and teacher recruitment exams suggest otherwise. Significant numbers of teachers have been found to perform poorly in subject knowledge tests pegged at the difficulty of the GCE O-level exam. Not surprisingly, tests of students show they are weakest in the same concepts as teachers (Perera 2011; World Bank 2011).

Absences

Another symptom of teacher management problems is teacher absences. The most obvious effect of teacher absence is lost instruction time for students; but whatever the operative pathways, higher teacher absence has been found to be associated with lower student test scores in a variety of settings (see, e.g., Herrmann and Rockoff 2012 for the United States; and Duflo, Hanna, and Ryan 2012 for India).

Teachers have the same leave allowances as other government employees (Aturupane 2009)—21 days of personal leave and 20 days of sick leave—but at 200 days they have a considerably shorter work year. If teachers take most or all of their leave during the school year, which appears to be the norm, the service loss experienced by beneficiaries of public education is more acute than for other public services.

In 2012, average leave taken per teacher was 30 days, though it varied by province from 23 to 33 days. Assuming that all leave days were taken during the school year, teacher absence would amount to 15 percent of the school year (Aturupane, Savchenko et al. 2014).[4] For a large, disparate set of middle- and low-income countries, estimates of teacher absence, whether or not officially authorized, vary from 11 to 30 percent (Chaudhury et al. 2006; Patrinos 2013).

Average teacher absence may be due to either a relatively uniform rate spread widely across the teaching force or to higher levels among certain segments of the teaching force (Glewwe, Ilias, and Kremer 2003). In Sri Lanka it is reported to be concentrated among teachers assigned to disadvantaged schools, perhaps reflecting the disutility that teachers experience from being assigned to these schools (Aturupane 2009).

Improving Teacher Effectiveness

The issues in teacher management and performance identified in Sri Lanka may be consistent with multiple causes related to the public school system generally and teachers more specifically. This section discusses policies and practices to raise teacher effectiveness in Sri Lanka in terms of specific, plausible causes for issues based on evidence from formative research from other countries. Recommendations for potential solutions are largely based on evidence from rigorous evaluations of interventions related to teachers and teaching from other countries.

Sri Lanka's social, economic, and public service context may differ in major ways from the contexts of the countries from which the evidence is drawn. To heighten the relevance, here the evidence is drawn from studies of public school systems that share many of the characteristics, and issues, of Sri Lanka's public schools, particularly with respect to teacher management. The evidence is drawn from studies of low-, middle-, and high-income countries; but even for the latter types, most of the evidence is from schools that cater to students from socioeconomically disadvantaged backgrounds.

Overcoming Deployment Difficulties

The Sri Lankan government has attempted to address difficulties in attracting and retaining teachers in rural schools by, for example, assigning new teachers to first serve in rural schools for a fixed term, providing cash hardship allowances and housing, and accelerating promotion. Other countries with rural schools with the same teacher deployment problems have attempted similar initiatives (Vegas 2005). However, these may not be successful if, for example, hardship allowances are modest or the disbursement of allowances is irregular or unfair; the quality of the housing offered is poor; faster promotion is not accompanied by an appreciable jump in position, prestige, and pay; or teachers lack confidence that the government will apply its rural school assignment and transfer rules in a transparent, objective, and fair manner—all concerns that may apply in Sri Lanka (Balasooriya 2012; IPS 2014). Even if such initiatives do overcome teacher unwillingness, they may not be as successful in preventing the loss in teacher motivation and effort from teaching in rural schools.

Improving working conditions may be central to attracting and retaining teachers in rural schools and promoting their motivation and effort. While they focus more on schools in poor urban neighborhoods than on rural schools, U.S. studies have examined the effects of different teacher-rated working conditions—both physical, such as facilities and resources, and social, such as school leadership, professional relations, professional authority and autonomy, engagement with school governance, relations with the community and parents, and school culture. After accounting for school, teacher, and student characteristics, they have found that better working conditions, especially social ones, are associated with higher teacher satisfaction and less likelihood that teachers will leave the school (Boyd et al. 2011; Ladd 2011; Johnson, Kraft, and Papay 2012).

To counteract the undesirability of teachers being assigned to rural schools far from their original residences, the Sri Lankan government has also preferentially recruited teachers from rural districts and assigned them to schools in those districts. This approach can be beneficial. An experimental evaluation in public primary schools in rural Kenya found that locally (community) hired teachers on short- and fixed-term, renewable contracts were considerably less likely to be absent from school than regular, centrally hired teachers on open-ended civil service contracts. Moreover, students assigned to contract teachers saw test score gains, while those assigned to regular teachers in the same schools did not, even though regular teachers were on average more qualified and experienced and received higher salaries (Duflo, Dupas, and Kremer 2015). Similarly, a study that randomly assigned locally hired contract teachers to public primary schools in rural India found that average student test scores went up (Muralidharan and Sundararaman 2013).

Since Sri Lanka's rural schools tend to have the lowest-performing students, providing effective teachers is critical if these students are to learn more. The undesirability of teaching in rural schools may be insurmountable, however, even with significant investments in these schools. It might be more cost-effective to permit teachers to travel daily from nearby towns to rural schools, either by providing transportation or subsidizing the transportation cost.

It might also be more cost-effective to bring students from rural communities to teachers, via residential public schools in towns. An added benefit is that residential urban schools can be better resourced, and data-driven practices for effective teaching identified in the international literature (see below) may be easier to implement. While in theory the effects of residential schooling on student academic and nonacademic outcomes are ambiguous, evaluations that take advantage of lottery-based admission of applicants to high-performing residential schools have found test score gains for students accepted in the United States (Curto and Fryer 2014) and for initially higher-achieving students among those accepted to these schools in France (Behaghel, de Chaisemartin, and Gurgand 2015).

Incentives for Better Performance

Teacher pay is chronically and acutely low in Sri Lanka, prompting constant calls for a substantial pay hike. Regardless of their magnitude, pay hikes can be designed to amplify the incentive effect of promotion on teacher performance by decompressing the pay scale, when the percentage hike in pay ratchets up with pay grade (rather than using the typical single percentage hike across the entire pay scale). Criteria for promotion would have to be revised to incorporate indicators correlated with teacher effectiveness, and new systems would be needed to gather regular, credible data on the chosen indicators.

Such adjustments in pay and promotion would incentivize more intensive effort by incumbent teachers and reward those who are more effective. It would also make teaching more attractive for prospective teachers who have better alternative employment options. As a side benefit, a pay adjustment can be structured so that the impact on public spending is less than that of an across-the-board, fixed-percentage hike. In any case, the public teachers' pay scale would need to be delinked from those of other public employees, which could be politically difficult.

Government monitoring through regular school inspections by local education officials can be effective in countering undesirable teacher behavior. Using village-level panel data, a study in India found that more frequent school inspections were associated with reductions in unauthorized teacher absences. However, the study also found that more community monitoring, measured by the number of parent-teacher association meetings, was not associated with fewer unauthorized teacher absences (Muralidharan et al. 2014).[5] The latter finding may be determined by the fact that parent-teacher associations in India lack the authority to manage public school teachers by, for example, sanctioning teachers for being absent—a position shared by Sri Lanka's counterpart institution, the school development committee.

Attracting and Supporting Effective Teachers

The Sri Lankan government recruits teachers based on academic credentials and invests in training new teachers. U.S. studies have found that academic and professional qualifications obtained before entering teaching are not good predictors of teacher effectiveness (Kane, Rockoff, and Staiger 2008; Harris and Sass 2011). Measures of cognitive ability and socioemotional ability (such as values, aptitudes, personality traits, and motivations) have been found to be somewhat better predictors (Dobbie 2011; Rockoff et al. 2011). Nevertheless, most of the variation in teacher effectiveness is still largely unexplained. This suggests that screening prospective teachers even based on evaluations currently viewed as state-of-the-art is unlikely to ensure that the teachers selected are effective.

In Sri Lanka new teachers undergo a three-year probation before being made permanent, but the conversion is essentially automatic. A probationary period can be useful, given that in the United States the effectiveness of teachers in the early years has been found to predict their effectiveness later (Kane, Rockoff, and Staiger 2008). This suggests that early-career teacher effectiveness can be used to screen out the least-effective teachers or target them for in-service training. While dismissing the least-effective teachers can raise aggregate recruitment and termination costs, these costs should be considered in terms of the costs of retaining less effective teachers: lost gains in learning and other longer-term outcomes for the child and the economy.

Teacher training in Sri Lanka needs to be reinforced. Training programs of various types, intensities, modalities, and timing during a teacher's career have been evaluated internationally. Evidence of their efficacy is mixed. In the United States, programs that have had a positive impact tend to be intensive; last a year or longer; and incorporate classroom observation and evaluation, feedback, and coaching. Weekly in-service mentoring by external trained mentors and programs that provided oversight of real teaching experiences were also found to be positively associated with teacher effectiveness (Rockoff 2008; Boyd et al. 2009).[6] Sri Lanka needs to ensure that its teacher training system includes all features of effective programs. School-based teacher development, which Sri Lanka has promoted, could be improved by demonstration lessons, peer coaching, school-based monitoring and assessment, individual consultations, visits to classrooms in other schools, and regular group teacher meetings.

Improvements in pay, benefits, and working conditions in public school teaching in Sri Lanka are overdue. The work attributes of teaching are becoming considerably less attractive over time, especially considering improvements in the attributes of private sector job alternatives in Sri Lanka and other countries. Pay, benefits, and working conditions matter in attracting and retaining effective teachers, and undoubtedly also for teacher motivation and effort; in the United States, after accounting for school, teacher, and student characteristics, better working conditions have been associated with higher teacher satisfaction and student test scores (Johnson, Kraft, and Papay 2012).

Evaluating Teachers

In Sri Lanka, reviews of teacher performance are basic and perfunctory. International evidence indicates that traditional teacher performance evaluations do not provide reliable information for identifying effective teachers, but well-designed and -implemented classroom observations, student perception surveys, and standardized student tests have been found to predict teacher effectiveness in the United States (Kane et al. 2011; Kane and Staiger 2012).

The research on measurement provides useful guidance for Sri Lanka:

- To learn how teachers perform, use multiple measures, such as classroom observations, student perception surveys, content tests of teachers, and student tests.
- Weigh all the information produced in a balanced way in making performance judgments (Mihaly et al. 2013).
- Make meaningful distinctions about the distribution of performance among teachers.
- Give teachers regular feedback and support based on performance data.

Basing teacher performance reviews on student scores on standardized tests and classroom observations could raise student academic achievement. Using rich, matched teacher-student panel data, a U.S. study evaluated the effects of a teacher performance review intervention conducted over a year and consisting of classroom observation, scoring, and oral and written feedback by a school administrator and a higher-performing teacher from another school. Review results were also used for promotion and tenure decisions. The study found that the intervention increased teacher effectiveness both during the evaluation period and in subsequent years (Taylor and Tyler 2012). In another U.S. study, reports of teacher effectiveness, based on student test score value added, were randomly provided to principals. It was found that principals adjusted views of individual teacher performance based on the information. In addition, in schools where principals received the value-added information, less effective teachers were more likely to leave and student test scores went up (Rockoff et al. 2012).

Supporting and Monitoring Student Learning

Assessment System

Quality education demands effective monitoring. An education system should assess learning and use the evidence for school and system improvement, accountability, educational planning, and policy development (Looney 2011; OECD 2013). In practice, an assessment system (figure 4.3) has three

Figure 4.3 Assessment System Structure

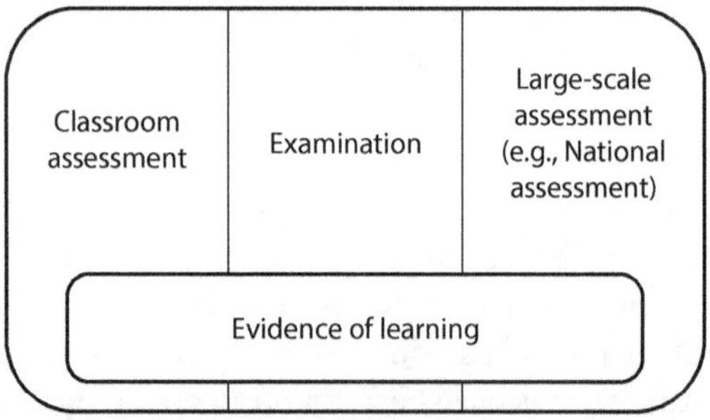

```
┌─────────────┬─────────────┬──────────────────┐
│ Classroom   │ Examination │ Large-scale      │
│ assessment  │             │ assessment       │
│             │             │ (e.g., National  │
│             │             │ assessment)      │
├─────────────┴─────────────┴──────────────────┤
│             Evidence of learning             │
└──────────────────────────────────────────────┘
```

Source: Adapted from Kanjee 2012.

interrelated components—classroom assessments, examinations, and large-scale, systemwide assessments (Kanjee 2012).

- *Classroom assessments* provide evidence of what students are learning in the classroom (Kellaghan and Greaney 2004). They can take such forms as observation, questioning and dialogue, marking of homework, use of portfolios, and diagnostic tests. Since they provide real-time information, they can be used to diagnose learning problems, improve instructional methods, provide feedback to or solicit feedback from students, and inform parents about their child's learning. They have been found to increase achievement and reduce the inequity of student outcomes (Black and William 1998).
- *Examinations* are the basis for certifying student achievement, selecting students to move on in the education system or into the workforce, and standardizing what is taught and learned in schools (Greaney and Kellaghan 2008; World Bank 2012). All eligible students are tested annually (more often where the system allows), and examinations cover the main subject areas in the curriculum. Generally, the stakes for examinations are high because they often condition access to particular education streams.
- *Large-scale, systemwide* are usually designed to give policy makers and educators information on how the education system as a whole is performing, how well students are learning, changes over time, and factors contributing to changes. They are often based on the results of tests of a sample of students and regularly cover a few subjects (e.g., every two to five years). They may be national, subnational, regional, or international (Greaney and Kellaghan 2008; World Bank 2012; Dundar et al. 2014).

Table 4.4 summarizes the differences between the three types of assessments. Because classroom assessments are mainly assessments *for* learning or *as* learning, they are primarily formative; examinations and systemwide assessments are mainly assessments *of* learning and are primarily summative (Airasian and Russell 2007; Greaney and Kellaghan 2008). In practice, the three types are not completely independent of each other (Clarke 2012).

Table 4.4 Differences between Assessment Types

Difference	Classroom	Examinations	Large-scale assessments	
			National	International
Type of assessment	Formative (assessment *for* and *as* learning)	Summative (assessment *of* learning)	Summative (assessment *of* learning)	
Purpose	Provide immediate feedback to support teaching and learning	Certify and select students	Assess performance against national standards and learning goals, and provide feedback to policy makers and educators	Assess performance against international standards, and provide feedback to policy makers and educators

table continues next page

Table 4.4 Differences between Assessment Types (continued)

Difference	Classroom	Examinations	Large-scale assessments	
			National	International
Frequency	Daily, weekly, monthly, quarterly, and annually	Annually, and more often where the system allows	For individual subjects, offered regularly (such as every 3–5 years)	
Who is tested?	All students	All eligible students	Usually, a sample of students at a particular grade or age	
Format	Varies (e.g., observation, questioning and dialogue, marking of homework, use of portfolios, diagnostic tests)	Usually, essay and multiple choice	Usually, multiple choice and short answer	
Coverage of curriculum	All subject areas	Covers main subject areas	Generally confined to a few subjects	
Additional information collected from students?	Yes, as part of the teaching process	Seldom	Frequently	Yes
Are students informed of results?	Yes	Yes	Seldom	
Scoring	Usually informal and simple	Varies from simple to statistically sophisticated techniques	Varies from simple to statistically sophisticated techniques	Usually involves statistically sophisticated techniques

Sources: Greaney and Kellaghan 2008; World Bank 2012.

Student Assessments in Sri Lanka

Recognizing the importance of assessment for monitoring student learning, Sri Lanka has put in place a student assessment system comprising all three components.

Classroom Assessments

In Sri Lanka classroom assessment is used to diagnose student learning issues, provide feedback to students on their learning, and inform parents about their child's learning. Results are disseminated to students and parents. They are also used as an input to the external examination program, although it is not clear whether classroom results are moderated before they are combined with scores on examination papers (World Bank 2012).

Teachers are given instruction manuals and assessment and evaluation guidelines that outline how students are expected to perform in different subjects at different grade and age levels. They are also given books with sample questions and guidance on scoring criteria. Moreover, the NCOEs and the NIE give preservice and in-service training to ensure that teachers build expertise in classroom assessment. Nevertheless, teachers still need help in integrating classroom assessment into their teaching practices.

A number of countries have established policies or provided guidelines to teachers to do classroom assessments more systematically. Their experience could be useful for Sri Lanka. For instance, the United Kingdom has introduced Assessment for Learning to encourage teachers to consider assessment as integral to teaching and learning. Italy requires teachers to use an evaluation form to track progress in student learning and to facilitate communication between students, parents, and teachers. Malaysia's new assessment system emphasizes continuous classroom assessment. Finland considers classroom assessment to be the main source of information on student learning and achievement (De Grauwe and Naidoo 2004).

National Examinations in Sri Lanka

Sri Lanka has a long history of public examinations. There are two main national secondary school examinations. The first is the GCE O-level examination at the end of grade 11, which directs students into science, technology, commerce, and arts streams. Students who pass can continue on to the next stage of education or enter the technical and vocational education and training (TVET) system. The second is the GCE A-level examination at the end of grade 13, which is a prerequisite for entrance into public university degree programs. The latter is highly competitive because the number of public university positions available is limited (see chapter 6). There is also a grade 5 scholarship examination. Its original purpose was to provide financial support for able but poor students, but apparently parents also use it to gain admission of their children to popular national schools (Little, Aturupane, and Shojo. 2013)

The country has a clear policy on national examinations. These are authorized by the Public Examination Act No. 25 of 1968 and conducted by the Department of Examinations (DOE). The act covers the purpose of examinations and their governance, distribution of power and responsibility, procedures for addressing problems, rules about preparing for examinations, grading and marking methodology, and use of the results. The government regularly allocates the necessary funding (World Bank 2012).

National examinations, the curriculum, textbooks, and teaching are all closely aligned, and examination objectives and content are carefully drafted. With the new curriculum reform, there will be a need to ensure close coordination between the DOE and the NIE to maintain the alignment.

Students are given resources to prepare for national examinations, such as sample examination questions, instructions on how to prepare, an explanation of what each examination measures, and an evaluation of each student's strengths and weaknesses. Compared to other South Asian countries, in Sri Lanka there is little inappropriate behavior related to national examinations. Students who do not pass can attend remedial or preparatory courses and retake the examination, or opt for less selective schools, universities, or tracks (World Bank 2012).

Although examinations are useful for monitoring learning, they cannot be the only source of evidence about the quality of student learning. Exam results provide insights into student achievement, but the information has its limitations;

the data are not as reliable a source of evidence on education quality as national assessments, mainly because over the years examination questions vary, and changes in pass rates may partly reflect differences in the difficulty of test questions rather than changes in education quality (Greaney and Kellaghan 2008; World Bank 2011).

National examinations have a powerful influence on the lives of students and on their future. Because of their high stakes, exams may exert considerable pressure on students and parents, often leading them to spend heavily on private tutoring (Aturupane, Savchenko et al. 2014). As a consequence, public debates have led many countries to initiate reforms (see box 4.1). However, reforming the examination system often requires changes to the entire education system. Major changes need to be introduced over several years, so that both schools and students can be properly prepared. It is recommended that the following

---

Box 4.1 Examination Reforms in Other Economies

- *United Kingdom:* With the introduction of comprehensive secondary education, the GCE O-level examinations were replaced by the General Certificate of Secondary Education (GCSE) examinations. The GCSE provides a uniform framework for assessment, with all candidates in all subjects graded from A* to G (with U as unclassified). Scotland has a different system; its examinations for standard grades, higher grades, and advanced higher grades are taken at different ages.
- *Queensland, Australia:* As higher secondary education was made available to all, Queensland discontinued both lower and senior secondary examinations in favor of school-based assessment of student performance in individual subjects. Entry to higher education is controlled through the school assessments, which are statistically moderated using scores on a general ability test all students take.
- *Hong Kong SAR, China:* After a fundamental review of the secondary education curriculum, in 2012 the Hong Kong Certificate of Education Examination and the Hong Kong Advanced Level Examination were replaced by a single examination, the Hong Kong Diploma of Secondary Education, given at the end of the 12th year.
- *Singapore:* The Ministry of Education revised its curriculum and assessment system in order for schools to better develop the creative thinking and learning skills that are now required, such as remembering; comparing and contrasting; classifying and categorizing; inferring and predicting; analyzing, interpreting, generating ideas, drawing conclusions, and distinguishing between fact, opinion, and judgment; and evaluating, synthesizing, making decisions, and solving problems. The examination format has been revised to factor in more thinking questions. Knowledge and inquiry (KI) has been introduced as a GCE A-level subject; it explores the nature of information and knowledge and different methods of inquiry in sciences, humanities, mathematics, and aesthetics.

Sources: Based on Hill 2013 for the United Kingdom, Hong Kong SAR, China, and Queensland and on Tan 2013 for Singapore.

considerations be kept in mind in bringing about changes to the examination system (Hill 2013):

- Examination reforms need to be linked to related reforms of the education system.
- Before any changes are made, it is advisable to communicate widely why they are needed, what changes they entail, and how the examination process will work once the changes have been made.
- Before changes are launched, it is important to engage in a comprehensive consultation process with all stakeholders to clarify and elaborate proposals and identify areas that generate resistance or are problematic.
- To avoid attempting too much change at one time, it is best to phase in change in a strategic way over several years.

Large-Scale, Systemwide Assessments

National Assessments. More and more countries are carrying out national assessments. Although national assessments are relatively new compared to examinations, the number went up from 12 in 1990 to 101 in 2013; in developing countries, only 8 were conducted in 1990, but there were 61 in 2013 (Benavot and Köseleci 2015). National assessments are designed to provide evidence of the performance of a country's education system and can be used to measure student learning both at one point in time and also over time. They allow analysis both of student strengths and weaknesses and of factors explaining disparities between subgroups of students.

National assessments were introduced in Sri Lanka in 2003, and several rounds have since been conducted. They are funded by the MOE and administered by the National Education Research and Evaluation Center (NEREC) at the University of Colombo. In 2012, new instruments were introduced to test cognitive skills in the first language (Sinhala or Tamil), English, and mathematics for grade 4 and in mathematics, science, and English for grade 8. Assessments cover the entire country; a multistage sampling approach enables analysis by province, type of school, gender, and medium of instruction.

The new national assessment of learning outcomes reflects curriculum objectives and sets competency standards. To ensure the quality of the assessment, all administrators are trained to a specific protocol; there is a standardized manual for administrators; administrators must record discrepancies; all booklets are numbered; to ensure high reliability, scorers are trained; data are processed twice; and there are internal and external reviewers. Specifically, observers of test administrators are appointed, as are monitors in addition to supervisors. Marking is also standardized to ensure fairness (World Bank 2012).

In addition to test scores, collecting data on schools, teachers, students, and parents would enable deeper analysis of what determines learning. In 2012, such data were collected, but the practice was discontinued in 2013 for budgetary reasons. Such information would be helpful not only to explain determinants of learning but also for policy design. For instance, the analysis could make it possible to identify which educational resources are more effective in increasing student learning—which in turn could suggest where spending on education should be directed. It would also permit disentangling the effects of schools and of family background. Many national and international assessments analyze factors associated with learning outcomes and apply the results in formulating educational policy.

More attention should be given to building up the capacity of examination-related experts and ensuring that assessments are done competently and on time. Assessments are complex; they call for expertise in test development, sampling, testing, and statistical analysis, all of which require high-level technical and operational skills. When these skills are not available, there is a risk of poor training of test coordinators, unclear guidelines for administering the assessment, errors in scoring, and limited secondary analyses (World Bank 2012).

Though not easy, ensuring that assessment findings reach all stakeholders and translate into policy and action is critical for improving teaching and learning. Unless the findings are widely disseminated, discussed at both system and school levels, and used to define educational policy, they are not likely to have any impact on teaching practices. Box 4.2 shows how some countries have done this successfully.

Box 4.2 Using National Assessment Results

Bangladesh in 2011 conducted the National Student Assessment (NSA), its first robust learning assessment, in Bangla and mathematics at grades 3 and 5. It was a nationally representative sample of students, with both government and registered nongovernment primary schools represented. In 2013, the NSA was extended to cover other types of schools. The NSA 2011 and NSA 2013 were intended to assess the learning achievement of students relative to learning outcomes and to examine the relationships between achievement and school and student factors. In addition to producing an analysis, the Ministry of Primary and Mass Education distributed an information brochure to education officials and teachers to enhance understanding of national assessment. The findings were widely shared and used especially to improve teaching and learning.

Chile's national assessment system, SIMCE (Sistema de Medición de la Calidad de la Educación), has carried out census-based assessments annually since 1988, collecting background information to identify important characteristics of students, teachers, classes, and schools. SIMCE publishes both national and school results. All schools are ranked, and their test scores are compared with those of other schools. SIMCE identifies the worst- and best-performing schools by test scores. Schools not performing well are given technical assistance. The results have generated policy debate but have also led to the improvement of education programs.

The Republic of Korea conducts the National Assessment of Educational Achievement (NAEA) for students in grades 6, 9, and 11 not only to measure achievement but also to

box continues next page

Box 4.2 Using National Assessment Results *(continued)*

provide information on which to base system improvement. Since 2008, the NAEA has been administered annually. Its objectives are to evaluate student achievement, address weaknesses and formulate strategic plans for enhancing achievement, obtain baseline data to be used in future assessments, identify factors that influence educational achievement, and give schools examples of effective assessment methods. To better manage the results, Korea launched the National Education Information System to enable electronic storage and management of the school achievement records of elementary, middle, and high school students. Teachers use this system to record student data electronically; students and parents can view school achievement records online, as can college admissions officers.

Sources: World Bank 2013 for Bangladesh; Ramirez 2012 for Chile; Baek 2010 for the Republic of Korea.

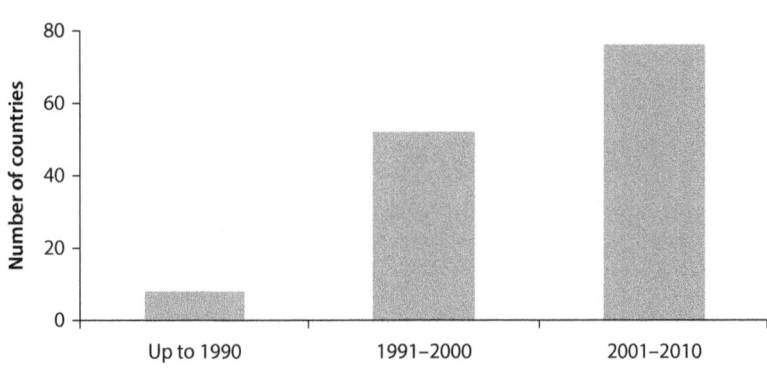

Figure 4.4 Developing-Country Participation in International Assessments

Source: Lockheed 2012.

Large-Scale International Assessments. More and more developing countries now participate in international assessments. These are designed to provide information both about a country's education system and about how its students compare with those of other countries. Participation in international assessments has grown considerably in recent decades. Between 2001 and 2010, more than 70 developing countries took part (figure 4.4).

The major international assessments are Trends in International Mathematics and Science Study (TIMSS), Progress in International Reading Literacy Study (PIRLS), and the Programme for International Student Assessment (PISA); table 4.5 summarizes the features of each. There are also regional assessments, such as the Southern and Eastern Africa Consortium for Monitoring Educational Quality (SACMEQ) in Anglophone Africa, the Latin American Laboratory for Assessment of the Quality of Education (LLECE) in South America, and the Programme for the Analysis of Education Systems of CONFEMEN (PASEC) in Francophone Africa. A regional assessment

Table 4.5 TIMSS, PIRLS, and PISA Compared

Aspect	TIMSS Trends in International Mathematics and Science Study	PIRLS Progress in International Reading Literacy Study	PISA Programme for International Student Assessment
Primary purpose	• Measures trends in student achievement in mathematics and science • Gathers information about learning contexts for mathematics and science • Gathers data about the mathematics and science curricula in each country • Provides countries with information to improve teaching and learning	• Measures trends in reading literacy in primary school to help build up the teaching and learning of reading skills • Measures changes in reading achievement • Investigates school and home experiences of children learning to read	• Evaluates education systems of various countries • Assesses the extent to which students have acquired the knowledge and skills necessary for participating fully in society • Provides a knowledge base for policy analysis and research • Measures trends over time in student and school characteristics
Subject areas tested	Mathematics, science	Reading	Reading, mathematics, science
Organization Responsible	IEA	IEA	OECD
Years of administration	1995, 1999, 2003, 2007, 2011, 2015 (planned)	2001, 2006, 2011, 2015 (planned)	2000, 2003, 2006, 2009, 2012, 2015 (planned)
Grade/age assessed	Grades 4 and 8	Grade 4	15-year-olds
Number of countries and economies participated	49 countries and 9 benchmarking participants	60 countries and 14 benchmarking participants	65 countries and economies
Type of test	Criterion-referenced	Criterion-referenced	Criterion-referenced
Achievement levels reported	Low, intermediate, high, advanced	Low, intermediate, high, advanced	Reading 1–5, Mathematics 1–6, Science 1–6

Source: Adapted from Di Giacomo, Fishbein, and Vanessa 2012.

initiative was launched recently in Southeast Asia. The Organisation for Economic Co-operation and Development (OECD) is working on a new PISA for Development (PISAfD) program (PISA was designed for developing countries), to make the PISA tests and background questionnaires more relevant to a broader range of contexts. Between 2015 and 2016 the first round of PISAfD was scheduled to be held in six countries: Ecuador, Guatemala, Paraguay, Senegal, Zambia, and Cambodia.

Participation in an international assessment would allow Sri Lanka to assess how its education system performs relative to other countries, monitor progress over time, and identify areas where it could be better aligned with other countries. Box 4.3 shows examples of countries that have accelerated education reforms based on the results of international assessments. International experience has also shown that participation can help build local technical and managerial capacity. The cost of participating in international assessments is high, but because the expected benefits are also high, Sri Lanka would gain commensurately.

Box 4.3 International Assessments and Education Reform

Poland's education reform began in 1999, when the country restructured the basic cycle of education and changed the curriculum. Concurrently, Poland decided to participate in the 2000 PISA in order to assess the quality of its education generally. Poland has now participated in five PISA rounds (2000, 2003, 2006, 2009, and 2012). Its students performed poorly at first, scoring well below the European Union average in mathematics, but the 2012 PISA ranked Poland 10th among participating countries for reading and science and 15th for mathematics. That suggests that changes introduced through the education reform boosted academic performance.

Germany's early performance in international assessments (e.g., TIMSS 1995 and PISA 2000) was unsatisfactory. That led the country to visit more successful countries to learn from their practices and identify areas for reform, which it then carried out. Since then it has seen a small but steady rise in its international test scores. Germany was ranked 16th for 4th grade mathematics in the 2011 TIMSS.

Vietnam first participated in the PISA in 2012. The results put Vietnam among the top-performing countries, with an education system that is more successful than those of such developed countries as Australia, Denmark, France, Norway, Switzerland, the United Kingdom, and the United States. Capitalizing on this performance, the government has embarked on further reforms in such areas as curriculum, teaching practices, and assessment.

Brazil has participated in PISA since 2000. It did badly on the early tests, but in 1995 it introduced a major reform to equalize educational opportunity for students from poor families and heighten educational quality in less-developed states. Brazil has also established an innovative Index of Basic Education Quality (IDEB), which combines achievement data with information on school attendance, repetition, and graduation rates. IDEB has made it possible to set targets and assess progress at the federal, state, municipal, and school levels. Its PISA scores have been going up steadily.

Singapore has participated in TIMSS since 1995, in PIRLS since 2001, and in PISA since 2009. Its main motivation for doing so is to benchmark its performance against other countries in order to improve student learning. Even though it regularly scores at or near the top on all international assessments, its education authorities constantly visit other countries to see what innovations Singapore can adopt. Its own education system has gone through three phases in its development: (a) survival-driven, 1969–78, when its primary concern was to expand opportunities for education to all; (b) efficiency-driven, 1979–96, when multiple pathways were created for retaining students, improving quality, and producing the more technically skilled labor force needed to achieve new economic goals; and (c) ability-based and aspiration-driven, since 1997, when the education system has been concerned with innovation, creativity, and research in order to build a knowledge economy.

Sources: World Bank 2010 for Poland; USAID 2012 for Germany, Brazil, and Singapore; http://gpseducation.oecd.org/CountryProfile?primaryCountry=VNM&treshold=10&topic=PI for Vietnam.

Governance and Accountability

The Governance Structure

General education has a complex governance structure, combining elements of decentralization, delegation, and devolution of functions and powers between the central government and the nine provincial councils. The central government is responsible for formulating national education policies; the provincial councils are primarily responsible for the management and delivery of education services. In fact, education is the most decentralized sector in the country, and education budgets typically account for more than half of all provincial spending. Policy makers and legislators have sought to combine the advantages of centralized academic systems, which facilitate goals such as nation-building, social cohesion, and uniform quality standards, and those of delegated management systems, such as increased proximity of administrative services to beneficiaries (World Bank 2011).

The central government is responsible for national policy, curriculum, textbook choices, providing incentives to increase attendance, administering national schools, human resource management and professional development for teachers and principals, conducting exams, and other initiatives, such as special education. Actual delivery of these services often combines central and provincial staff, with the latter operating within a matrix management structure.

About 9,000 schools (97 percent of public schools and 88 percent of all schools) are administered by the nine provincial councils, mainly through 97 zonal education and 365 divisional education offices. Provincial councils draw up education plans and budgets and employ and deploy provincial education administrators, principals, and teachers. Zonal authorities transfer and deploy principals and teachers within zones.

Accountability

The basic institutional foundation to deliver good public education is in place. Already established are such characteristics of good public services as (a) input-oriented, line-item budgeting; (b) cadres of public education officials, such as principals, teachers, education administrators, teacher educators, and university academic staff; (c) opportunities for professional development and career progression for both academic and administrative staff; (d) cash accounting systems; (e) formal performance auditing by the Auditor General's Department; and (f) internal education system audits. The government is currently constructing other important components of good-quality service delivery, such as medium-term program budgeting with a multiyear planning horizon and systems for appraising the performance of principals, teachers, and education administrators.

The incentive system, however, is feeble. Although government institutions have explicit performance incentives through such rewards as appointment to higher-status positions, promotions, greater responsibility, job security, more interesting and stimulating work, and decreased supervision, two factors undermine the actual operation of the incentive system for all public employees: (a) The financial incentives for better performance are minimal. Because the government wage and salary structure is highly compressed and annual increments are small, nonperformance has little opportunity cost. (b) Promotions are still mainly based on seniority, with performance incentives having at best a secondary role. Those two elements are likely to be a drain on teacher effectiveness.

There is also anecdotal evidence from civil society and newspaper reports suggesting that the good governance principles of the general education system may sometimes be violated by (a) the influence of political patronage on appointment of school principals and education officials, transfers of teachers, and student admissions to popular schools; and (b) informal payments for admission of students to popular schools. The magnitude of these problems is unknown, although Transparency International has estimated that side payments for student admissions occurred in 2 percent of schools.

Accountability in Schools

The government is seeking to make individual schools more accountable in two ways: monitoring schools through quality assurance (QA), and empowering schools and local communities through school-based management.

Sri Lanka's QA model is based on the U.K. and Scottish models. It assesses school performance in eight areas: (a) student achievement; (b) learning, teaching, and assessment; (c) curriculum management; (d) co-curricular activities; (e) student welfare; (f) leadership and management; (g) physical resource management; and (h) how the school relates to the community.

Internal QA is the bedrock of modern systems. Its objective is to promote within schools a culture of continuous quality improvement and self-evaluation. Feedback from schools and principals to internal QA has been very positive, and QA is considered useful for monitoring school performance and improving quality. The system is in place. The government should now encourage all schools to conduct annual self-evaluations and feed the information from these into school development plans, as well as sharing the self-evaluations with divisional and zonal offices (to see how such a system works in Scotland, see box 4.4).

External QA monitoring supports the improvement of the school system as a whole. Internal and external QA are complementary and mutually reinforcing. The first step is an external review of annual internal QA self-assessments. The external review panel then seeks to validate the self-assessment findings and also looks at dimensions of quality that go beyond the internal reviews. Sri Lanka needs to tighten the link between internal and external QA. External reviews by government education administrators generally occur every three to five years. Given that school performance varies among schools, good practice would be for external reviews to be tailored to school needs: High-performing schools would normally be reviewed about once every five years, middling schools about once every three years, and low-performing schools every 12–18 months.

Box 4.4   School Internal Quality Assurance in Scotland

Scotland is among Europe's QA leaders. Its system combines internal and external reviews.

Internal Quality Assurance

Scottish schools undertake annual internal self-evaluations. The theme, *Getting It Right*, has three dimensions: *How are we doing? How do we know? What are we going to do now?* School self-evaluations look at such aspects of school performance as student attendance, teacher performance, student learning, curriculum delivery and assessment, extra- and co-curricular activities, school management and leadership, student welfare, physical resources, and school-community relationships. The findings are shared with the local education authority and the Inspectorate of Schools, which conducts external assessments, and are posted on school websites. Feedback from schools suggests that the internal self-assessment process is extremely useful.

External Quality Assurance

Education Scotland assures the quality of Scottish education and promotes improvement and innovation to enhance learners' experiences and outcomes. Each year, a sample of primary and secondary schools is selected for review. A particular interest is development of the skills and understanding of children and young people so that they can learn the most possible. Schools identified as high performers are normally reviewed about once every five years, average performers about once every three years, and low performers every year to year-and-a-half. The results are shared with the schools and with government authorities for future action.

Source: http://www.gov.scot/gettingitright/Publications.

Sri Lanka is also seeking to make individual schools more accountable through a school-based management initiative, the Program for School Improvement (PSI). This initiative, which began in 2006, was influenced by reforms in developed countries, such as the United States and the United Kingdom, and in developing countries in East and South Asia. The objective is to enable schools to become self-managing, with deep community involvement, and to improve the delivery of education services.

The PSI has been very popular with principals, teachers, parents, and members of the local community; support for it has been nearly universal. Principals and teachers state that they feel more empowered and motivated and that the active involvement of parents, past pupils, and other local community representatives has invigorated their schools. This was found to be particularly important in small and remote rural communities. Being involved in school affairs gave parents a greater sense of ownership and commitment to the education of their children. Past pupils saw their support as "giving something back" to schools from which they had benefited. This echoes findings elsewhere; in El Salvador (Sawada and Ragatz 2005) local community members expressed a sense of greater efficacy and commitment to their school.

This initiative was found to have a positive impact on learning outcomes. A rigorous impact assessment based on a randomized design found that for grade 4 students, participation in PSI was associated with higher scores on mathematics and English language tests (Aturupane, Glewwe et al. 2014). Similar reforms were also found to have positive results in El Salvador, Kenya, Mexico, and Nicaragua (see Barrera-Osorio, Fasih, and Patrinos 2009). Experience with charter schools in OECD countries has also been positive (see box 4.5) and offers some useful lessons.

A number of factors were found to have contributed to the favorable effects of PSI in Sri Lanka (Aturupane, Kellaghan, and Shojo 2013). The leadership provided by dynamic and motivated school principals was of central importance, as was increased teacher and parental involvement in the education process, at school and at home. School development committees directed their efforts to bringing in more resources, both cash and in-kind, for their schools. The resources were used for co-curricular and extracurricular activities, such as drama and literary events, and athletics and games, as well as such curriculum-related activities as the purchase of books for the library and field trips for children to places of cultural or historical interest.

Box 4.5 Charter Schools and Effective School-Based Management

Charter schools are public schools that are publicly funded but privately managed. The greater operational freedom of charter schools is accompanied by more accountability for results, with performance standards stipulated in the contract. In the United States, charter schools typically offer preprimary through secondary education and are tuition-free. Charter schools are also found in other OECD countries, such as Norway, Sweden, Canada, and the United Kingdom.

Rigorous studies of charter schools consistently find robust evidence that school quality can raise student academic achievement. High-performing U.S. charter schools have been found to produce large test score gains for all but deeply disadvantaged students, reducing achievement gaps (see, e.g., Angrist et al. 2010; Abdulkadiroglu et al. 2011; Dobbie and Fryer 2011). High-performing charter schools have also been found to improve longer-term education outcomes, such as secondary school graduation and college enrollment, again particularly for disadvantaged students (see, e.g., Dobbie and Fryer 2013b; Angrist et al. 2016).

In line with evidence from numerous school types and systems, inputs such as class size, per-student expenditures, teacher certification, and teacher training have not been found to be correlated with the effectiveness of high-performing charter schools. However, five educational practices were found to explain about half of the variation in effectiveness in high-performing charter schools in New York City (Dobbie and Fryer 2013a). These practices were then tested in chronically low-performing public schools, typically attended

box continues next page

Box 4.5 Charter Schools and Effective School-Based Management *(continued)*

by socioeconomically disadvantaged students, in Houston, Denver, and Chicago and were found to markedly raise average test scores in primary and secondary grades (Fryer 2014). The five practices are:

(1) *Frequent teacher feedback*: Regular feedback and intensive support from school administrators for teacher professional development based on student assessment data, classroom observation, and parental and student perceptions heighten the quality of instruction.
(2) *Use of data to guide instruction*: Conducting regular student assessments linked to minimum learning standards and using student assessment data allows school administrators and teachers to adjust instruction to the learning needs and goals of the individual student.
(3) *Intensive tutoring*: Regular provision of intensive, free, personalized tutoring by students in higher grades relieves remedial needs determined by student assessments and other measures of student engagement and effort.
(4) *Increased instruction time*: Significantly more hours per school day and more days per school year help, with additional instructional time customized to the needs of students, such as more classes or tutoring in a subject with which the student struggles.
(5) *High expectations*: Building and sustaining a culture of high expectations for student success is effective, with parents, school administrators, teachers, and peers encouraging individual learning and education goals; it typically results in students preparing for and going to college (Brookings Institution 2012).

The payoffs to introducing these practices in public schools will hinge on schools having capable principals and teachers. They will also depend on determining the appropriate intensity mix of practices to administer at the school rather than the system level, and adjusting the mix as the school learns how well certain practices work for it and for changing teacher and student composition.

Effective application of these proven practices requires significant public spending and efficient systems for collecting, processing, and reporting school performance data. With budgets limited, investing in these practices will likely mean altering the composition of outlays. One possible direction is to allocate away from areas where the evidence on effects is unfavorable, such as teacher certification, teacher training, and school infrastructure.

Cost and Financing of Schools in Sri Lanka

Public expenditures on primary and secondary education have increased. In 2013, nominal and real public spending on primary education was LKR 121.38 billion, and on secondary education LKR 48.78 billion (base year 2002). Both nominal and real general public spending has gone up since 2011. Figure 4.5 shows the annual rate of change of public spending on primary and secondary education, and since the civil conflict ended, there has been an upturn in public

Figure 4.5 Public Spending on Primary and Secondary Education, 2004–13

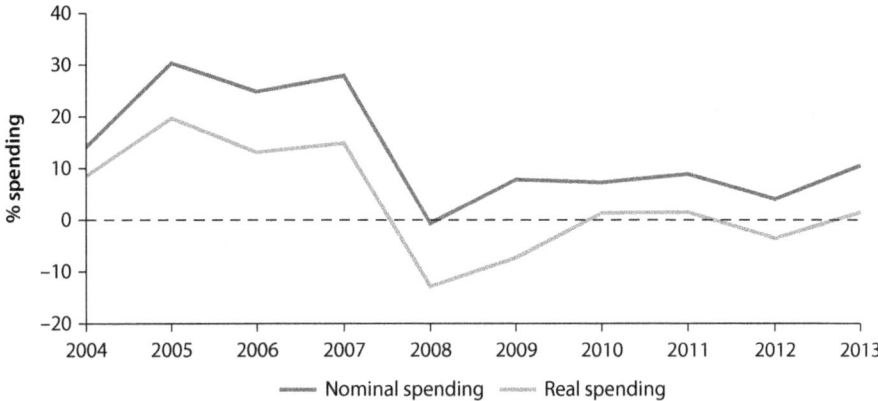

Source: Aturupane et al. 2014.

spending generally, including on education, though even as recently as 2013 spending was below its 2007 level (87 percent in real terms).

Although it is now spending more on education in both nominal and real terms, Sri Lanka still invests less in education than other countries at similar levels of development. Annual public investment in education has been less than 2 percent of GDP for the past several years, compared to an average of over 4 percent for lower-middle-income countries and 5 percent for upper-middle-income countries.[7] Even spending on public education as a percentage of total government spending, at about 10 percent, is among the lowest.

Redistributive Funding

Public investment in primary and secondary education favors the most disadvantaged provinces. The government funding policy is based on a formula that seeks to promote balanced regional development. Figure 4.6 shows that public education spending per student is greater in the poorer Northern, Eastern, and Uva provinces than in the wealthier Western, Central, and Southern provinces. The aim is to provide additional support to the poor provinces where learning outcomes and student performance are low. For instance, the Northern Province, which had the lowest GCE O-level pass rate in 2012, spent about LKR 9,500 per student, while the Western Province, which had the highest pass rate, spent about LKR 6,000. However, the relationship between pass rates and per-student expenditures is still negative, probably because factors like poverty and underdevelopment also influence learning.

Equity Funding

Sri Lanka has also tried equity funding of schools in other ways. Since 2000, the government's Education Quality Inputs Scheme (EQI) has been attempting to equalize resources across schools. About 2 percent of recurrent expenditures

Figure 4.6 GCE O-Level Pass Rates and Provincial Investment in Education, 2012

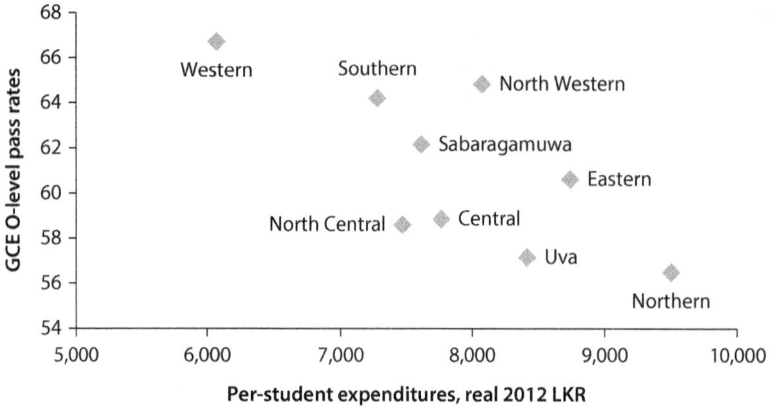

[Scatter plot showing GCE O-level pass rates (y-axis, 54–68) vs. Per-student expenditures, real 2012 LKR (x-axis, 5,000–10,000). Data points: Western (~6,000, 67); Southern (~7,300, 64); North Western (~8,100, 65); Sabaragamuwa (~7,700, 62); Eastern (~8,800, 61); North Central (~7,200, 59); Central (~7,700, 59); Uva (~8,500, 57); Northern (~9,500, 56.5).]

Source: Aturupane et al. 2014.

are to be allocated according to a formula that gives greater weight to smaller schools, which are more likely to be in rural and remote locations and not as well supported by community contributions or school development societies as larger, more urban schools.

Experience with EQI has been mixed, although small, poor schools seem to have derived some benefits. The EQI has suffered from such drawbacks as nonavailability of funds, delays in the release of funds, nonreleases in some years and some provinces, and the inability of smaller schools to comply with the rules for use of the funds. However, there is some evidence that it has allowed poorly resourced schools to purchase teaching and learning materials and consumables and has contributed to better attendance of students and greater student learning in smaller schools (Arunatilake and Jayawardena 2013).

Sri Lanka has also tried to use a systemwide school-funding formula. The government in the early 2000s introduced the Norm-Based Unit Cost Resource Allocation Mechanism (NBUCRAM). Its objective was to provide an equitable and rational basis for the allocation of resources to schools: The recurrent budget was allocated based on norms like STRs, estimated learning costs of different subjects and grades, number of students in a school, and the grade levels covered by schools of each type. The capital budget was allocated according to a stock-adjustment principle, which takes into account changes over time in the capital stock of schools relative to a desired level (determined according to defined standards for capital works, equipment, and technology). One component of the reform was a quality input grant that would flow directly to schools to speed up resource utilization and be more sensitive to local school needs. This system heightened the equity of resource allocation and utilization; children from low-income households benefited particularly

(Arunatilake and Jayawardena 2010). However, with spending on education low for the past four to five years, the formula fell into disuse. It needs to be restored because it provides a sound basis for equitable public investment in education.

Household Spending

Household spending on education is substantial, even though state education is free. It goes to supplemental expenditures, such as books and stationery, transportation, private tuition fees, and the costs of attending private and international schools, boarding schools, colleges, and universities.

Even though public schooling is free, private tuition is a growing phenomenon, constituting the largest item in the household education budget (36 percent). Private tutoring—fee-based supplemental instruction in academic subjects—is widespread, with high rates of take-up in all socioeconomic groups. Several possible reasons have been posited for this, such as compensating for shortcomings and distortions in the delivery of school services. Whatever the reason, the decision to obtain tutoring can be viewed as rational and potentially efficient. Some studies in Sri Lanka and elsewhere indeed suggest that tutoring has positive effects on student academic achievement; others that explored the effects for different population subgroups found larger effects for poorer households than for richer ones. However, tutoring is also said to engender risks; it can, for example, distort the efforts of regular teachers, dampen demand for reforms, reduce student engagement at school, and heighten socioeconomic disparities in education outcomes.

Because studies have not yet conclusively identified the net effect of tutoring on learning achievement, more and better research on its benefits and risks is needed. Nevertheless, it seems that a policy that promotes open competition in the tutoring market could be welfare-enhancing and that subsidizing tutoring for poorer households could also help raise their welfare gains.

Conclusion and Policy Options

This chapter reviewed critical constraints that interfere with the improvement of the quality of school education and proposed policy options to address them. The main options can be summarized as follows:

Education Offerings and Curriculum
- Actively pursue the expansion of senior secondary education opportunities across the country, widening the range of education streams offered to students. Particular attention should be given to increasing opportunities to access the science and technology streams and to learn foreign languages. This should be accompanied by effective measures, adapted to specific situations, to addressing teacher shortages in new subject areas.

- Upgrade the school curriculum to reflect international trends in curriculum practices, and especially facilitate the acquisition of both cognitive and soft skills, which are both important for students' personal development and in high demand in the labor market.

Teacher Effectiveness
- Ensure that recruitment, deployment, and promotion are not subject to political influence.
- Address deployment issues. A variety of measures could be considered and possibly combined, depending on the circumstances: (a) improvement in work conditions in rural areas; (b) provision of transportation or a subsidy for it from teachers' homes to schools; (c) direct recruitment of teachers from rural districts; (d) establishing residential schools for rural students in urban areas; and (e) providing hardship allowances or offering faster promotion.
- To motivate teachers, decompress the pay scale and design pay hikes to reward performance, and revise promotion criteria to incorporate indicators of performance. These adjustments could both provide incentives for current teachers to perform better and make teaching more attractive for higher-caliber teacher prospects. If necessary, the revised pay scales for teachers could be delinked from the scales for other government employees.
- Improve teacher performance evaluation with additional information, such as classroom observation and student test scores.
- Ensure regular inspections of schools with credible penalties and rewards, fairly applied, to improve teacher presence, punctuality, and time-on-task.
- Use the probation period to test the effectiveness of new teachers. Do not convert it automatically into a regular teacher contract. How teachers perform in the first two to three years of service has been found to be a strong predictor of their future effectiveness. Ineffective young teachers can be screened out, to be targeted for remedial training or simply not given a long-term contract.
- Strengthen teacher training, after a full review of course content, delivery modes, proficiency, and the performance of trainers. Shortfalls in teacher performance may be partly due to shortcomings in their training at entry and during service. Monitor and evaluate the impact of reform, once introduced.

Monitoring Student Learning
- Provide additional support to teachers for integrating classroom assessment into teaching practices through guidelines, materials, in-service training, etc.
- In national assessments, collect data not only on test scores but also on schools, teachers, students, and parents. This would permit a more thorough analysis of what determines learning. Such an analysis would contribute to the design of more effective policies.
- Ensure that assessment findings are widely disseminated and contribute to policy design. Full integration of national assessments into the policy

environment will ensure that findings reach all stakeholders and are utilized at both the system and the school levels.
- Consider participation in international assessments, such as PISA and TIMMs. This would permit international benchmarking for student learning and measurement of progress over time relative to the group of middle- and high-income countries that Sri Lanka aspires to join.

Governance and Accountability
- Strengthen QA mechanisms. Internal QA helps to promote a culture of continuous quality improvement and self-evaluation within schools. External QA and monitoring support improvement of the entire school system. Both are mutually reinforcing and critical for improving teaching and learning.
- Improve the accountability of schools through the school-based management initiative, the Program for School Improvement (PSI), by promoting a combination of periodic social audits and rigorous evaluations and expanding its implementation.

Financing of General Education
- Pursue funding policies that promote equity. Consider reintroducing the norm-based, unit-cost resource allocation mechanism. Monitor and evaluate the impact of these policies at the school level.
- Undertake a study to measure the benefits and risks of private tutoring.

Notes

1. The primary education cycle corresponds to grades 1–5, junior secondary to grades 6–9, and senior secondary to grades 10–13.
2. In 2012, a pilot initiative for on-site training and support, the School-Based Teacher Development Program, was formally introduced. Administered jointly by zonal in-service advisors (ISA), school principals, and teachers themselves, the program has now been scaled up across the country, with guidebooks circulated to schools (MOE 2013).
3. The study, however, did find effects on measures of school management by principals.
4. The pattern of absences across provinces mirrors the pattern of provincial leave levels.
5. In India parent-teacher associations are now called school management committees.
6. For example, in the United States, an experimental evaluation of in-service training to improve the extent and quality of teacher-student interactions found that the intervention increased student test scores. The training consisted of cycles of observation, reflection, and consultation based on videos of the teacher's classroom practice (Allen et al. 2011). Among a small set of program features examined, teacher preparation and certification programs that provided oversight of real teaching experiences and formal opportunities for teachers to conduct research on teaching and learning while teaching their students were also found to be associated with teacher effectiveness (Boyd et al. 2009).
7. Public education spending here includes spending on general (primary and secondary) education, higher education, and vocational education and training.

References

Aaronson, D., L. Barrow, and W. Sander. 2007. "Teachers and Student Achievement in the Chicago Public High Schools." *Journal of Labor Economics* 25 (1): 95–135.

Abdulkadirogglu, A., J. Angrist, S. Dynarski, T. J. Kane, and P. Pathak. 2011. "Accountability and Flexibility in Public Schools: Evidence from Boston's Charters and Pilots." *Quarterly Journal of Economics* 126 (2): 699–748.

Airasian, P., and M. Russell. 2007. *Classroom Assessment: Concepts and Applications.* New York: McGraw Hill.

Allen, J. P., R. C. Pianta, A. Gregory, A. Y. Mikami, and J. Lun. 2011. "An Interaction-Based Approach to Enhancing Secondary School Instruction and Student Achievement." *Science* 333 (6045): 1034–37.

Anderson, P., and G. Morgan. 2008. *Developing Tests and Questionnaires for a National Assessment of Educational Achievement.* Vol. 2 of *National Assessments of Educational Attainment.* Washington, DC: World Bank.

Angrist, J. D., S. R. Cohodes, S. M. Dynarski, P. A. Pathak, and C. R. Walters. 2016. "Stand and Deliver: Effects of Boston's Charter High Schools on College Preparation, Entry, and Choice." *Journal of Labor Economics* 34 (2): 275–318.

Angrist, J. D., S. M. Dynarski, T. J. Kane, P. A. Pathak, and C. R. Walters. 2010. "Inputs and Impacts in Charter Schools: KIPP Lynn." *American Economic Review: Papers and Proceedings* 100: 1–5.

Arunatilake, N., and P. Jayawardena. 2010. "Formula Funding and Decentralized Management of Schools—Has It Improved Resource Allocation in Schools in Sri Lanka?" *International Journal of Educational Development* 30 (1): 44–53.

———. 2013. "School Funding Formulas in Sri Lanka." Background Paper Prepared for the *Global Monitoring Report 2013/14: Education for All.* Paris: UNESCO.

Assessment Reform Group. 2002. *Assessment for Learning: 10 Principles.* http://www.hkeaa.edu.hk/ DocLibrary/SBA/HKDSE/Eng_DVD/doc/Afl_principles.pdf.

Aturupane, H. 2009. "The Pearl of Great Price: Achieving Equitable Access to Primary and Secondary Education and Enhancing Learning in Sri Lanka." Research Monograph 29, Consortiums for Research on Educational Access, Transitions, and Equity. Institute of Education, University of London, London, U.K.

Aturupane, H., P. Glewwe, R. Ravina, U. Sonnadara, and S. Wisniewski. 2014. "An Assessment of the Impacts of Sri Lanka's Programme for School Improvement and School Report Card Programme on Students' Academic Progress." *Journal of Development Studies* 50 (12): 1647–69.

Aturupane, H., P. Glewwe, and S. Wisniewski. 2013. "The Impact of School Quality, Socioeconomic Factors, and Child Health on Students' Academic Performance: Evidence from Sri Lankan Primary Schools." *Education Economics* 21 (1): 2–37.

Aturupane, H., T. Kellaghan, and M. Shojo. 2013. "School-Based Education Improvement Initiatives: The Experience and Options for Sri Lanka." South Asia Human Development Sector Discussion Paper Series 58, World Bank, Washington, DC.

Aturupane, H., Y. Savchenko, M. Shojo, and K. Larsen. 2014. "Sri Lanka: Investment in Human Capital." South Asia Human Development Unit Discussion Paper Series 69, World Bank, Washington, DC.

Baek, S. 2010. *Case Study on Korea's Educational Assessment System.* Seoul: Seoul National University.

Balasooriya, B. M. J. 2012. "Teacher Recruitment and Teacher Mobility in Sri Lanka." In *Commonwealth Education Partnerships 2012/13 by Commonwealth Secretariat*. Cambridge: Nexus Strategic Partnerships.

Barrera-Osorio, F., F. Fasih, and H. Patrinos. 2009. *Decentralized Decision-Making in Schools: The Theory and Evidence on School-Based Management*. Washington, DC: World Bank.

Behaghel, L., C. de Chaisemartin, and M. Gurgand. 2015. "Ready for Boarding? The Effects of a Boarding School for Disadvantaged Students." Warwick Economics Research Paper Series 1059, Department of Economics, University of Warwick, Warwick.

Benavot, A., and N. Köseleci. 2015. "Seeking Quality: Growth of National Learning Assessments, 1990–2013." Background Paper for EFA Global Monitoring Report 2015. Paris: UNESCO

Black, P., and D. Wiliam. 1998. "Assessment and Classroom Learning." *Assessment in Education: Principles, Policy and Practice* 5: 7–74.

Boyd, D., P. Grossman, H. Lankford, S. Loeb, and J. Wyckoff. 2009. "Teacher Preparation and Student Achievement." *Educational Evaluation and Policy Analysis* 31 (4): 416–40.

Boyd, D., P. Grossman, M. Ing, H. Lankford, S. Loeb, and J. Wyckoff. 2011. "The Influence of School Administrators on Teacher Retention Decisions." *American Educational Research Journal* 48 (2): 303–33.

Brookings Institution. 2012. *Learning from the Successes and Failures of Charter Schools*. Hamilton Project Policy Brief 2012–06. USA: Brookings Institution, Washington, DC.

Chaudhury, N., J. Hammer, M. Kremer, K. Muralidharan, and F. H. Rogers. 2006. "Missing in Action: Teacher and Health Worker Absence in Developing Countries." *Journal of Economic Perspectives* 20 (1): 91–116.

Chetty, R., J. N. Friedman, and J. E. Rockoff. 2013. "Measuring the Impacts of Teachers I: Evaluating Bias in Teacher Value-Added Estimates." *American Economic Review* 104 (9): 2593–632.

———. 2014. "Measuring the Impacts of Teachers II: Teacher Value-Added and Student Outcomes in Adulthood." *American Economic Review* 104 (9): 2633–79.

Clarke, M. 2012. "What Matters Most for Student Assessment Systems: A Framework Paper." SABER–Student Assessment Working Paper 1, World Bank, Washington, DC.

Curto, V. E., and R. G. Fryer Jr. 2014. "The Potential of Urban Boarding Schools for the Poor: Evidence from SEED." *Journal of Labor Economics* 32 (1): 65–93.

De Grauwe, A., and J. P. Naidoo. 2004. *School Evaluation for Quality Improvement*. Paris: UNESCO.

Di Giacomo, F. T., B. G. Fishbein, and W. Vanessa. 2012. "International Comparative Assessments: Broadening the Interpretability, Application and Relevance to the United States." *Research in Review*: 2012–15.

Dobbie, W. 2011. "Teacher Characteristics and Student Achievement: Evidence from Teacher for America." http://scholar.princeton.edu/sites/default/files/wdobbie/files/dobbie_tfa_2011.pdf.

Dobbie, W., and R. Fryer. 2011. "Are High-Quality Schools Enough to Increase Achievement among the Poor? Evidence from the Harlem Children's Zone." *American Economic Journal: Applied Economics* 3 (3): 158–87.

———. 2013a. "Getting Beneath the Veil of Effective Schools: Evidence from New York City." *American Economic Journal: Applied Economics* 5 (4): 28–60.

———. 2013b. "The Medium-Term Impacts of High-Achieving Charter Schools on Non-Test Score Outcomes." NBER Working Paper 19581, National Bureau of Economic Research, Cambridge, MA.

Duflo, E., P. Dupas, and M. Kremer. 2015. "School Governance, Teacher Incentives and Pupil-Teacher Ratios: Experimental Evidence from Kenyan Primary Schools." *Journal of Public Economics* 123: 92–110.

Duflo, E., R. Hanna, and S. P. Ryan. 2012. "Incentives Work: Getting Teachers to Come to School." *American Economic Review* 102 (4): 1241–78.

Dundar, H., T. Béteille, M. Riboud, and A. Deolalikar. 2014. *Student Learning in South Asia: Challenges, Opportunities, and Policy Priorities.* Washington, DC: World Bank.

Fryer, R. G. 2014. "Injecting Charter School Best Practices into Traditional Public School: Evidence from Field Experiments." *Quarterly Journal of Economics.* 129 (3): 1355–1407.

Glewwe, P., N. Ilias, and M. Kremer. 2003. "Teacher Incentives." NBER Working Paper 9671, National Bureau of Economic Research, Cambridge, MA.

Goldhaber, D., and M. Hansen. 2013. "Is It Just a Bad Class? Assessing the Long-Term Stability of Estimated Teacher Performance." *Economica* 80: 589–612.

Greaney, V., and T. Kellaghan. 2008. *Assessing National Achievement Levels in Education.* Vol. 1 of *National Assessments of Educational Attainment.* Washington, DC: World Bank.

Guerra, N., K. Modecki, and W. Cunningham. 2014. "Developing Social-Emotional Skills for the Labor Market—The PRACTICE Model." World Bank Policy Research Working Paper 7123, World Bank, Washington, DC.

Hanushek, E. A., and S. G. Rivkin. 2006. "Teacher Quality." In *Handbook of the Economics of Education*, Vol. 2, edited by E. Hanushek and F. Welch, 1051–78. Amsterdam: Elsevier.

Harris, D. N., and T. R. Sass. 2011. "Teacher Training, Teacher Quality and Student Achievement." *Journal of Public Economics* 95: 798–812.

Herrmann, M., and J. Rockoff. 2012. "Worker Absence and Productivity: Evidence from Teaching." *Journal of Labor Economics* 30 (4): 749–82.

Hill, P. 2013. "Examination Systems." Asia-Pacific Secondary Education System Review Series 1, UNESCO, Bangkok.

Hoxby, C. E. 2002. "The Cost of Accountability." NBER Working Paper 8855, National Bureau of Economic Research, Cambridge, MA.

IPS (Institute of Policy Studies). 2014. *Sri Lanka: State of the Economy 2014—Rising Asia-Opportunities and Challenges for Sri Lanka.* Colombo: Institute of Policy Studies.

Jackson, C. K., J. E. Rockoff, and D. O. Staiger. 2014. "Teacher Effects and Teacher-Related Policies." *Annual Review of Economics* 6: 801–25.

Johnson, S. M., M. A. Kraft, and J. P. Papay. 2012. "How Context Matters in High-Need Schools: The Effects of Teachers' Working Conditions on Their Professional Satisfaction and Their Students' Achievement." *Teachers College Record* 114 (10): 1–39.

Kane, T. J., J. E. Rockoff, and D. O. Staiger. 2008. "What Does Certification Tell Us about Teacher Effectiveness? Evidence from New York City." *Economics of Education Review* 27 (6): 615–31.

Kane, T. J., and D. O. Staiger. 2012. "Gathering Feedback on Teaching: Combining High-Quality Observations with Student Surveys and Achievement Gains." MET Project Research Paper, Bill & Melinda Gates Foundation, Seattle.

Kane, T. J., E. Taylor, J. Tyler, and A. Wooten. 2011. "Identifying Effective Classroom Practices Using Student Achievement Data." *Journal of Human Resources* 46 (3): 587–613.

Kanjee, A. 2012. "Options for Developing Integrated Assessments Systems to Improve Learning and Teaching." *Compare: A Journal of Comparative and International Education* 42 (3): 509–45.

Kellaghan, T., and V. Greaney. 2004. *Assessing Student Learning in Africa*. Washington, DC: World Bank.

Kellaghan, T., V. Greaney, and T. S. Murray. 2009. *Using the Results of a National Assessment of Educational Achievement*. Vol. 5 of *National Assessments of Educational Attainment*. Washington, DC: World Bank.

Ladd, H. F. 2011. "Teachers' Perceptions of Their Working Conditions: How Predictive of Planned and Actual Teacher Movement?" *Educational Evaluation and Policy Analysis* 33 (2): 235–61.

Little, A. W., H. Aturupane, and M. Shojo. 2013. "Transforming Primary Education in Sri Lanka: From a 'Subject' of Education to a 'Stage' of Education." South Asia Human Development Working Paper 61, World Bank, Washington DC.

Lockheed, M. 2012. "Policies, Performance and Panaceas: The Role of International Large-Scale Assessments in Developing Countries." *Compare: A Journal of Comparative and International Education* 42 (3): 509–45.

Looney, J. W. 2011. "Integrating Formative and Summative Assessment: Progress toward a Seamless System?" OECD Education Working Paper 58, OECD, Paris.

McCaffrey, D. F., T. R. Sass, J. R. Lockwood, and K. Mihaly. 2009, "The Intertemporal Variability of Teacher Effect Estimates." *Education Finance and Policy* 4 (4): 572–606.

Mihaly, K., D. F. McCaffrey, D. Staiger, and J. R. Lockwood. 2013. *A Composite Estimator of Effective Teaching*. RAND External Publication. http://www.rand.org/pubs/external_publications/EP50155.html.

MOE (Ministry of Education). 2011. *Education Sector Development Framework and Program (ESDFP) 2012–16*. Colombo: Ministry of Education.

———. 2013. *Guidebook on School-Based Teacher Development*. Colombo: Ministry of Education.

———. 2014. *Our School: How Good Is It? Process of Evaluation and Monitoring for Assuring the Quality in Education*. Colombo: Ministry of Education.

Ministry of Public Administration and Home Affairs. 2010. *Revision of Salaries and Allowances of the Public Service in Terms of Budget Proposals 2011*. Public Administration Circular 28/2010. Colombo: Ministry of Public Administration and Home Affairs.

Muralidharan, K., J. Das, A. Holla, and A. Mohpal. 2014. "The Fiscal Cost of Weak Governance: Evidence from Teacher Absence in India." NBER Working Paper 20299, National Bureau of Economic Research, Cambridge, MA.

Muralidharan, K., and V. Sundararaman. 2013. "Contract Teachers: Experimental Evidence from India." NBER Working Paper 19440, National Bureau of Economic Research, Cambridge, MA.

NEREC (National Education Research and Evaluation Centre). 2014. *National Report: National Assessment of Achievement of Students Completing Grade 4 in Year 2013*. Colombo: NEREC, University of Colombo.

OECD (Organisation for Economic Co-operation and Development). 2013. *Synergies for Better Learning: An International Perspective on Evaluation and Assessment*. Paris: OECD.

———. 2015. *The Experience of Middle-Income Countries Participating in PISA 2000-2015*. Paris: OECD.

Papay, J. P., and M. A. Kraft. 2015. "Productivity Returns to Experience in the Teacher Labor Market: Methodological Challenges and New Evidence on Long-Term Career Improvement." *Journal of Public Economics* 130: 105–19.

Patrinos, H. A. 2013. "The Hidden Cost of Corruption: Teacher Absenteeism and Loss in Schools." In *Global Corruption Report: Education*, edited by G. Sweeney, K. Despota, and S. Linder, 70–73. New York: Routledge; Berlin: Transparency International.

Perera, M. E. S. 2011. *Status of English Language Teaching in Sri Lanka*. Colombo: Ministry of Education, Sri Lanka. Processed.

Pillay, H., I. A. Muttaqi, Y. R. Pant, and N. Herath. 2015. *Teacher Professional Development*. TA-6637 REG: Development Partnership Program for South Asia: Subproject 11: Innovative Strategies for Accelerated Human Resources Development in South Asia. Manila: Asian Development Bank.

Ramirez, M. 2012. "Developing the Enabling Context for Student Assessment in Chile." SABER Working Paper 2, World Bank, Washington, DC.

Rivkin, S. G., E. A. Hanushek, and J. F. Kain. 2005. "Teachers, Schools, and Academic Achievement." *Econometrica* 73 (2): 417–58.

Rockoff, J., D. Staiger, T. J. Kane, and E. Taylor. 2012. "Information and Employee Evaluation: Evidence from a Randomized Intervention in Public Schools." *American Economic Review* 102 (7): 3184–213.

Rockoff, J. E. 2004. "The Impact of Individual Teachers on Student Achievement: Evidence from Panel Data." *American Economic Review, Papers and Proceedings* 94 (2): 247–52.

———. 2008. "Does Mentoring Reduce Turnover and Improve Skills of New Employees? Evidence from Teachers in New York City." NBER Working Paper 13868, National Bureau of Economic Research, Cambridge, MA.

Rockoff, J. E., B. A. Jacob, T. J. Kane, and D. O. Staiger. 2011. "Can You Recognize an Effective Teacher When You Recruit One?" *Education Finance and Policy* 6 (1): 43–74.

Sawada, Y., and A. Ragatz. 2005. "Decentralization of Education, Teacher Behavior, and Outcome: The Case of El Salvador's EDUCO Program." In *Incentives to Improve Teaching: Lessons from Latin America*, edited by E. Vegas. Washington, DC: World Bank.

Tan, E. 2013. *Assessment in Singapore: Assessing Creativity, Critical Thinking and Other Skills for Innovation*. http://www.oecd.org/edu/ceri/07%20Eugenia%20Tan_Singapore.pdf.

Taylor, E. S., and J. H. Tyler. 2012. "The Effect of Evaluation on Teacher Performance." *American Economic Review* 102 (7): 3628–51.

UNESCO. 2015. *EFA Global Monitoring Report 2015*. Paris: UNESCO.

USAID (U.S. Agency for International Development). 2012. "Examining the Role of International Achievement Tests in Education Policy Reform: National Education Reform and Student Learning in Five Countries." USAID Policy Paper. http://www.epdc.org/sites/default/files/documents/Examining%20the%20Role%20of%20International%20Achievement%20Tests.pdf.

Vegas, E. 2005. *Incentives to Improve Teaching Lessons from Latin America*. Washington DC: World Bank.

Walker, M. 2011. *PISA 2009 Plus Results: Performance of 15-Year-Olds in Reading, Mathematics and Science for 10 Additional Participants*. Melbourne: ACER Press. http://research.acer.edu.au/pisa/1/.

Wehella, M. M., and B. M. J. Balasooriya. 2014. "Free Education Policy and Its Challenges: Sri Lanka." In *Commonwealth Education Partnerships 2014/15 by Commonwealth Secretariat*. Cambridge: Nexus Strategic Partnerships.

Whelan, F. 2009. *Lessons Learned: How Good Policies Produce Better Schools*. London: Fenton Whelan.

Wiswall, M. 2013. "The Dynamics of Teacher Quality." *Journal of Public Economics* 100: 61–78.

World Bank. 2010. *Successful Education Reform: Lessons from Poland*. Knowledge Brief 34. Washington, DC: World Bank.

———. 2011. *Transforming School Education in Sri Lanka: From Cut Stones to Polished Jewels*. Washington, DC: World Bank.

———. 2012. *Sri Lanka: Student Assessment SABER Country Report*. Washington, DC: World Bank.

———. 2013. *Bangladesh Education Sector Review 2013*. Washington, DC: World Bank.

CHAPTER 5

Technical and Vocational Education and Training: The School-to-Work Transition

Introduction

While Sri Lanka outperforms other South Asian countries in terms of achievements in general education, its relative advantage dissipates at the levels of technical and vocational education and training (TVET) and, as will be seen in the next chapter, higher education. On average, Sri Lankan students complete about 10 years of school, considerably above the regional average of 6 years. However, opportunities to pursue studies or acquire job-specific skills beyond secondary education are very limited. Of a cohort of about 450,000 students who sit for General Certificate of Education Ordinary Level (GCE O-level) exams every year, only 20 percent will move on to higher education and only about one-third of the rest will enroll in TVET programs.[1] This leaves half the students leaving secondary schools with no opportunity for further education or training.

An additional concern is that the TVET programs currently offered are of questionable quality and lack labor market relevance, which means that graduates enter the labor market with skills that do not match the demand. This skills mismatch arises from (a) poor alignment of curricula with competences required to qualify for specific occupations; (b) a disproportionate number of students pursuing trades for which there is little demand; and (c) a training system unable to adjust to changes in the demand for skills fueled by growth and technological change.

Both skill shortages and skill mismatches undermine productivity growth and the prospects for Sri Lanka to join the group of upper-middle-income countries. To build a solid human capital base, the country needs to direct particular efforts to TVET and put in place a flexible skills development system that can adjust rapidly to changes in demand and give a larger proportion of students leaving general education opportunities to build their cognitive and noncognitive skills.

This chapter first examines how Sri Lanka's rapid economic transformation is affecting the demand for skills and what changes can be expected in coming years. It also reviews the skills constraints now confronting employers and their critical views of the products of the training sector, especially preemployment training. The chapter then examines the current structure and limitations of TVET before discussing in detail a range of reforms that could transform it into a demand-driven, flexible skills development system.

The Workforce for a Middle-Income Sri Lanka

Demand for Skills

Sri Lanka is on a path of rapid economic transformation—modernizing agriculture, deepening industrial development, and expanding services. As it moves forward, human capital is critical to ensure that the country can compete in a globalized world where higher-order skills and competences are crucial for attracting foreign investment and enabling domestic entrepreneurship. With technological advances and the global sourcing of skills, foreign investment, which is highly mobile, can be selective about where to invest, and the quality of skills available is critical to investment decisions, particularly in the service sector, where English and information communications and technology (ICT) skills are central.

As the economy becomes more diversified and more specialized, so too will the technologies and skills required and the infrastructure for skills delivery. The Republic of Korea and other countries that have achieved economic transformation have recognized this (box 5.1). As economies shift from being factor-based to efficiency-based and eventually innovation-based, the types of workers required change from low-skilled and low-cost manufacturing labor to technicians to engineers and scientists. Schools deliver basic skills, but as economies require more advanced and specialized skills, the locus of that training shifts to colleges and universities.

The rapid changes in demand for skills will continue well into the 21st century (figure 5.1) as, over time, even routine manual skills become more complex and higher-order skills for analytical thinking and communication take precedence. As innovation picks up, the quality of a country's workforce is integral to industrial upgrading. In addition to technical competencies, employers also desire soft skills, such as problem-solving, resilience, confidence, and judgment. Many of these skills, both cognitive and noncognitive, can be acquired through TVET if the programs have the flexibility to adjust to changing needs and have supportive infrastructure and instructors. In an environment of consistently evolving skills needs, on-the-job training (OJT) and lifelong learning also become critical.

Developing the right skill mix for Sri Lanka will be affected by a number of challenges, especially the new demographic challenge. Sri Lanka's demographic dividend peaked in 2005 and is likely to end by 2017. Both declining fertility (down from 3.4 percent in 1981 to 2.4 percent in 2011) and increasing life expectancy are changing the age structure of the labor force. Fewer youth

Box 5.1 The Republic of Korea: How Economic Development Changed Investment in Skills

Skills needs and policies for skills development depend on a country's stage of economic development and its goals. As economies transition from being factor-driven to efficiency-driven (Schwab and Sala-i-Martin 2012), the skills they need change. The Republic of Korea experienced a similar transition between the mid-1970s and the mid-1990s (figure B5.1.1). As the period began, the Korean economy was labor-intensive, most workers were low-skilled, and policies emphasized simple vocational (ADB 2012) and basic on-the-job training. As the economy grew more sophisticated and more capital-intensive and the need arose for better-skilled workers, the focus shifted to the acquisition of more advanced technical skills, which led to the expansion of junior technical colleges. Workplace training was then mandated, with an emphasis on expanding skills. Since the mid-1990s the Korean economy has become innovation-driven and knowledge-based. Skills policies have shifted from producing technicians to producing engineers and scientists. With active industry cooperation, university education has expanded to accommodate the demand for more sophisticated skills, and firms have committed to lifelong competency development for their workers

Figure B5.1.1 How Economic Development Drove Changes in TVET in the Republic of Korea

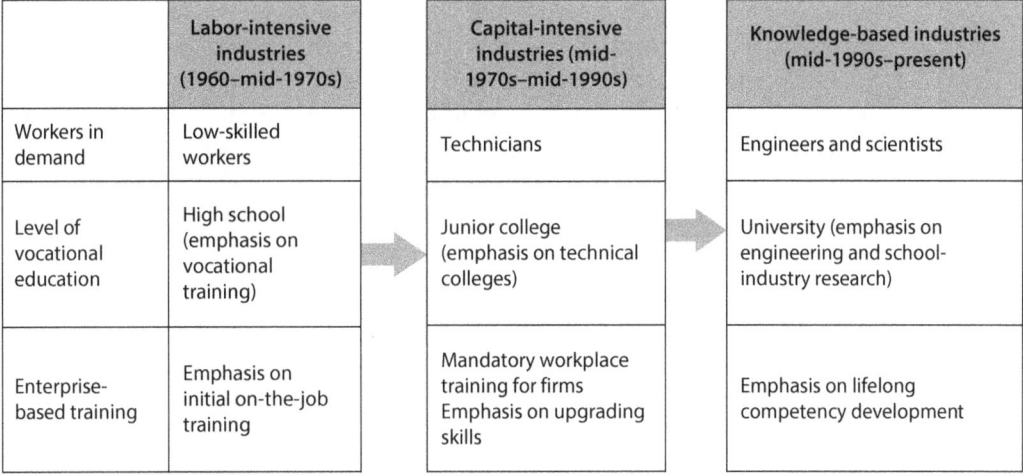

	Labor-intensive industries (1960–mid-1970s)	Capital-intensive industries (mid-1970s–mid-1990s)	Knowledge-based industries (mid-1990s–present)
Workers in demand	Low-skilled workers	Technicians	Engineers and scientists
Level of vocational education	High school (emphasis on vocational training)	Junior college (emphasis on technical colleges)	University (emphasis on engineering and school-industry research)
Enterprise-based training	Emphasis on initial on-the-job training	Mandatory workplace training for firms Emphasis on upgrading skills	Emphasis on lifelong competency development

Sources: ADB 2012, adapted from Kwon 2011.

(aged 15–24) are entering the labor force, and the proportion of young women dropped from 8.1 percent in 2002 to 4.6 percent in 2013 and of young men from 12.9 to 7.9 percent. Meanwhile, the proportion of male workers aged 40 and up rose from 28.4 to 34.1 percent (IPS 2015). These trends suggest that the labor market is tightening. They also suggest that efforts to upgrade skills need to be directed not only to youth but also to adults in the labor force.

Figure 5.1 Changes in Skills Needs, 1970–Present

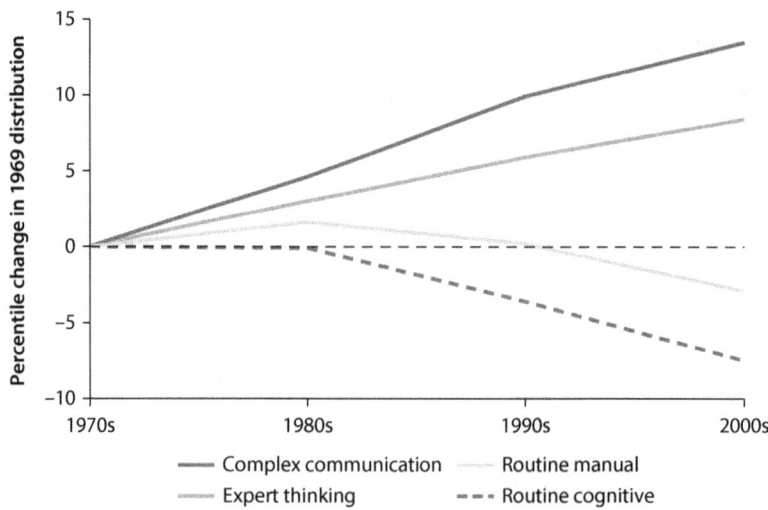

Sources: Levy and Murnane 2004; World Bank 2008.

Another challenge is the low female labor force participation rate (LFPR), which both affects the raw labor force supply and limits the prospects for a large skilled workforce, as well as the prospects for high returns to investments in training women. Even though more women participate in the labor force in Sri Lanka than in other South Asian countries, the Sri Lankan female LFPR compares poorly with other middle-income countries like Vietnam and Malaysia (figure 5.2). In 2013, it was 35.6 percent and the male rate was 74.9 percent. Participation rates are higher among two groups of women: those with the least education, and those with the most. In 2012 the LFPR of women with General Certificate of Education Advanced Level (GCE A-levels) was 17 percentage points higher than for women with GCE O-levels, and those with a bachelor's degree or more were employed at rates 36 percentage points higher than those with A-levels. However, the difference in the participation of highly educated women and those with less education is narrowing, though slowly. Encouraging more women to acquire job-specific skills through TVET programs and then seek paid work will be critical to expanding the supply of skilled labor.

Overseas employment may also drain potential skilled workers from domestic industry at a time when labor markets are tightening. Emigration is both a boon and a liability for workforce development in Sri Lanka. In 2014 remittances from migrant labor accounted for the largest share of the country's foreign exchange earnings, an estimated US$7 billion, equivalent to 10 percent of gross domestic product (GDP). However, an estimated 300,000 Sri Lankans leave each year for opportunities abroad. Historically, 40 percent of these have been women, of whom 80 percent are domestic workers (IPS 2015), but in recent years higher-skilled workers have represented a larger share.

Figure 5.2 Female Labor Force Participation in Developing Countries, 1990–2012

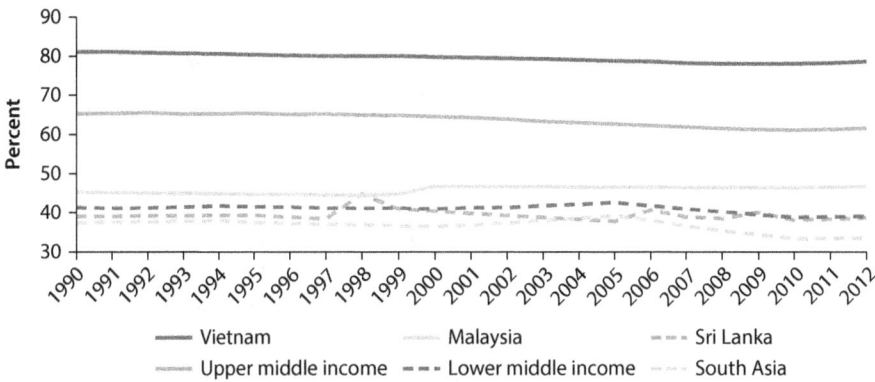

Source: World Bank 2016.
Note: Percentage of the female population aged 15–64.

Skills development programs will also have to take into account the aspirations of youth, which can lead to distortions in the labor market and contribute to youth unemployment. In Sri Lanka, where the proportion of youth aged 15 and up with secondary education is high (comparable to Malaysia and higher than in Korea) and family size is relatively small, parents have high expectations for what children can achieve; few are attracted to blue-collar professions. In Sri Lanka, queuing for white-collar jobs is a recognized phenomenon (box 5.2) that is partly driven by the duality of the labor market, where those formally employed—particularly those in the public sector—enjoy more desirable benefits and social protection.

Skill Shortages and Mismatches

In a labor market subject to rapid changes, two types of skill constraints seem to be hurting the economy: (a) employers do not find enough skilled labor to meet their needs; and (b) firms, particularly those in modern high-value-added industries, complain that the quality of training provided to TVET graduates is inadequate.

Sri Lankan firms see skills shortages as a major barrier to their productivity and growth; the post-2009 growth dividend has exacerbated the problem. As shown in figure 2.26, this constraint seems most severe in Sri Lanka. Compared to Indonesia (4.5 percent), the Philippines (7.8 percent), and Nepal (5.9 percent), a larger proportion of firms in Sri Lanka (16 percent) found the lack of well-trained workers to be a major constraint. In Sri Lanka, among other parameters—such as connectivity to global knowledge, access to finance, pressure from foreign competition, and infrastructure inadequacies—the productivity of firms (output and value added by worker) is closely correlated with access to skills (Dutz and O'Connell 2013).

In the Skills Toward Employment and Productivity (STEP) Employer Survey, among a range of labor factors that affect firm operations and growth, firms

Box 5.2 Why Educated Youth Are Unemployed

High unemployment rates of educated youth are a common phenomenon in Sri Lanka, partly because the public sector is considered the most attractive place to work. Although the national unemployment rate fell to 3.9 percent in 2013, the rate for those aged 15–24 was still 19.1 percent. Moreover, for those with GCE A-levels and above, the unemployment rate was 8.6 percent (DCS 2013). Reasons cited for this have been (a) educated youth have the wrong skills for the labor market; (b) unemployment is the result of queuing as young people wait for public jobs to open up; and (c) unemployment is a function of restrictive labor market policies that prevent firms from creating jobs (Arunatilake and Jayawardena 2010). Seers (1971), who first identified this problem, suggested that youth have high expectations but not the skills demanded in the labor market, and concluded that the problem was essentially the skills mismatch. Glewwe (1987) and Dickens and Lang (1991) empirically demonstrated the mismatch. By comparing actual earnings with reservation wages for youth with different amounts of education, however, Rama (1999) rejected the hypothesis and showed that educated youth queue for public jobs where the benefits and social protection are more attractive.

---

identified worker TVET skills as third most important after previous work experience and employee turnover. Notably, 33 percent of firms considered TVET skills to be important—more than twice the 16 percent that identified the general education of workers as a problem. Firms also highlighted that in the 12 months preceding the STEP survey, the overwhelming challenge when recruiting workers in almost all job categories except the most elementary was the lack of job-specific skills (figure 5.3).

Even when TVET graduates are available, firms question the quality of programs currently imparted by the TVET sector (figure 2.24). Over 50 percent of firms in the STEP survey stated that the TVET system did not produce the type of graduates they seek. A similar percentage stated that the sector does not offer practical skills and does not produce workers with up-to-date knowledge of methods, materials, and technology. Employers are also dissatisfied with university and general education. Indeed, dissatisfaction with general education, which feeds into TVET quality, is particularly high.

This lack of satisfaction with the qualifications and competences of graduates, the skills mismatch, can also be measured by comparing the educations and skills of individuals reported in a household survey against employer perceptions of what high- and low-skilled workers need: While 56 percent of employers think that highly skilled workers should have passed GCE A-levels, just over 40 percent of high-skilled wage earners and 30 percent of the self-employed have done so (figure 5.4). Similarly, while 40 percent of employers think a low-skilled worker should have passed GCE O-levels, only 20 percent of low-skilled wage earners and less than 30 percent of the self-employed have done so. TVET shows a similar mismatch: Almost 60 percent of employers

Figure 5.3 Skills Shortages, by Job Category

Source: Dundar et al. 2014, based on STEP Survey.

Figure 5.4 Labor Force Skills Stock and Employer Requirements

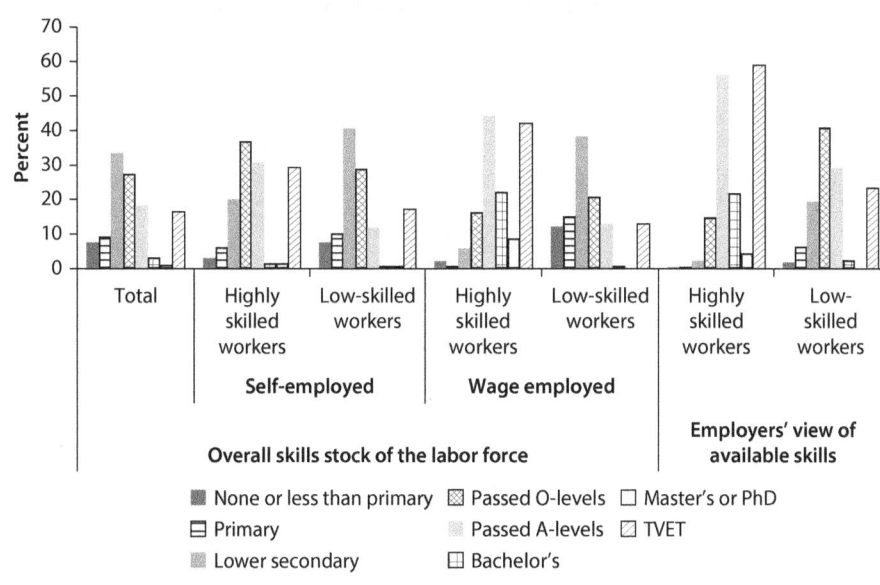

Source: Dundar et al. 2014.
Note: TVET = technical and vocational education and training.

expect that a high-skilled worker would have completed TVET, and 24 percent expect the same of low-skilled workers. Yet only 40 percent of high-skilled and 16 percent of low-skilled workers have such qualifications.

There is in particular evidence that the job-specific skills that employers value are in short supply. For example, 80 percent of employers expect a higher-skilled worker to know English and 40 percent expect that of less-skilled workers. Similarly, 75 percent of employers think an average higher-skilled worker should have computer skills, and 38 percent expect the same of lower-skilled workers (figure 5.5, panel B). However, only 20 percent of Sri Lankans are fluent in English and only 15 percent know how to use computers. The supply and demand differences are less stark in workers who are formally employed; the informal sector is far behind.

There is also some evidence of imbalance, with the population being overskilled for low-end jobs but underskilled for high-end jobs. Currently there are no substantial mismatches between supply of and demand for cognitive skills in low-skilled jobs, thanks to the expansion of primary and secondary education. On average, 71 percent of Sri Lankans use reading skills, 67 percent use writing skills, and about 87.5 percent use numeracy skills (figure 5.5, panel A). On average, those currently employed have substantially higher skills than employers need for low-skilled occupations but not enough skills to qualify for high-skilled occupations. Also, compared to other countries that participated in the STEP survey, the likelihood of Sri Lankans using reading and writing skills is lower, although their use of numeracy skills is similar.[2]

Figure 5.5 Labor Force Cognitive, English, and Computer Skills and Employer Requirements

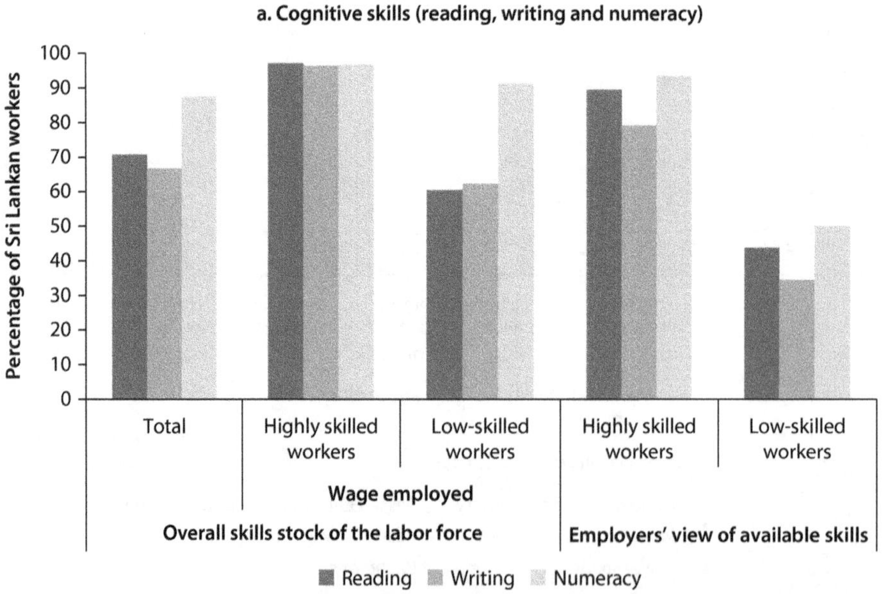

a. Cognitive skills (reading, writing and numeracy)

figure continues next page

Figure 5.5 Labor Force Cognitive, English, and Computer Skills and Employer Requirements *(continued)*

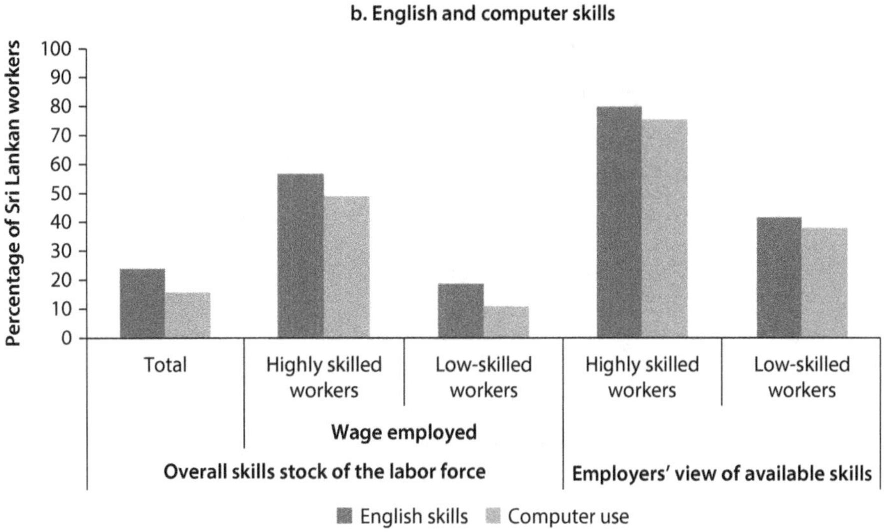

b. English and computer skills

[Bar chart showing percentage of Sri Lankan workers with English skills and Computer use across categories: Overall skills stock of the labor force (Total, Highly skilled wage-employed workers, Low-skilled wage-employed workers) and Employers' view of available skills (Highly skilled workers, Low-skilled workers). Approximate values — Total: English 24, Computer 16; Highly skilled wage: English 57, Computer 49; Low-skilled wage: English 19, Computer 11; Highly skilled (employers): English 80, Computer 76; Low-skilled (employers): English 42, Computer 39.]

Source: Dundar et al. 2014.

The view that inadequate skills depress national productivity and competitiveness is reflected in Sri Lanka's current rankings on international indexes. The Creative Productivity Index ranks Sri Lanka 18th of 24 regional economies generally and 12th out of 24 on human capital (ADB 2014). On the World Economic Forum Global Competitive Index, between 2014 and 2015 Sri Lanka's ranking among more than 170 countries dropped from 65th to 72nd (WEF 2014). Underlying these low and relatively stagnant rankings are, among other factors, problems in higher education and training and in labor market efficiency (Chandrasiri and Gunatilake 2015).

The TVET Sector: Organizational Structure and Shortcomings

The TVET sector in Sri Lanka is complex, fragmented, and poorly coordinated. The public sector consists of more than 30 statutory boards and 15 ministries (figure 5.6). The Ministry of Skills Development and Vocational Training (MSDVT) is responsible for more than 70 percent of publicly provided training, delivered through several agencies, each with its own board and procedures. Among them, the most important are the Department of Technical Education and Training (DTET), the National Apprentice and Industrial Training Authority (NAITA), the Vocational Training Authority (VTA), and the University of Vocational Technology (UNIVOTEC). The MSDVT, with support from the Tertiary and Vocational Education Commission (TVEC), formulates skills and youth development policies, coordinates institutions within its purview, and manages program administration and monitoring and evaluation (M&E). Specialized training (the other 30 percent of public training) is offered by other ministries, such as the Ministry of Health and the Ministry of Tourism.

Figure 5.6 Structure of the TVET Sector, 2016

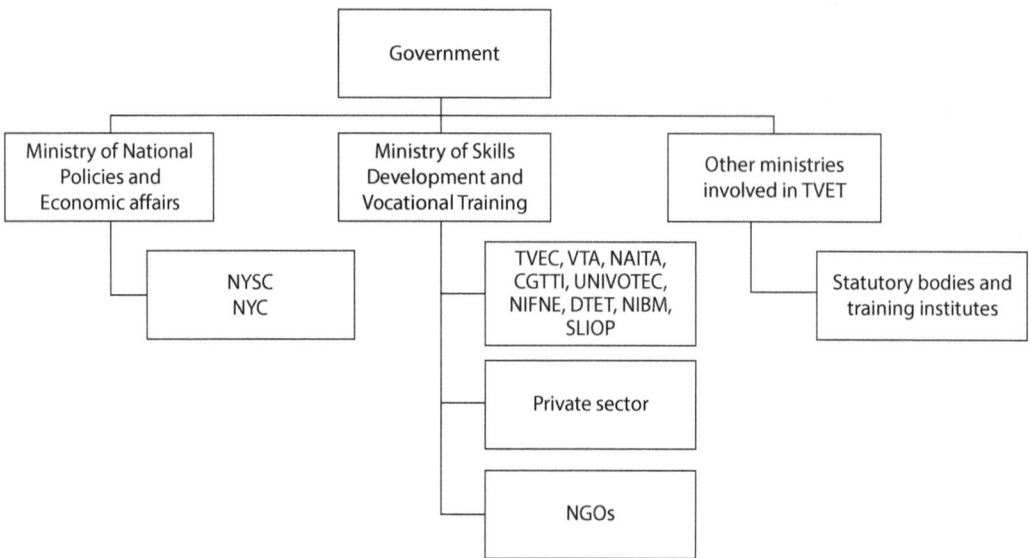

Source: Based on information obtained from the Sri Lankan government.
Note: Note: CGTTI = Ceylon-German Technical Training Institute; DTET = Department of Technical Education and Training; NAITA = National Apprentice and Industrial Training Authority; NGO = nongovernmental organization; NIBM = National Institute of Business Management; NIFNE = National Institute of Fisheries and Nautical Engineering; NYSC = National Youth Services Council; NYC = National Youth Corps; SLIOP = Sri Lanka Institute of Printing; TVEC = Tertiary and Vocational Education Commission; TVET = technical and vocational education and training; UNIVOTEC = University of Vocational Technology; and VTA = Vocational Training Authority of Sri Lanka.

Private institutions have a more significant role in providing training services than they have in general or higher education. About 29 percent of TVET students attend private institutions, and about 3 percent nongovernmental organization (NGO)–financed institutions. This may even be an underestimate because the data are drawn only from institutions registered with TVEC. Private training is provided through fee-based professional associations, some of which offer certificate, diploma, and degree courses, and through institutes set up under the Companies Act of 2007. Religious and voluntary NGOs offer craft training to unemployed youth, rural women, school leavers, and semiskilled or unskilled workers; most of their programs are free or charge only a nominal fee.

Sri Lanka's public sector is nevertheless still the primary provider of pre-employment training. Although the number of private and public registered institutes delivering training is roughly the same (519 public, 562 private and NGO in 2013), the public programs attract about 70 percent of students. Upon completion of training, students receive a national certificate or a diploma. UNIVOTEC offers a bachelor's degree. Of the programs listed in the TVEC training guide, 63 percent target school leavers with less than GCE O-levels, 29 percent require O-levels, and 8 percent require A-levels. Public TVET programs are effectively free for school leavers, though fees are charged to employed students taking part-time courses.

The TVEC is responsible for registering training providers and accrediting programs. While all public institutions are subject to this control, a large proportion of private institutions are neither registered nor accredited and have no incentive to do either.

Employers have identified both the shortage of TVET graduates and the inadequacy of the training they receive as major constraints. The problems are in large part caused by shortcomings related to its organization and management; the most important are the following:

- The fragmentation of the sector, with several ministries involved, a variety of agencies with their own statutory boards and procedures, and many private providers that are neither registered nor accredited. The lack of coordination not only can lead to duplication of efforts and inefficiencies; it also complicates the design and enforcement of an overall skills development plan.

- The alignment of training standards and competencies with the needs of the labor market is proceeding slowly. In 2005 Sri Lanka introduced a qualification (National Vocational Qualification [NVQ]) system to help define training standards based on occupational requirements. Based on the standards, curriculum and course content are supposed to be continually updated. The objective is to make it easier for employers to identify the specific qualifications of youth entering the labor market. Implementation is still problematic. Although the NVQ system is mandatory for public institutions, it is only partially used by the private sector. Any updating that does occur often happens slowly. Not all trades are covered, and soft skills are not always added to training content. As a result of varied or lagging application or incomplete information, many private employers still do not use the NVQ system in recruiting workers.

- Although employers should have a central role in ensuring that vocational training is relevant, they are still only minimally involved in the design and delivery of training programs. Potentially they could, for example, contribute to the development and upgrading of competency standards, endorse curricula, train instructors for specific industries, and provide part-time trainers. However, their relative lack of involvement is largely responsible for the disconnect between those programs and labor market demand, as well as for limited use of the NVQ framework. The government is now attempting to address this issue by setting up industrial sector skills councils (ISSCs) in priority sectors (box 5.3). The objective is to strengthen the links between the public and private sectors and for the councils to directly review and validate competency standards and training program design. However, although one ISSC was recently set up in the construction sector, the pace of establishing the councils is still very slow.

- There is little capacity for generating information on labor market outcomes and monitoring outcomes of the TVET system. There is also little capacity for regular assessment of labor market trends and changes in employer needs by analyzing labor market and firm surveys and tracer studies, which makes it hard to anticipate changes in demand or adjust training programs to new needs. Further, there is not enough information to measure how well

Box 5.3 Industrial Sector Skills Councils

The government is launching industrial sector skills councils (ISSCs) for priority sectors, starting with tourism, construction, light engineering, and information communications and technology (ICT). The councils are to be independent, employer-led organizations working with trade unions, professional bodies, and chambers of commerce and responsible for building up the skills of all those employed in their sector. They are to (a) undertake or validate skills gaps analysis and identify priority training needs; (b) set up a program of interventions to close the gaps, where necessary revising, formulating, and validating competency standards, training packages, and quality assurance mechanisms; and (c) provide assistance for skills certification and job placement. The councils can be a useful means to coordinate industry knowledge and views and feed the information into the skill development system.

---

programs, centers, and graduates perform. There is a dearth of information on staffing, teacher performance, program financing, and postprogram student employment status, which means there is little limited ability to evaluate outcomes or to engage feedback loops for program or system improvement.

- TVET in general suffers from a shortage of qualified teaching staff, especially staff with industrial experience. Unattractive salaries, few performance incentives, and minimal career progression structures undermine teacher motivation and make retention difficult. In the vast majority of cases, the lack of instructional materials, equipment, and facilities that are up to date further demoralize teaching staff. The result is an underskilled and unstable teaching base. Few instructors have much industrial experience, and there are few conduits for them to upgrade their skills through in-service training. As a result, many TVET institutions rely extensively on contract instructors.

- The quality assurance (QA) system is at an incipient stage of development: Registration and accreditation requirements have been formulated, and a unit has been set up within TVEC to apply them. However, a significant number of private institutions and courses are not even registered, much less accredited; TVEC has little capacity to verify the information given or enforce procedures; and training center adoption of a quality management system is either tentative or has faced difficulties or delays due to complicated reporting procedures. Regular monitoring of teacher performance and employment outcomes of graduates is also lacking. The monitoring challenge is compounded by fragmentation and variance, particularly in the private sector, which reduces opportunities to scale up quality programs.

There are nevertheless indications that the internal efficiency of Sri Lanka's TVET system has been improving. Internal efficiency is usually measured by retention and completion rates. Data up to 2010 on TVET institutions run by MSDVT, or its predecessor agency, suggest that while recruitment stagnated in 2004–07, after 2008 it improved, as did completion rates. While in 2004–07 the completion rate averaged in the mid-40s, it reached 76 percent in 2010 (Dundar et al. 2014). Data for 2014 indicate that these trends have continued. Although a high completion rate does not guarantee that graduates have the skills the labor market is looking for, it does indicate that students are completing courses of study.

There is also some comforting evidence that despite the shortcomings of the system, investing in skills pays off in Sri Lanka. Analysis of STEP survey data found that a TVET course of study has an estimated rate of return of 17 percent—nearly double the return on an additional year of formal education. Return on TVET went up from about 12 percent in 2000 to 21 percent in 2004 (figure 5.7, panel a), but by 2012 it had dropped slightly, to 17 percent. TVET returns are higher for graduates who are self-employed; in 2012 the TVET premium was

Figure 5.7 Wage Premiums in Sri Lanka, by Education and Skill Type

Source: Dundar et al. 2014.

Note: The first bar for each year (panel a) reflects the wage premium for completed primary education relative to no or incomplete primary education, and the next-to-the-last bar reflects the premium for completing bachelor's and above relative to passing A-levels. The last bar is the premium for TVET relative to non-TVET. The wage premiums represent differences in the coefficients of a regression of log hourly wage on basic controls (education, TVET, gender, urban, province, age, and age squared). TVET = technical and vocational education and training.

25 percent for the self-employed and 12 percent for formal wage earners. However, Sri Lankans with technology skills, computer knowledge, and English (figure 5.7, panel b) and soft skills like openness and emotional stability earn more than those without them, signaling their importance. This suggests that competencies rather than qualifications per se earn the greatest premium. This evidence supports the view that TVET is a profitable investment in Sri Lanka, and that the country could benefit from well-designed reforms that could improve sector efficiency and reach.

Sri Lanka's Skills Supply System: Areas for Potential Reform

Given the clear indications provided by the labor market and the current shortcomings of the training sector, now well identified, Sri Lanka needs to embark on a wide range of reforms related to (a) sector governance and accountability; (b) the quality of inputs; (c) the cost and financing of TVET; (d) private sector involvement; and (e) information and social perception.

Governance and Accountability

Although, in recent years, Sri Lanka has made progress in realigning its workforce development strategy with its economic development plan, and has given skills development a high priority, current skills development programs are not yet fully integrated with the government's economic development plan. Preparation of the Skills Sector Development Program (SSDP) in 2014 was a major achievement, but it needs to be periodically reviewed and updated to reflect and adjust to changes in economic conditions and priorities. Sector-specific and regional TVET plans are also being prepared, but an overarching workforce development plan has yet to be drafted in consultation with key stakeholders, especially employers. Implementing such a plan would stimulate national development.

Better coordination between providers would greatly facilitate the workforce development process. Given the large number of actors in the sector, interministerial coordination is necessary to both monitor progress and define strategic directions. The Inter-Ministerial Sector Coordination Committee (IMSCC) has been set up to coordinate national policies and programs, but it is not yet functional. To use resources efficiently, course offerings also need to be rationalized, and both physical and human resources redeployed as needed across all public TVET institutions.

Providing greater institutional autonomy and greater institutional accountability could lead to better performance. Because the central authorities exercise tight control, public training units are not fully accountable for performance and have little incentive to respond to—let alone anticipate—potential demand. Consequently, public institutions have neither the freedom nor any incentive to replace obsolete training courses, change curricula, or bring the private sector into decision making to foster responsiveness to labor market needs. Nor do they have any incentive to help graduates find employment. Increased institutional autonomy does not mean a smaller role for government but a changed one, where, in exchange for funding, the government sets expectations and defines the outcomes. The benefit of decentralized institutional decision-making autonomy is that skills would be better matched with labor markets and costs would be lower because of flexible governance structures and local information.

Another critical element is the need for wider dissemination of labor market information. No planning and strategy design can be effective without it. The planning process needs to regularly ascertain national and regional demand based on information from employers. It requires timely and accurate information about the current demand for skills and the training opportunities available, as well as reliable forecasts of potential needs. Currently, labor market information is mostly gained from reading newspaper job advertisements; there is no systematic use of all the data that labor market and firm surveys elicit. Lead ministries lack analytical capacity. Within the training system, there is also a need for more careful and systematic monitoring of how providers and instructors are performing through systematic analysis of data collected for each training provider and through periodic tracer studies. Efforts to build such monitoring capability have been launched, but they are still tentative and timid and need to be accelerated.

Assuring the quality of TVET programs also needs to be reinforced. QA systems involve institutional registration, course accreditation, and committed quality management. They also require the capacity to verify the information received and to enforce requirements. Building up QA implies not only ensuring the quality of public institutions but also extending the registration and accreditation process to cover more private providers. Gathering information on private and public TVET institutions and making it transparently available would improve the confidence in the system of potential consumers of TVET and help them make important investment decisions.

Quality of Inputs

Currently there is a significant disconnect between the skills of instructors and the technical competencies needed in the labor market. Further, vacancy rates for instructors average 32.5 percent across TVET institutions and are as high as 50 percent for a few institutions, such as DTET and NAITA. This lack of professionals entering TVET instruction, which is detrimental to training quality, is a function of cumbersome and lengthy recruitment processes, lack of preservice training or opportunities to upgrade skills, minimal career progression structure, and low salaries.

Creating opportunities for the professional development of instructors would enhance the quality of TVET instruction and make skills development more responsive to labor market needs. There needs to be a better balance between academic credentials and professional experience for instructors in vocational training centers and teachers in technical colleges. Similarly, teaching staff must not only be qualified in their own technical field but should also have mastered the pedagogical tools they need to efficiently transmit knowledge and practices.

Partnering with industry to train instructors on the current state of technology would be the most effective way of upgrading instructor skills. In some priority sectors, such as tourism, there is already great willingness to train instructors because there is a recognized need for a continuous supply of good-quality entrants. Efforts to upgrade instructor skills can be facilitated through ISSCs, and more generally, through greater involvement of the private sector in training.

In addition to greater opportunities for upgrading skills, there should be prospects for career progression and salary increases linked to performance. There is currently little incentive for instructors to focus on the timely graduation of their students or worry about their career paths after completing a skills program. An incentive structure that rewards instructors for such outcomes will encourage instructors to actively engage not only with students but also with industry to ensure that their students perform well. There has been a pilot attempt to introduce performance-based funding for training institutions, but this requires regular collection of output as well as input data and data on outcome indicators, such as the introduction of courses for which labor market demand is high and where graduates are employed. This pilot has to be thoroughly evaluated for feasibility and impact before it can be considered scalable.

Ensuring that centers also have up-to-date equipment and instructional materials would facilitate the work of instructors and improve the quality of training. Many TVET centers lack equipment that trainees can use to practice what they are being taught. As a result, employers are often reluctant to recruit graduates who have no hands-on experience; they prefer to hire youth with a good general education and build their technical skills in house on their own equipment and machinery.

Cost and Financing of TVET

For public institutions, TVET is mainly financed from the national budget, and each year the inflation-adjusted allocation is based on the previous year's budget.[3] The bulk of the budget is allocated to the main ministry, MSDVT, which spends most of it on centers run by the 10 agencies within its purview. In recent years, TVET public spending has been rising in real terms (figure 5.8), and 58 percent has gone to capital expenditures (Dundar et al. 2014); only 42 percent is spent on recurrent expenditures. It might be advisable to begin introducing monetary incentives to attract and retain qualified instructors.

About two-thirds of Sri Lanka's investment in TVET comes from the public sector, with the rest provided by the private sector and households. Although its fragmentation makes it difficult to get full information on sector costs and revenues, it is estimated that Sri Lanka allocates a total of 0.23–0.34 of GDP to TVET.

Public institutions rely on public funding and rarely recover their costs, despite modest fees for specific audiences. They rarely seek alternative sources of revenue from productive activities because they are not authorized to retain those revenues.

Diversifying TVET revenue sources and encouraging greater revenue self-generation (with accompanying autonomy) would encourage a more effective

Figure 5.8 Spending by the Ministry of Skills Development and Vocational Training

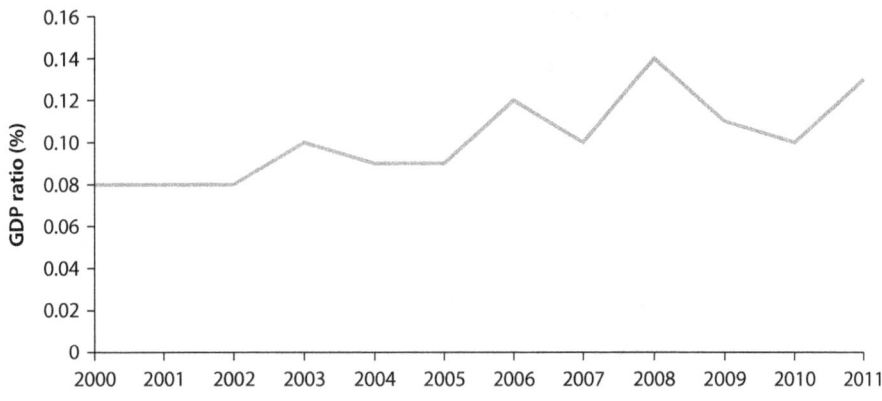

Sources: MOF budget estimates; Central Bank.

utilization of resources. Although, given the priority the government has given skills development, public funding for TVET institutions is likely to go up, it may not be enough to respond to the rising needs. TVET institutions should be encouraged to diversify their funding sources and generate resources themselves; that would force them to connect more with external partners and focus more on returns. This should, of course, be accompanied by the right to retain those revenues.

Introducing a voucher scheme could be a way to induce more youth to acquire job-specific skills and to make training delivery more efficient. A voucher is a demand-based financing mechanism that offers consumer choice, personal advancement, the promotion of competition, and equal opportunity (West 1997). The main driver of the efficiency argument for vouchers is that, through them, public and private institutions can compete for students, which in turn leads to both improvements in quality and cost and innovation as institutions seek to attract students. International evidence on voucher effectiveness is mixed, however, and certain prerequisites need to be considered before launching such a program (box 5.4).

Management of resources would also be more efficient if the system of budgetary allocations based on previous allocations were replaced by a more transparent system through which each institution requests funds based on identified needs and commits to achieving specific results. This would help ensure that funds are allocated more effectively, particularly if institutions are given incentives to maximize performance.

Private Sector Involvement

The TVET sector is still heavily supply-driven, taking into account neither the demand from employers nor the needs of the informal sector. In principle, the private sector helps to define occupational standards and is asked to offer placement to trained students. Industry is represented on public TVET boards and

Box 5.4 The Efficiency of Vouchers

The Sri Lankan government has expressed interest in providing vouchers to households to expand their technical education opportunities. A voucher is a publicly funded promissory coupon that households can use to defray the cost of attending a private school that participates in the program. The premise is that public financing need not imply public provision of education, and that governments can combine funding with quality assurance and take advantage of the competition between schools induced by school choice to achieve their efficiency and efficacy aims for education.

While voucher programs can be introduced at any level of education, they are usually found at the preprimary, primary, and secondary levels. Vouchers may be universal or targeted at disadvantaged households. In both cases, they offer disadvantaged households education opportunities beyond what would have been possible given their circumstances (e.g., low-income or poor local public schools).

In theory, all students can benefit from vouchers if private schools initially perform better (i.e., are more effective in a value-added sense) than public schools and public schools raise their performance in response to vouchers. If programs control the ability of private schools to screen voucher students, this can encourage students to exert more effort and select higher-performing private schools. And this can also encourage private schools to build their reputation based on performance (rather than screening success).

Evidence on the effect on voucher students: Typically, voucher programs in the United States have been found to have small or no positive effects on the test scores of voucher students (see Wolf et al. 2010 for Washington, DC; and Witte et al. 2012 for Milwaukee). There is some inconsistent evidence that voucher programs raise test scores for African-American students, who are traditionally disadvantaged (see Peterson et al. 2003 for New York City, Dayton, and Washington, DC). More consistent evidence suggests that voucher programs raise school progression, particularly for African-American students (see Chingos and Peterson 2015 for New York City; and Cowen et al. 2013 for Milwaukee). In rural Andhra Pradesh, India, private school vouchers provided to public school students as part of a small-scale experiment were generally found to have no positive effects on test scores. Although average test scores were comparable between voucher winners and losers, however, private schools had on average substantially lower expenditures than public schools, mainly due to lower teacher pay, which indicates that private schools were more cost-effective in producing academic achievement (Muralidharan and Sundararaman 2015).

Evidence on the effect on public school performance: Vouchers can induce competition between private and public schools and thereby induce higher public school performance. The evidence suggests that higher exposure to competition from vouchers, measured variously, induces gains in test performance in public schools in a variety of settings such as, in the United States, Milwaukee (Hoxby 2000; Chakrabarti 2008) and Florida (Figlio and Hart 2010); in Canada, Ontario (Chan and McMillan 2009); and in Sweden (Sandstrom and Bergstrom 2005).

Evidence on the aggregate effect: The aggregate or general equilibrium effects are ambiguous due in part to potential negative spillovers on the academic achievement of non-voucher students in both public and voucher schools. Estimates of aggregate effects of

box continues next page

Box 5.4 The Efficiency of Vouchers *(continued)*

vouchers from reduced-form and structural estimations using data from Canada, Chile, and Sweden vary from negative to null to positive (Epple, Romano, and Urquiola 2015). The most credible evidence on potential negative spillovers comes from rural Andhra Pradesh, India, where eligibility for private school vouchers was first randomized across villages and then randomized across applicants within villages. Test scores were found not to differ on average between nonvoucher students in voucher villages and nonvoucher villages, suggesting the absence of negative spillovers on nonvoucher students. These effects were examined separately for those who did not apply to the voucher program, applicants who lost the lottery for vouchers, and students in private schools before the voucher program (Muralidharan and Sundararaman 2015).

Recommendations:

- To start, the government would need to assess the existing level and variation in performance across private institutions, and, importantly, relative to public institutions. The desirability of a voucher program increases with the initial quality advantage possessed by private institutions.
- Voucher values should be high enough to attract adequate numbers of high-quality private institutions and of students. This benefit has to be traded off against the cost of the program in absolute terms and relative to per-student expenditures in public institutions.
- A robust, fair accreditation system for private institutions would be necessary, along with a robust quality assurance system for both public and private institutions.
- Information on the characteristics and performance of private and public institutions should be widely and regularly disseminated to help households in their selection of institutions.
- A robust, efficient, and fair grievance collection and resolution system for a voucher program is desirable.
- Some handholding support can be beneficial for disadvantaged households.
- What households can use vouchers for and what institutions can use voucher earnings for would need to be determined. In most programs, households can only use vouchers to pay for tuition and major fees, and institutions are required to use these earnings only for expenditures that benefit voucher students.

---

other committees, but this is mostly ad hoc; the industry representatives are a minority, with little influence on decisions made. They have no incentive to participate actively.

Design and implementation of a demand-driven TVET sector will not be successful, however, without industry ownership and full employer participation. Employers can ensure the quality and relevance of courses by endorsing competency standards and contributing to the design of course curricula. Occupational standards and training programs at all levels of qualification are now being revised to make them consistent with the qualification framework introduced in 2005. In 2013, only 114 occupations out of 400 (corresponding to NVQ 1–4) had been covered, and only 18,000 graduates out of 150,000 trained in accredited public and private institutions obtained NVQ certificates. Covering the whole spectrum of occupations will take time and constant updating. Involving employers in this process is critical not only to make course offerings more relevant but also to facilitate private sector recognition and use of training certificates and diplomas. By helping define competency standards at each qualification level, employers are more likely to consider NVQ certificates as providing useful information for their recruiting.

Employers can also greatly improve the quality of training by providing their assessment of labor market needs, offering industry training possibilities for both instructors and trainees, and participating in collaborative training programs (box 5.5).

Box 5.5 Examples of Employer Involvement in Training

Brazil. The mismatch between demand for and supply of skills in Brazil was bridged by employer-owned and -managed training. The National Industrial Apprenticeship Service (SENAI), created in the 1940s, is operated by the Federation of Industries. SENAI was followed by four other specialized services: commerce (SENAC), rural areas (SENAR), small enterprises (SEBRAE), and transportation (SENAT). All have the same basic structure and legal framework. Chambers of employers finance training programs through a 1 percent payroll levy and run the services with full independence. SENAI, now a network of 500 training institutions, trains 2 million workers a year. SENAR and SEBRAE were originally government bureaucracies; but because of inefficiencies, lack of responsiveness, and inflexibility, they were recreated with ownership, management, and budgets were transferred to employer associations. SENAT, the newest service, took a different path: It created an extensive satellite network to train employees of more than 1,000 firms throughout the country.

Australia. The industry skills councils (ISCs) in Australia are nonprofit companies financed by the government but governed by independent industry-led boards. Their mission is to bring together industry, training providers, and governments to work on a common industry-led agenda for workforce development. The ISCs

- provide integrated industry intelligence and advice on workforce development and skills needs to the Australian Workforce and Productivity Agency, the government, and enterprises.
- support the development, provision, and continuous improvement of training and workforce development products and services, such as Industry Training Packages.
- provide independent advice on skills and training to enterprises, matching identified training needs with appropriate solutions—they work with enterprises, employment service providers, registered training organizations, and government to allocate training places in the Enterprise-Based Productivity Places Program.

box continues next page

Box 5.5 Examples of Employer Involvement in Training *(continued)*

- in states and territories, engage with governments, industry advisory bodies, and peak representative bodies in their area of industry coverage.
- coordinate closely with the National Workforce Development Fund.

Sources: OECD 2012; World Bank 2008; www.isc.org.au.

The Government of Sri Lanka is fully aware of the need for greater involvement of the private sector and has made it a priority. It is launching ISSCs in four priority sectors: tourism and hospitality, construction, light engineering, and ICT over the next five years. Each council would have a majority of representatives from the industry and would be responsible for conducting or reviewing sectoral labor market studies (skills gap analysis), identifying training needs, revising and endorsing competency standards and course contents, and facilitating the apprenticeship and employment of trainees. Nevertheless, implementation of this initiative is proceeding slowly, mostly because of lengthy procedures. Government support is now critical to ensure that the councils are established swiftly and effectively.

Information Dissemination and TVET Brand Perception

Currently, too few youths opt for vocational training, despite its economic returns and demand from employers for more graduates with technical skills. Branding of TVET is not easy because higher education qualifications have more social status. Ignorance about the job and earnings opportunities TVET offer are also a significant factor. Moreover, social taboos are associated with certain sectors, such as tourism. For example, many Sri Lankans in rural areas who associate tourism with Western values actively discourage their children from entering that sector.

There is thus a definite need for both students and the population as a whole to become more aware of the work opportunities that a TVET qualification unlocks. Changing their perceptions requires disseminating more information: Families and youth need to be made aware of the employment and earnings prospects of TVET programs and about career paths in technical areas. Detailed information about the offerings of training providers (duration, content) and of their relative success in facilitating trainee employment would be useful for parents. Lead ministries and TVET institutions must therefore build up their analytical, monitoring, and reporting capacity and launch a dissemination strategy. The information could be made readily accessible through a variety of media, such as TV and radio programs (box 5.6).

Career counseling in secondary schools could also be a major channel to provide information on technical and professional options and types of careers. Schools need to be proactive in sharing information about technical and vocational career opportunities. This requires linkages between general education providers and TVET institutions so that the former can serve as a bridge to the latter.

Box 5.6 Benefits of Information Sharing

Households make decisions about career opportunities based on perceived returns to education; those decisions will be poor when their information is incorrect. Poorer families are more likely to be misinformed because they lack access to networks where they can find advice on schooling and career choice. One simple policy intervention would be to share information on the returns to different types of study and training programs to update what families believe about TVET and associated opportunities. There is some evidence that providing such information can have an impact on both educational attainment and learning outcomes (Jensen 2012; Avitabile and de Hoyos 2015).

Information provided in career counseling or recruitment can also be effective. In India, one experiment to attract female employees used recruiters from the business processing outsourcing (BPO) industry to share information with households, communities, and schools. The recruiters visited local community leaders in villages as well as schools.

For three years, recruiters provided information on the BPO industry to randomly assigned villages, giving an overview of the industry, the types of jobs available and how much they paid, specific firms seeking workers, how to apply for jobs, interview skills, mock interviews, and English assessment and hosting question-and-answer sessions. Ultimately, the experiment (a) increased household investments in women; (b) increased the employment of women; and (c) delayed their marriage and childbearing. Investments in women aged 15–21 increased in the treatment villages, with more women paying to enroll in courses like English and computer science. Also, women in the treatment villages were 4.6 percent points more likely to work in the BPO industry than those in comparison villages, and 2.4 percentage points more likely to work at all outside the home for pay.

Introduction of a technology stream in secondary schools should help to build this bridge. Students should have access to resources where they can learn about career choices and different paths to those careers.

Conclusion and Policy Options

The Government of Sri Lanka, which has long recognized that lack of a skilled labor force would make it impossible to achieve its inclusive growth goals, is embarking on a series of reforms motivated both by awareness of how an effective TVET sector could contribute to growth and by the desire to provide skill-building opportunities to a larger proportion of young Sri Lankans who cannot access higher education.

Summarizing the discussion on ways to improve the efficiency of the sector and meet the needs of Sri Lanka for skilled labor, the main recommendations are to

- ensure effective coordination among the various stakeholders and periodic updating of the skills development strategy.
- give agencies and centers more decision-making autonomy and use performance-based financing to promote accountability.

- strengthen quality assurance and apply it to the whole sector, public and private.
- build up labor market information systems and closely monitor the performance of TVET agencies.
- pursue professional development programs for instructors, with an emphasis on industry experience.
- reward good performance by instructors.
- encourage agencies to diversify revenue sources and let agencies keep self-generated revenues for their own use.
- more actively engage the private sector to make training truly demand-driven.
- ensure that ISSCs are established and operational.
- upgrade equipment and instructional materials, in line with technology improvements, whenever needed.
- actively disseminate information about employment and earnings prospects and about the offerings and performance of training providers.
- rely on the private sector for further expansion through public-private partnerships (PPPs).

Notes

1. See figure 6.1 for more detailed figures and data sources.
2. Bolivia, Laos, Vietnam, and Yunnan Province of the People's Republic of China.
3. Most spending in the provinces is channeled through funds levied at the center.

References

ADB (Asian Development Bank). 2012. *Innovative Strategies in Technical and Vocational Education and Training for Accelerated Human Resource Development in South Asia.* Manila: ADB.

———. 2014. *Creative Productivity Index: Analysing Creativity and Innovation in Asia.* Manila: ADB.

Arunatilake, N., and P. Jayawardena. 2010. "Explaining Labor Market Imbalance in Sri Lanka: Evidence from Jobsnet Data." In *The Challenge of Youth Employment in Sri Lanka,* edited by R. Gunatilaka, M. Mayer, and M. Vodopivec, 69–89. Washington, DC: World Bank.

Avitabile, C., and R. de Hoyos. 2015. "The Heterogeneous Effect of Information on Student Performance: Evidence from a Randomized Control Trial in Mexico." World Bank Policy Research Working Paper 7422, World Bank, Washington, DC.

Chakrabarti, R. 2008. "Can Increasing Private School Participation and Monetary Loss in a Voucher Program Affect Public School Performance? Evidence from Milwaukee." *Journal of Public Economics* 92: 1371–93.

Chan, P. C. W., and R. McMillan. 2009. *School Choice and Public School Performance: Evidence from Ontario's Tuition Tax Credit.* Mimeo, University of Toronto.

Chandrasiri, S., and R. Gunatilake. 2015. *The Skill Gap in Four Industrial Sectors in Sri Lanka.* Colombo: International Labour Organization.

Chingos, M. M., and P. E. Peterson. 2015. "Experimentally Estimated Impacts of School Vouchers on College Enrollment and Degree Attainment." *Journal of Public Economics* 122: 1–12.

Cowen, J. M., D. Fleming, J. F. Witte, P. J. Wolf, and B. Kisida. 2013. "School Vouchers and Student Attainment: Evidence from a State-Mandated Study of Milwaukee's Parental Choice Program." *Policy Studies Journal* 41 (1): 147–68.

DCS (Department of Census and Statistics). 2013. *Sri Lanka Labour Force Survey Annual Report 2013*. Colombo: Department of Census and Statistics.

Dundar, H., B. Millot, Y. Savchenko, T. A. Piyasiri, and H. Aturupane. 2014. *Building the Skills for Economic Growth and Competitiveness in Sri Lanka*. Washington, DC: World Bank.

Dickens, W., and K. Lang. 1991. "An Analysis of the Nature of Unemployment in Sri Lanka." NBER Working Paper 3777, National Bureau of Economic Research, Cambridge, MA.

Dutz, M. A., and S. D. O'Connell. 2013. "Productivity, Innovation and Growth in Sri Lanka: An Empirical Investigation," World Bank Policy Research Working Paper 6354, World Bank, Washington, DC.

Epple, D., R. E. Romano, and M. Urquiola. 2015. "School Vouchers: A Survey of the Economics Literature." NBER Working Paper 21523, National Bureau of Economic Research, Cambridge, MA.

Figlio, D. N., and C. M. D. Hart. 2010. "Competitive Effects of Means-Tested School Vouchers." NBER Working Paper 16056, National Bureau of Economic Research, Cambridge, MA.

Glewwe, P. 1987. "Unemployment in Developing Countries: Economists' Models in Light of Evidence." *International Economic Journal* 1 (4): 1–17.

Hoxby, C. M. 2000. "Does Competition Among Public Schools Benefit Students and Taxpayers?" *American Economic Review* 90 (5): 1209–38.

IPS (Institute of Policy Studies of Sri Lanka). 2015. *Sri Lanka: State of the Economy*. Colombo: IPS.

Jensen, R. 2012. "Do Labor Market Opportunities Affect Young Women's Work and Family Decisions? Experimental Evidence from India." *Quarterly Journal of Economics* 127: 753–92.

Kwon, D. -B. 2011. "TVET in Korea: History of Challenges and Responses and the Future. Korean Research Institute for Vocational Education and Training." Presentation at the World Bank, February 24.

Levy, F., and R. Murnane. 2004. "Key Competencies Critical to Economic Success." In *Defining and Selecting Key Competencies*, edited by Rychen, D. S., and L. H. Slaganik. Cambridge, MA: Hogrefe and Huber.

Muralidharan, K., and V. Sundararaman. 2015. "The Aggregate Effect of School Choice: Evidence from a Two-Stage Experiment in India." *Quarterly Journal of Economics* 130 (3): 1011–66.

OECD (Organisation for Economic Co-operation and Development). 2012. *Better Skills, Better Jobs, Better Lives: A Strategic Approach to Skills Policies*. Paris: OECD.

Peterson, P., W. Howell, P. J. Wolf, and D. E. Campbell. 2003. "School Vouchers: Results from Randomized Experiments." In *The Economics of School Choice*, edited by C. Hoxby, 107–44. University of Chicago Press.

Rama, M. 1999. "The Sri Lankan Unemployment Problem Revisited." Policy Research Working Paper 2227, World Bank, Washington, DC.

Sandstrom, M., and F. Bergstrom. 2005. "School Vouchers in Practice: Competition Won't Hurt You." *Journal of Public Economics* 89: 351–80.

Schwab, K., and X. Sala-i-Martin. 2012. *Global Competitiveness Report 2012–13*. Geneva: World Economic Forum.

Seers, D. 1971. *Matching Employment Opportunities and Expectations*. Geneva: International Labour Organization.

Tan, H., and S. Chandrasiri. 2004. "Training and Labor Market Outcomes in Sri Lanka." World Bank Institute Working Paper. World Bank, Washington, DC.

UNP (United National Plan). 2015. *The Five-Point Plan*. Colombo: UNP.

WEF (World Economic Forum). 2014. *The Global Competitiveness Report 2014-2015*. Zurich: WEF.

West, E. 1997. "Education Vouchers in Principle and Practice." *World Bank Researcher Observer* 12 (1): 83–103.

Witte, J. F., D. Carlson, J. M. Cowen, D. J. Fleming, and P. J. Wolf. 2012. *The MPCP Longitudinal Educational Growth Study Final Year Report*. School Choice Demonstration Project Report 29. Fayetteville: University of Arkansas.

Wolf, P., B. Gutmann, M. Puma, B. Kisida, L. Rizzo, N. Eissa, and M. Carr. 2010. *Evaluation of the DC Opportunity Scholarship Program Final Report, Executive Summary*. Washington, DC: National Center for Education Evaluation and Regional Assistance, Institute of Education Sciences, U.S. Department of Education.

World Bank. 2008. *School and Work in the Eastern Caribbean: Does the Education System Adequately Prepare Youth for the Global Economy?* Washington DC: World Bank.

———. 2014. *Skills Development Project-Project Appraisal Document*. Washington, DC: World Bank.

———. 2016. *Sri Lanka: A Systematic Country Diagnostic—Ending Poverty and Promoting Shared Prosperity*. Washington, DC: World Bank.

CHAPTER 6

Higher Education: From Intakes to Outcomes

Introduction

In Sri Lanka, as in any other country, higher education is the most complex segment of the education pyramid because it has several missions: delivering quality teaching, equipping students with market-relevant skills, producing useful research, and contributing to social well-being. It is also expected to offer students academically selective but socially neutral access. To reach these objectives, which all contribute to economic development, higher education needs to have adequate resources, to use the resources efficiently, and to be effectively and transparently managed, with full and clear accountability. Because achievement of several of these missions is not satisfactory in Sri Lanka, the country's huge human resources potential cannot be fully realized.

Despite significant improvements in the last decade, higher education in Sri Lanka is not performing on a par with the group of upper-middle-income countries Sri Lanka aspires to join. One reason is the heritage from lower levels of education; another reason is the policies and practices of the authorities in charge of higher education. Only a holistic approach that deals with both will bring success.

This chapter first examines who has access to which types of higher education institutions (HEIs) and programs and analyzes the performance of the system (the quality and relevance of inputs, outputs, and outcomes). It then deals with how the system is financed, how the financial resources are utilized, and how higher education is governed, before at last discussing policy options.

Overview of the Higher Education Sector

In 2014, Sri Lanka had 15 public universities, 18 other higher education institutes under the University Grant Commission (UGC), 13 private HEIs, and one Sri Lanka Institute of Advanced Technological Education (SLIATE) that comprises 13 advanced technical institutes. An estimated 630,000 students were enrolled (table 6.1), about 80 percent of them in public institutions and almost half of

Table 6.1 Enrollment in Higher Education, by Institution, 2014

Type of institution	Number of institutions	Enrollment	Share (%)
Public universities	15	130,439	21
Postgraduate and other institutes	18	13,810	2
Open universities	1	36,922	6
External degree programs (EDPs)	–	298,801	48
SLIATE	1	15,294	2
Private higher education institutions[a]	13	123,489	20
Students abroad[b]	–	10,000	1
Total		628,755	100

Sources: UGC 2014; MOHE 2014.
Note: – = not applicable.
a. Institutions recognized by MOHE.
b. Estimate.

those in external degree programs (EDPs).[1] EDP students do not attend classes in universities and use distance learning methods, which are often outdated. Though their number has been decreasing recently, they are still the single largest group of students.

Access to Higher Education

Enrollment in higher education in Sri Lanka is comparable to the average in low-income countries, and lower than in middle-income countries. Although enrollment in almost all segments has increased in recent years, there has been no "explosion" of the kind many other countries have experienced, partly because of pre-university bottlenecks. The flow of entrants into higher education consists of students who have passed the GCE A-levels, a number that has not changed much for the last four years. The number of students taking the exam has gone up by only 3 percent and the pass rate itself has stagnated at about 60 percent. This is the first clear illustration of the heritage from the earlier stages of education, though it is compounded by demographic trends.

In addition, the public higher education subsector cannot even tap the pool of youths who, having passed the hurdles of secondary education, in principle have the credentials for postsecondary study, and the largely unregulated private sector is too small to bridge the gap. Hence, large cohorts of young people have neither prospects for continuing on to higher education nor the qualifications necessary to join the labor force. An estimated three out of four youths who finish secondary education leave the general education system soon after (figure 6.1). Of those who do pursue postsecondary education, few have access to public universities, which constitute the elite segment of higher education.

Of the 240,000 students who sat for the GCE A-level exam in 2014 (figure 6.1), some 144,000 passed, in theory becoming eligible to attend an "HEI"; of these, about 47,000 entered a public institution, 14,000 became EDPs, and 26,000 entered a private university. The remaining 57,000 (almost 40 percent) left the education system.

Figure 6.1 Paths to Higher Education in Sri Lanka, 2014

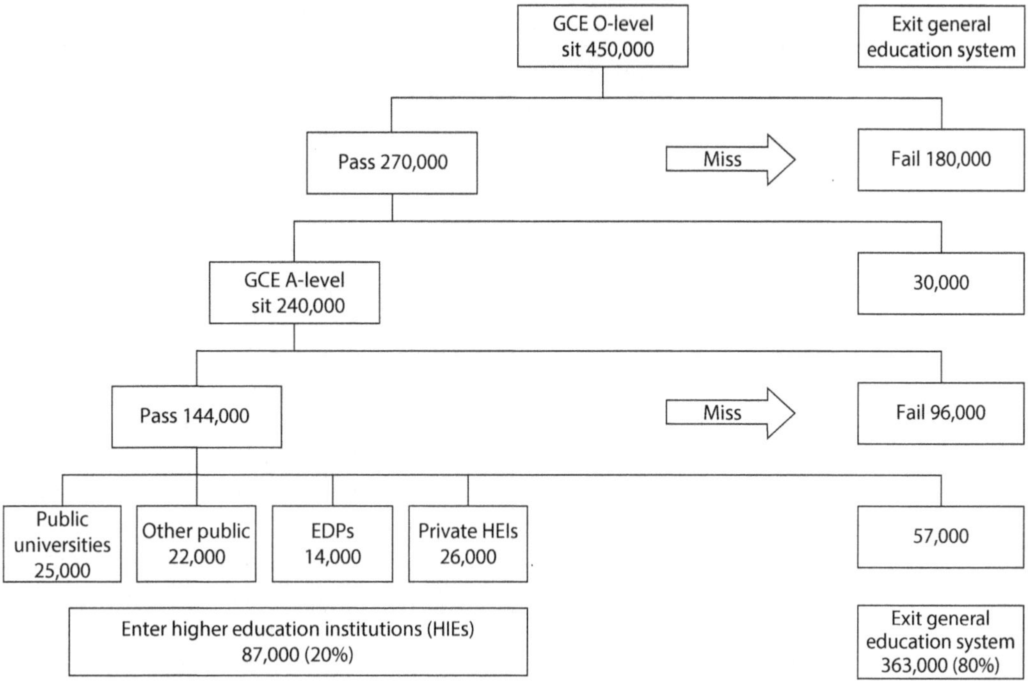

```
                    GCE O-level              Exit general
                    sit 450,000              education system

        Pass 270,000      → Miss →    Fail 180,000

        GCE A-level                     30,000
        sit 240,000

        Pass 144,000      → Miss →    Fail 96,000

  Public    Other public   EDPs    Private HEIs        57,000
universities   22,000     14,000     26,000
  25,000

     Enter higher education institutions (HIEs)    Exit general
              87,000 (20%)                      education system
                                                   363,000 (80%)
```

Sources: Data from MOHE 2014 and UGC 2014.
Note: EDP = external degree program; GCE = General Certificate of Education; and HEIs = higher education institutions.

The legacy of problems with secondary education is also reflected in the program choices of those entering higher education. The lack of appetite among GCE candidates for reputedly difficult scientific subjects is reflected in a similar reluctance among university students to attack the science, technology, engineering, and mathematics (STEM) disciplines. Also, although university admission criteria take into account geographic location as well as merit, enrollment rates by province differ substantially.

Where They Enroll

An estimated 26,500 students who could not find a seat in a public institution enrolled in a private one ("nonstate" in Sri Lanka). Private higher education is still largely informal; the MOHE recognizes 13 providers as degree-awarding institutes, and an unknown but larger number of other institutions operate without MOHE control or support. Considering only the 13 formally recognized providers, Sri Lanka appears to have one of the lowest shares of private higher education providers in the world; it falls into the group of countries which combine low private participation and a low higher education GER. Less than 5 percent of higher education students are enrolled in private HEIs; meanwhile, private HEIs enroll 79 percent of students in Japan, 80 percent in the Republic of Korea, 85 percent in Chile, and 86 percent in Israel—all countries that boast of high higher education enrollment rates.[2]

What happens to the 57,000 students eligible for but not enrolled in an HEI is not known precisely. Some enroll in a TVET institution, and others enter the labor market. An estimated 10,000 or less have the luxury of studying abroad—though Sri Lanka's outbound mobility ratio is very low. Thus, there is obviously a substantial pool from which higher education could draw to expand; an even larger source of expansion is secondary students who fail to qualify for the GCE A-levels—almost a third of those who take the GCE O-levels.[3]

Admissions are based on both merit and district quotas, but their weight differs from one discipline to another. In the arts and humanities, only merit is supposed to be taken into account, but in reality up to 20 percent of admissions are also based on historical district quotas. In all other disciplines, the weight of merit varies between 32 and 38 percent. Although the quota system was installed for laudable equity reasons, it has been so politically manipulated that ultimately it has had perverse effects. Many bright students are barred from universities because the system favors students on the basis of the district where they live, irrespective of their academic level. Hence, the "elite" public universities are not necessarily composed of the most meritorious students.

Looking at the broad higher education sector—"tertiary" education—allows for international comparisons. It is clear that the main source of increased enrollment in that sector for 2010–12 was by far in the short general cycles, regrouped in the ISCED 5 category.[4] Despite the spectacular ISCED 5 jump, their share in total enrollment is still much lower than in the comparator countries (table 6.2).

Participation

In 2013, the higher education GER in Sri Lanka was 18.8 percent. Sri Lanka was 86th out of 127 countries in 2012 and 71st of 97 in 2013. The Philippines, Vietnam, and India—which all have significantly lower GDP per capita than Sri Lanka—had GERs of 25 to 34 percent. In 2012, the GER for Indonesia, with the same GDP per capita, was almost double Sri Lanka's. Of the ASEAN countries with which Sri Lanka aims to compete, Malaysia's GER was 20 points higher and Thailand's was 35 points higher than Sri Lanka's (figure 6.2). Basically, Sri Lanka's higher education GER is lower than it should be, given its GDP per capita (figure 6.3).[5]

Table 6.2 Tertiary Education: Changes and Shares of Enrollment, by ISCED Levels, Selected Countries, 2010–12
Percent

	Change in enrollment			Share of enrollment			
	ISCED 5	ISCED 6, 7, and 8	All	ISCED 5	ISCED 6 and 7	ISCED 8	All
Malaysia	−4	5	1	40	57	3	100
Korea, Rep.	5	2	3	24	74	2	100
Sri Lanka	84	0	4	8	90	1	100
Thailand	−8	2	0	14	85	1	100

Source: UIS.

Figure 6.2 Tertiary Education Gross Enrollment Rate, Selected Countries and Groups of Countries, 2013

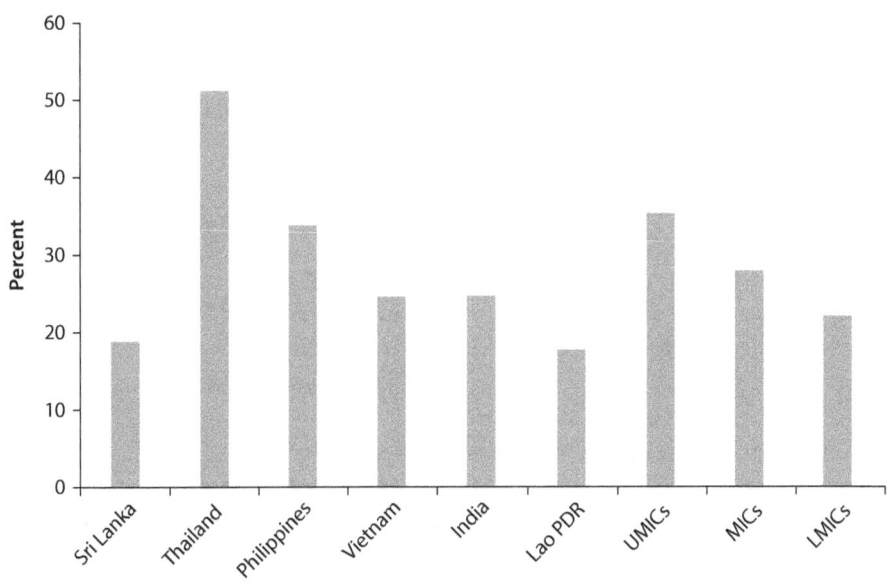

Source: UIS.
Note: LMICs = lower-middle-income countries; MICs = middle-income countries; and UMICs = upper-middle-income countries.

Figure 6.3 Higher Education Gross Enrollment Rate and GDP per Capita, International Comparisons, 2012

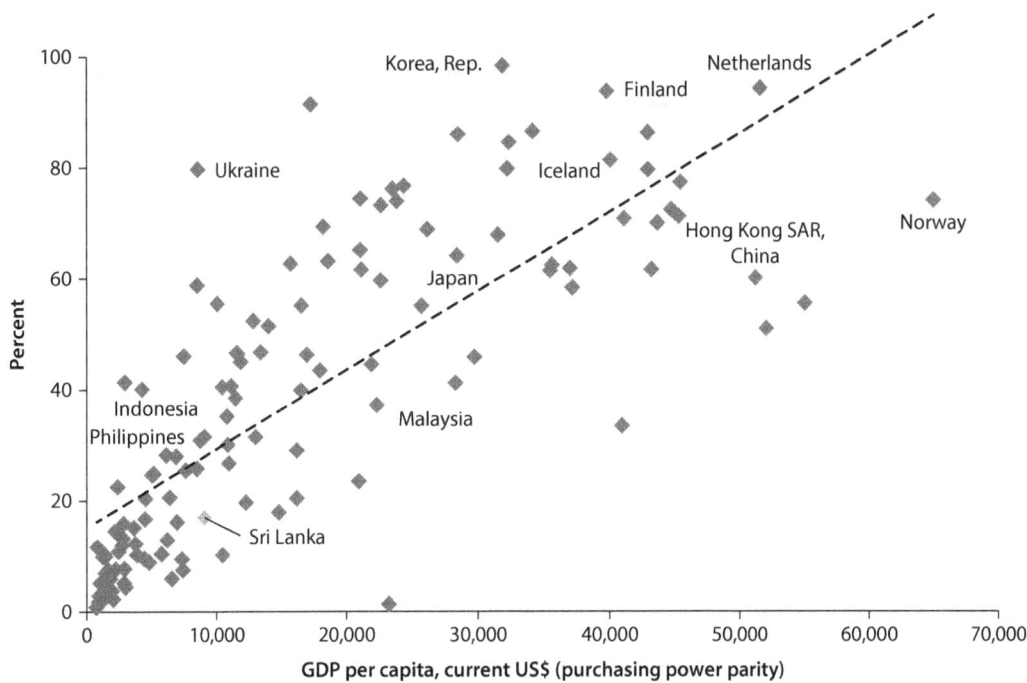

Source: WID.
Note: GDP per capita expressed in purchasing power parity, current international $.

From a dynamic perspective, Sri Lanka's 2013 higher education GER corresponds to the one lower-middle-income countries averaged in 2010, middle-income countries in 2006, and upper-middle-income countries in 2002. Thus, to catch up with the upper-middle-income country group, Sri Lanka must bridge a gap of at least 11 years (figure 6.4).

Some additional observations are needed to complete the analysis of enrollment rates:

- The GER estimated from administrative sources may be inflated to the extent that it takes into account students enrolled in EDPs. A large, but not precisely known, proportion of those students are working adults or the unemployed who seek to upgrade their qualifications, and students enrolled in regular programs who want to beef up their résumés with additional degrees. Adding such part-time students to full-time ones confuses categories and may lead to incorrect conclusions.
- Data from the Household Income and Expenditure Surveys (HIES), as in many other countries, yield even lower GERs than data from administrative sources. The aggregate GER estimated from the 2012/13 HIES barely reaches 15 percent.
- The admissions process is excruciatingly slow, because of extended negotiations between universities and UGC, political interference, and sheer technical inefficiency. After they take the GCE A-levels exam, it can take up to two years for students to start attending courses. These delays severely and unfairly penalize students, who must be idle for long periods of time, lose studying habits, and often miss the foundation courses offered by universities.

Figure 6.4 Tertiary Education Gross Enrollment Rate, Sri Lanka and Countries Grouped by Income, 1999–2013

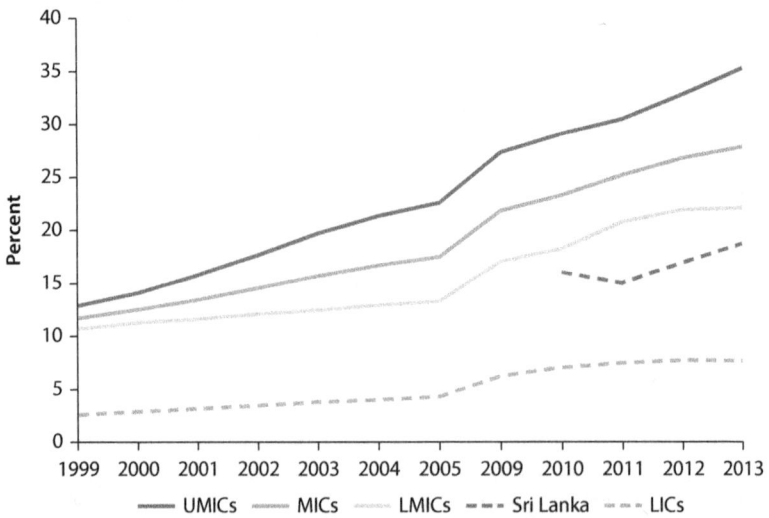

Source: UIS.
Note: LICs = low-income countries; LMICs = lower-middle-income countries; MICs = middle-income countries; and UMICs = upper-middle-income countries.

Fields of Study

The distribution of students in public institutions by field of study is highly skewed toward the arts and the social sciences. Together, arts, law, management, and commerce accounted for 55 percent of total undergraduate enrollment in 2014, and science, engineering, architecture, and computer science accounted for only 28 percent (table 6.3).

This pattern is not surprising, given the distribution of the pool of those who pass GCE A-levels and are eligible for university. The secondary school distribution by streams is a strong predictor of specialization in university, for both intakes and total enrollment (table 6.4).

The easier the discipline, the more students it attracts (figure 6.5). It can be assumed that students will use the same low-risk strategy in their choices of both further studies and job markets. This illustrates the qualitative dimension of the heritage, and its far-reaching consequences. The distribution of postgraduate enrollment not only mechanically reproduces but even amplifies what is observed at the undergraduate level (table 6.3). The bias is most extreme in the EDPs: about 68 percent of EDP students are in arts programs and just 10 percent in physics programs.

This attraction to soft disciplines is certainly not unique to students in Sri Lanka, but here again Sri Lanka has a special, and unenviable, position. It is ranked first of 106 countries for the proportion of its students in humanities and arts but is only 79th of 99 countries for the proportion in science and

Table 6.3 Undergraduate and Postgraduate Enrollment, by Discipline, Public Universities and Institutions, 2014

Disciplines	Undergraduate enrollment	Share (%)	Postgraduate enrollment	Share (%)
Arts	25,873	31	9,332	29
Management, commerce, and law	19,741	24	8,968	28
Medicine, dental, veterinary, indigenous med., paramedical	10,201	12	2,839	9
Agriculture	3,884	5	1,190	4
Science, IT, engineering, and architecture	23,509	28	7,054	22
Education			2,335	7
Total	83,208	100	31,718	100

Source: UGC 2014.

Table 6.4 Student Distribution, by Discipline Groups, 2014
Percent

	GCE A levels	University undergraduate admissions	University undergraduate enrollment
Social sciences	73	50	55
STEM	26	33	28

Source: UGC 2014.
Note: GCE = General Certificate of Education; and STEM = science, technology, engineering, and math.

Figure 6.5 GCE A-Levels: Pass Rates and Distribution, by Discipline Groups, 2014

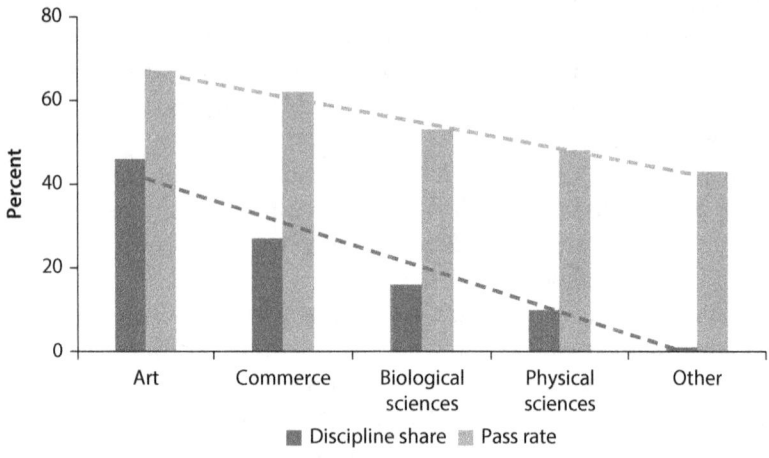

Source: MOHE 2014.

engineering (table 6.5). For engineering alone, it fares even worse, at 92nd of 103 countries.[6] The consequences will be discussed later, but at this point, it is worth observing that Sri Lanka has more in common with the Lao People's Democratic Republic than with Singapore, Korea, or Vietnam.

Student Profile

Among the various factors affecting how equitable the higher education sector is, three—gender, location, and economic background—can be observed quantitatively.

Sri Lanka can rightly boast of its gender parity in primary and secondary education. Parity is not lost in higher education: the higher education GER estimated from the HIES data was 12.3 percent for males and 17 percent for females in 2012–13. However, it tends to erode as students move up the university ladder. The female lead at the GCE A-level exam is dented at the undergraduate admission stage and gradually disappears by postgraduate study (table 6.6).

High as it is, the participation of women in higher education is not evenly distributed across programs. While women account for 73 percent of students of the arts, law, management, and commerce, their participation drops to 42 percent in scientific fields (table 6.7). In postgraduate studies, they are a solid majority in education (71 percent), and are still fully dominant in the arts (55 percent), but are a minority in management (35 percent) and engineering (26 percent). In SLIATE, 36 percent of the students are women.

Sri Lanka's gender patterns are not unique; those in Eastern Europe, the Middle East, and Latin America are similar. In 2013, as many as 99 countries had achieved gender parity. However, Sri Lanka outperforms most South and East Asian comparators (figure 6.6). This is an asset for Sri Lanka. It should be preserved as enrollment continues to grow. The question, however, is what

Table 6.5 Higher Education Enrollment, by Discipline Groups, Selected Countries, 2012 or Closest Year

Discipline group and country	%	World rank[a,b]
Humanities and arts		
Sri Lanka	**49.7**	**1**
Korea, Rep.	18.2	15
Lao PDR	12.8	36
Argentina	12.5	39
Uzbekistan	11.6	42
Turkey	9.6	54
Singapore	9.4	57
Malaysia	8.5	68
Thailand	7.4	80
Kyrgyz Republic	6	83
Vietnam	5.7	87
India	5.6	89
Indonesia	0.5	105
Science, engineering, manufacturing, and construction		
Singapore	40	3
India	38.8	4
Korea, Rep.	35.2	5
Malaysia	34.8	6
Uzbekistan	25.7	27
Indonesia	24.2	38
Vietnam	23.6	41
Argentina	18.5	68
Thailand	18.2	71
Honduras	17.9	77
Turkey	17.7	78
Sri Lanka	**17.2**	**79**
Lao PDR	13.8	90

Source: UIS.
a. Number of countries ranked = 106.
b. Number of countries ranked = 99.

Table 6.6 Female Participation in Higher Education, by Level, 2014

Level of participation	Females	Total	Females/total (%)
Qualified (GCE A/L)	93,557	143,740	65
Admissions, undergraduate programs, public universities	15,694	25,200	62
Enrollment, undergraduates, public universities	43,839	80,408	55
Enrollment, postgraduates, public universities	16,498	33,084	50

Sources: UGC 2014; MOHE 2014.
Note: GCE A/L = General Certificate of Education, Advanced Level

Table 6.7 Female Undergraduate Admissions, by Discipline, 2014
Percent

Discipline	Females/total	Distribution (females)
Arts	81	38
Law	84	2
Management and commerce	61	19
Medicine, dental, veterinary, indigenous med., paramedical	68	11
Agriculture	70	7
Science	47	15
Engineering	24	2
Architecture	45	1
Computer science	45	4
Total	62	100

Source: UGC 2014.

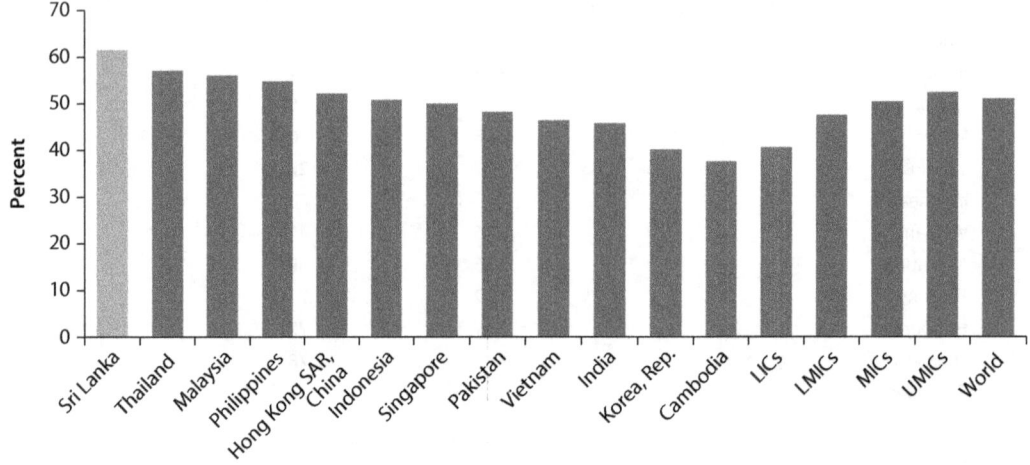

Figure 6.6 Female Enrollment in Higher Education, Selected Economies and Groups, 2013

Source: UIS.
Note: LICs = low-income countries; LMICs = lower-middle-income countries; MICs = middle-income countries; UMICs = upper-middle-income countries.

women make of their investment in higher education and how they recoup it on the labor market.

The issue of geographical equity of access cannot be addressed in the same way for higher education as for lower levels, not only because the number of sites is more limited but also because higher education students are likely to have considerably more mobility than younger students. Nevertheless, the wide regional disparity of the GER is telling; in 2012/13 it was three times higher in the Western Province than in the North Central or the Eastern Province (figure 6.7). Similarly, the GER in rural areas was just 14.2 percent, compared to 20.8 percent in urban areas.[7]

Figure 6.7 Tertiary Education Gross Enrollment Rate, by Province and Gender, 2012–13

Source: HIES 2012/13.

Figure 6.8 Tertiary Education Gross Enrollment Rate, by Quintile and Gender, 2012–13

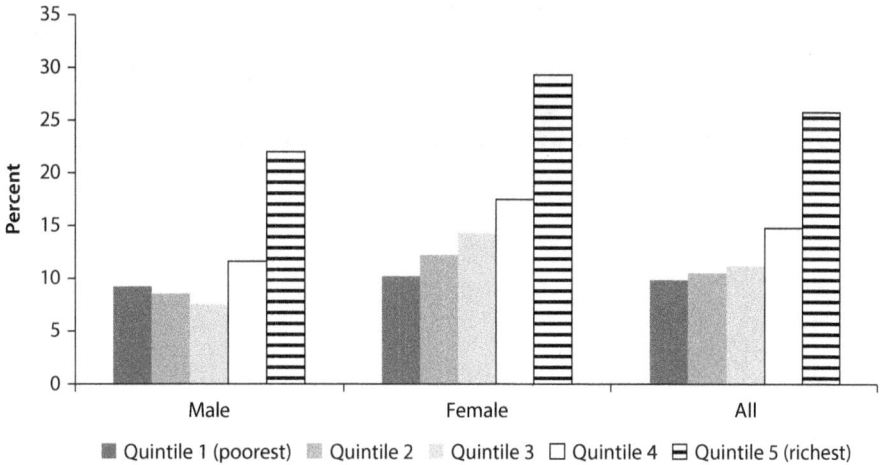

Source: HIES 2012/13 data.

Economic background significantly affects participation. The GER is 2.7 times higher for students from the richest quintile than for those from the poorest one (figure 6.8). While this is a familiar pattern in many countries, it is more intriguing in the case of Sri Lanka, where in secondary education the GER for the richest students is only 1.3 times that of the poorest ones. Here the legacy of secondary education does not play out as well as it does for gender. The economic selection at the university level, pronounced for both men and women, is indeed a matter of concern.[8]

Performance: Inputs, Processes, Outputs, and Outcomes

Measuring higher education performance is difficult due to data limitations. The access issues already discussed are a first indicator, but others can also be used. Here attention is given first to inputs, the most important being HEI human resources. We then move to quality assurance (QA) processes, labor market outcomes, and research. The section concludes with how Sri Lanka fares in international rankings.

Human Resources

Arguably, among the many factors that affect the quality of higher education learning and research, faculty members are the most important. Are there enough? Are they properly qualified? Do they use teaching techniques adapted to the modern world? Answers to these critical questions are possible only for the public universities and other HEIs managed by the MOHE.

These institutions employ about 5,000 full-time faculty, of whom 4,500 are in the 15 public universities.[9] On average, the student-teacher ratio (STR) is 29:1—extremely high for tertiary education and not compatible with quality student-centered teaching. Indeed, in 2012, the higher education STR in Sri Lanka, then estimated at 45:1, was the fourth highest in the world; in Malaysia it was 19:1; and in Korea it was 14:1. Sri Lanka belongs to the small group of countries with both extremely high STRs and very low GERs (figure 6.9). This serious deficit in

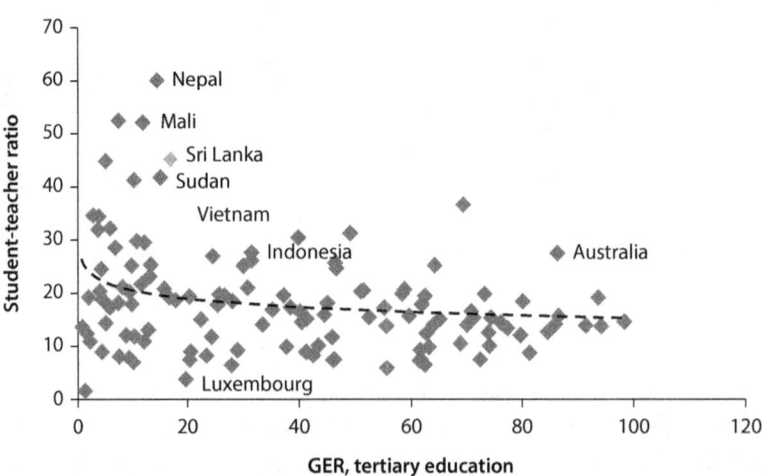

Figure 6.9 Higher Education Student-Teacher Ratios and International Gross Enrollment Rates, 2012 or Closest Year

Source: UIS.
Note: GER = gross enrollment rate.

the number of faculty members available is all the more perturbing in view of the need to increase enrollment; if the situation is to improve, faculty numbers will have to go up faster than enrollment. This will be a major challenge, both financially and organizationally.

Moreover, the average STR hides disparities between universities, and even more between disciplines. As might be expected, STRs are higher in arts and humanities and in management and business programs, but are not much lower in scientific programs. The only disciplines where the STRs seem manageable are agriculture and medicine.

Unfortunately, while STRs are exceptionally high, so are faculty vacancies. The ministry estimates that the vacancy rate was 28 percent in 2014, with about 3,100 positions to be filled (MOHE 2014). The problem seems particularly acute in the medical faculties. Reasons range from a lack of candidates to high attrition and pure administrative issues. If only 2,000 of the vacancies were filled, the average STR would drop to 16:1.

A positive point, however, is that full-time teaching staff constitute 89 percent of the pool of faculty members. To some extent this compensates for the fact that there are so few teachers overall. Another positive point is that as many as 45 percent hold a PhD (up from 40 percent in 2008) and another 39 percent an MPhil or other Master's degree. The proportion of faculty members with a doctorate is important for postgraduate teaching and critical for research. From this point of view, the faculties of engineering, medicine (a special case), agriculture, and science are well-equipped. However, faculties in social sciences, arts and humanities, management, and law-, where the majority of students and faculty members are concentrated, fare much worse (figure 6.10).

Figure 6.10 Public Higher Education Faculty Members, by Academic Qualification and Discipline, 2012

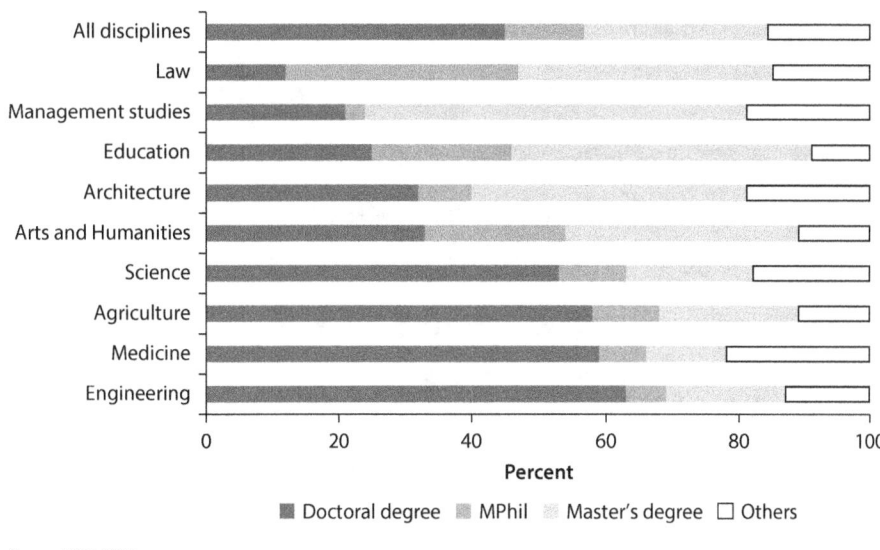

Source: UGC 2014.

Overall, 44 percent of all faculty members are women, but they are not evenly distributed across the academic hierarchy.[10] As lecturers, they recover the edge they have over men as undergraduates and lose as postgraduates. Yet as they move up the pyramid, they become a smaller and smaller minority and are less than a third of all professors (figure 6.11).

Having recognized the need to heighten the proficiency of teachers, in the last 10 years the ministry and the UGC have launched several campaigns for continuing education of the faculty members who are currently employed. The main vehicle has been sending master's-educated faculty members to reputable foreign universities to get a PhD. To minimize the brain drain and the number of vacant positions, current schemes prioritize programs split between local and overseas institutions. Each university has a staff development center (SDC) to coordinate such activities; but the competence and the activity of the SDCs are quite uneven, and only a few (e.g., the University of Colombo) are adding real value. Yet more efforts are needed to update faculty members' subject knowledge and to adopt a more student-centered pedagogical approach. In addition, though there is a consensus that graduates lack IT, English, and soft skills, the academic staff members who are supposed to teach these skills often have not mastered them enough to transmit them to students.[11]

The distribution of faculty members by qualifications does not match their distribution by academic status. Very few hold a professorship; most are lecturers (table 6.8). As this pattern has basically not changed since 2007, it may be that the possibilities of moving up in an academic career are limited. If so, incentives for progress are also limited—an obvious concern, especially since many more faculty members will be needed.[12]

Public universities and HEIs employ about 11,000 nonteaching staff, of whom 4 percent are administrative and other executive staff. On average, there

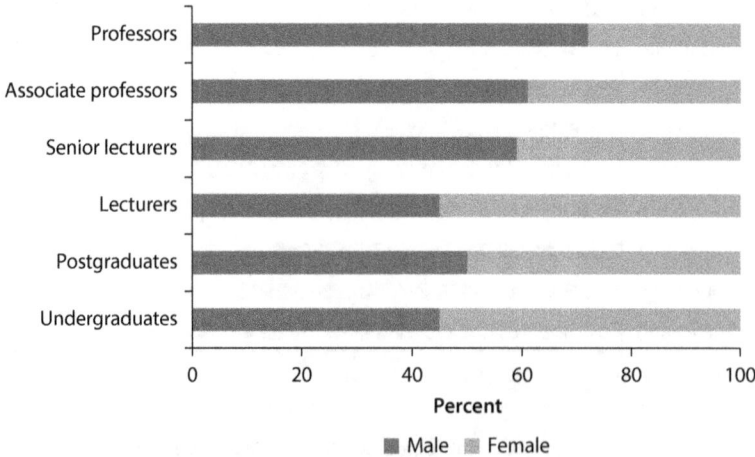

Figure 6.11 Structure of Student and Faculty, 2014

Source: UGC 2014.

Table 6.8 Distribution of Faculty Members, by Academic Status, 2007 and 2014

Type of faculty member	Number (2014)	Share, % (2014)	Share, % (2007)
Professor	580	7	10
Associate professor	89	2	2
Senior lecturer	2,588	48	47
Lecturer	1,767	44	41
All	5,024	100	100

Sources: UGC 2007, 2014.

are 2.1 such staff for each faculty member. This ratio is moderate; American public 4-year universities average 4.6 nonteaching staff for every faculty member. These figures suggest that the operations of public universities are reasonably efficient. The high proportion of temporary nonteaching staff (67 percent) may in the future allow the flexibility needed to adapt to changes in enrollment numbers and composition and to mission diversification.

Within the nonteaching staff, senior managers—about 500 in public universities—are of special concern. They determine the life of universities, adapting their institutions to constant changes and to the outside world. Many lack necessary skills in such areas as strategic planning, human resources, facilities and equipment management, QA, finance, and student affairs. Recognizing this as a problem, with donor support the government has launched a program of short-term training. The challenge is to sustain this timely program and scale it up to continue to build institutional capacity.

Physical Environment and Equipment: Qualified faculty members—in particular those who earned higher degrees from and have been exposed to good universities abroad—perform better and are more committed when the physical environment is supportive and they have the resources they need to teach and do research. Similarly, the importance of a good learning environment in which students can excel cannot be underestimated. Over the last decade a considerable number of facilities have been built, for both universities and ATIs, but they often still lack up-to-date laboratories, equipment, and material. At many campuses Internet connections and full free wireless connection are limited. Dormitories, cafeterias, and meeting areas often do not encourage the blossoming of the academic community. Facility maintenance is also often deficient.

Quality Assurance

Having enough appropriately qualified staff and keeping programs and curricula up to date are necessary conditions if HEIs are to fulfill their missions, but in Sri Lanka they are often not met. Equally necessary is a permanent system to monitor and enhance the quality of higher education. This section examines the extent to which such a system exists in Sri Lanka, and how effective it is.

For the past decade, Sri Lanka has been gradually building the foundations of a solid and comprehensive QA system staffed with the necessary expertise. Ten years ago, QA was not part of the academic culture, and there was often resistance to the introduction of instruments to review and assess institutional and faculty members' performance. Today, it is no longer viewed as an external threat to academic freedom. However, the private sector is still not much affected by the QA institutions and instruments that public HEIs now accept. Rules for the accreditation of private universities deserve immediate attention.

Several measures have been put in place to assure the quality of public universities, among them

- the UGC Quality Assurance and Accreditation Council (QAAC), which has the mandate for external QA of public universities.
- internal quality assurance units (IQAUs) established in each public university.
- a credit and qualifications framework, codes of practice, subject benchmarks, and procedures for internal and external QA of universities and other HEIs.
- a procedure for regular internal review of program, departmental, and subject quality.
- an external quality review process based on nationally agreed-on criteria and benchmarks, in which trained assessors periodically review programs, subjects, departments, and institutions.
- a mechanism for the QAAC to draw on international expertise and experience to keep abreast of current developments and thinking. Financing, however, has been a problem.
- adoption of the Sri Lanka Qualification Framework (SLQF), with which nearly all the bachelor's, master's, and doctoral degrees now comply.

The QA process has made an excellent start in public universities, but it is now urgent to expand it to all Sri Lankan HEIs, including private ones, as is being done in more and more countries. Malaysia, Thailand, and Indonesia all have QA and accreditation agencies that deal with both public and private HEIs. Such an agency should be autonomous. It could be formally linked to the ministry but operate independently.[13] In addition, the expertise developed by the UGC QAAC members notwithstanding, combining quality control and funding decisions in a single body as is now done is a potential source of conflicts of interest.

Despite the indisputable progress the SLQF has made, university and ATI proposals for new degree programs are still not formally based on it.[14] Few IQAUs are heralding the SLQF, even though they should be its natural champions in HEIs. IQAU directors are expected to be formally given the responsibility for the QA of the SLQF in their universities. Similarly, at the central level, the SLQF is not yet part of the QAAC's responsibility, as it should be, but this situation is expected to change in the near future.

A fully empowered QA/accreditation body could be used for such purposes as

- assessing HEI degree-awarding capacity
- ranking HEIs

- approving the entry of foreign HEIs
- recognizing degrees by third parties
- assessing credit transfers between accredited HEIs
- determining eligibility for direct or indirect government funding and scholarships
- other rights, such as eligibility for reduced regulation.

The QAAC could apply its current external review processes to the private sector, which is currently under the purview of the MHEH (although, in fact, many private HEIs operate without any official recognition). Private HEIs would presumably pay for the reviews, which would avoid burdening the state. If the reports from both institutional and subject reviews were published, the public could have greater confidence in the quality of private higher education provision.

Students, governments, institutions, and employers could all benefit from external quality reviews of private Sri Lankan and international providers. Students and governments would have some assurance that the programs meet certain standards. Employers would have useful information on the quality of the degrees job seekers have obtained. Finally, accreditation gives governments a useful instrument on which to base institutional registration, funding, and regulatory decisions.

It is important that the QA and accreditation system for private HEIs be flexible enough to allow for the parallel system of "private" accreditation, so that private HEIs could either be accredited by the QAAC or an equivalent body or their partner's foreign accreditation could be accepted, such as the UK Quality Assurance Agency or the Australian Universities Quality Agency, once recognized by the QAAC. In other words, the domestic QA system should complement, not replace, the existing system of institutional affiliations. The role of the QAAC would be to accredit accreditation agencies and international partners, rather than institutions themselves. This concept of private accreditation has been used in a number of jurisdictions.[15]

Graduation

In 2014, Sri Lanka's public HEIs were graduating some 38,000 students, of whom 29,000 earned bachelor's degrees and the rest master's or higher. Although not a direct measure of quality, graduation is both an expected output of the higher education system and an indicator of its internal efficiency (although not a perfect one, since it can be easily manipulated by lowering or raising either the difficulty of the examinations or the severity of the scoring).

Even if the data do not allow for a precise estimate of how efficient public universities are at producing graduates (overall, there were as many bachelor's graduates in 2014 as students admitted in 2011/12), they shed light on differences between disciplines. The estimated graduation rates shown in table 6.9 for the STEM group of disciplines are much lower than those in arts and

Table 6.9 Undergraduate Admissions, Graduation, and Ratios, 2011–14

Disciplines	Undergraduate admissions (2011)	Bachelor's degrees (2014)	Graduates 2014/ admitted 2011
Arts and law	9,860	14,875	1.5
Management and commerce	5,466	5,726	1.0
Medicine, dental, veterinary, indigenous med., paramedical	2,894	1,843	0.6
Agriculture	1,332	867	0.7
Science	5,495	2,295	0.4
Engineering and architecture	2,260	1,652	0.7
Computer science	1,475	947	0.6
Total	28,782	28,205	1.0

Source: UGC 2014.

humanities, law, business, and management. This pattern echoes that at the GCE A level, and confirms that STEM streams are less attractive to students because they are more difficult than the "soft" disciplines. Given the higher graduation rates for soft disciplines, these crowd out STEM disciplines at graduation even more than at admission.

In 2014, EPD programs graduated about 11,700 students—a very small number considering total enrollment is 299,000. This low productivity may be attributed to a combination of very different factors: high dropout rates midstream and, for students who do take the exam, a low pass rate. Both cases raise questions about the role, function, and efficiency of EDPs that need to be thoroughly examined.

The distribution of graduates by gender amplifies the gender patterns of new students. Women outperform and outnumber men, at both the undergraduate and postgraduate levels (figure 6.12).

This pattern is found in a number of countries; the aggregate share of females among Sri Lankan graduates is almost exactly equal to the world average. It is also close to most comparators in East Asia, and even higher than in many of them (figure 6.13).

Reportedly, students in Sri Lanka take longer than is usually needed to graduate. "The main reason is not longer courses of study but inefficiencies in transition from one level of education to the next and disruptions due to university closures" (IPS 2015). The problem starts in secondary school. On average, half a year is wasted between taking the GCE O-levels and beginning the A-level course because of delays in release of the results of the former. The same problem recurs between release of A-level scores and admission to universities. Up to one-year gaps have been reported. Such gaps prevent freshmen from attending the foundation courses they need most.

Once in university, students also face many curriculum, political, and other disruptions, so that many are 24 when they receive their first degree—which

Figure 6.12 Students Admitted and Graduated, by Gender, 2014

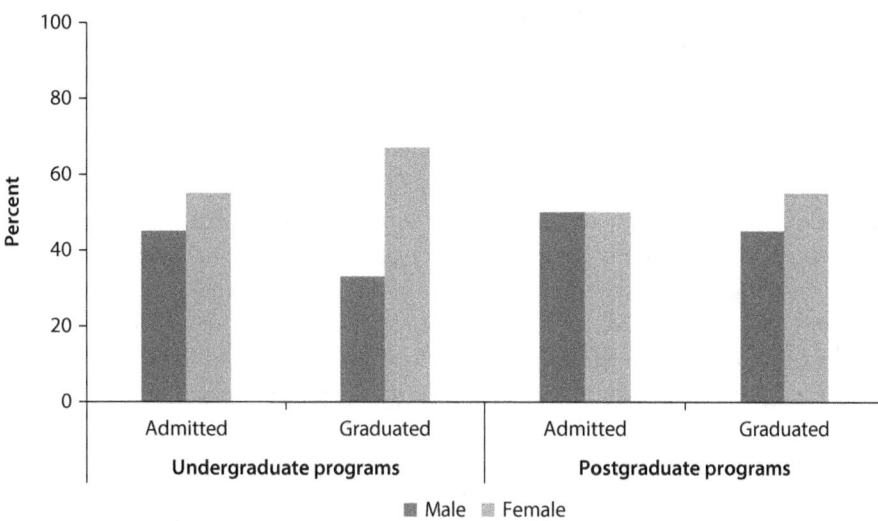

Source: UGC 2014.

Figure 6.13 Tertiary Education Graduates, by Gender, Selected Countries, 2013 or Closest Year

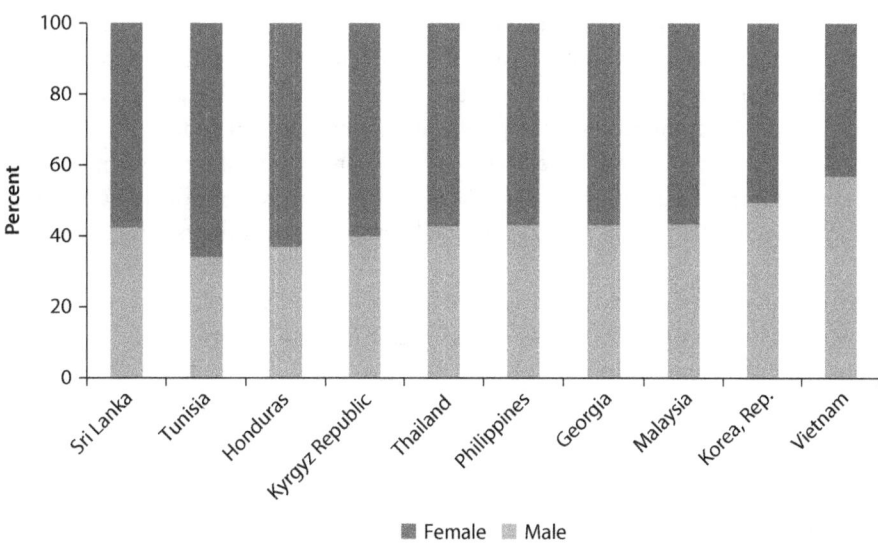

Source: UIS.

means a delay in their joining the labor force. Finally, time also elapses between graduation results and convocation, adding another damaging delay, often of several months. These wastages are costly for students. Since a substantial part of them are under government control, this is area where change can come quickly.

Learning Outcomes

Learning assessments measure the extent to which HEIs succeed in equipping students with the skills and knowledge they expect to receive. Public universities have established mechanisms for midterm and year-end examinations and continuous assessment; but practices differ by university, and there is no formal benchmark for either universities or disciplines. Assessments need to be improved and harmonized so that they can really help faculty members to teach better, provide feedback to students, and adjust curricula to make them more effective.

Two areas where deficiencies are often flagged by the authorities and even more by employers (see the next section) are English and IT proficiency. In response, the ministry has embarked on a large-scale effort to boost, and assess, student performance in these two areas. Students were tested after a first round of special programs (table 6.10), with priority given to application of the skills rather than just theoretical knowledge. Because graduates from secondary school who access university at best have been exposed only marginally to these two subjects, this type of program will have to be scaled up.

The EDPs are definitely one of the major challenges for the government. It is widely recognized that the EDP quality is substandard. EDP students are formally enrolled in public universities, of which three (Peradeniya, Sri Jayewardeneepura, and Kelaniya) are responsible for 86 percent of the enrollment and 90 percent of the graduates. However, the universities give little support or academic guidance to these students, who must rely heavily on self-study or external training institutions (ETIs).[16] Tutorial classes are either nonexistent or of poor quality. The main mode of teaching is through lecturing, with little engagement and few practical lessons. The sponsoring universities render only administrative services, which consist mainly of examinations. Revenue from examination fees seems to be the main reason for universities to accept—and for a few of them, even welcome—EDP students. The UGC has set up a standing committee to tackle this issue; already (a) the number of new registrations has been educed—in 2014 only 8 of the 15 public universities had any; (b) EDP centers have been organized into more operational centers for open and distance learning; (c) specific QA manuals for EDPs have been drafed; and (d) there is closer collaboration between the ETIs in charge of delivering the programs.

Table 6.10 University Tests for Student IT Competency and Teaching of English, 2012–13

UTEL	No. of students registered	No. of students sat	No. of students pass UTEL reading 5	% pass	No. of students pass UTEL listening 5	% pass
	24,365	10,426	7,966	76	6,637	64
UCTIT	No. of students registered	No. of students sat	No. of students pass UCTIT basic level	% pass	No. of students pass UCTIT intermediate level	% pass
	23,606	10,581	6,842	65	2,157	20

Source: HETCedps.
Note: UTEL = Teaching of English test; and UCTIT = Test for Student IT Competence.

However positive these actions are, they are not proportionate to the magnitude of the problem EDPs pose. The new centers have not yet managed to generalize the outcome-based education (OBE) approach, and negotiations with the ETIs are dragging. Student admissions have resumed without the core problems being tackled. With universities already overburdened with internal students and thin resources, the most realistic approach would be (1) to rely more on ETIs, most of which are private, while giving the students genuine academic support, and (2) to explore the potential of massive open online courses (MOOCs). MOOCs may be particularly appropriate for older students, part-time students, and adults—categories that constitute the majority of EDP students. Experience elsewhere has shown that adults benefit most from this type of distance learning. That implies, however, that the year-end examinations, which are incompatible with distance learning practices, be replaced by flexible quizzes, given as students progress.

Labor Market Outcomes

Producing graduates is a primary goal of HEIs. Making sure they have acquired skills and knowledge is, however, an even more important goal than simply churning out graduates—although more difficult to achieve, let alone gauge. The ultimate test of HEI performance is how graduates fare in the workplace and apply what they have learned.

Labor market outcomes have not always been considered central to the university mission. Even today, there are pockets of resistance to the idea. Skepticism comes from those in the academic community who see the "merchandisation" of a university as a threat to humanistic academic ideals. There is also ideological resistance from those who consider monetization of degrees to be evidence of aggressive capitalism. Both types of resistance have tended over time to dissolve, especially the second. China, Vietnam, Lao PDR, and other communist/socialist countries have all come to recognize that helping students to become employable, and employed, is not only a prime responsibility of HEIs but is also fully compatible with socialist ideals. Following these examples, Sri Lanka's government is now fully on board with this reality, although it is not abandoning missions such as nation and community building, for which no price can be calculated. Finally, students themselves are now concerned with their employability.

The Aggregate Picture

The rates of labor force participation, unemployment, and underemployment are the indicators usually used to sketch a preliminary picture of the labor market situation. Sri Lanka is characterized by a combination of very low labor force participation (55 percent), moderate unemployment (4.4 percent), and high underemployment (18 percent). These rates are close to those common in lower-middle-income countries (table 6.11).[17] The very low female LFPR[18] is striking,[19] considering that they outnumber males at all levels of education. Another characteristic is a high youth unemployment rate. Here, Sri Lanka is more similar to high-income and Middle Eastern countries than to lower-middle-income countries (figure 6.14).

Table 6.11 Labor Force Participation and Unemployment Rates, Selected Countries and Groups, 2013

Country or group	Labor force participation rate, total (% of total population aged 15+) (modeled ILO estimate)—2013	Labor force participation rate, female (% of female population aged 15+) (modeled ILO estimate)—2013	Unemployment, total (% of total labor force) (national estimate)—2013
Sri Lanka	55	35	4.4
Malaysia	59	44	3
Singapore	68	59	2.8
Thailand	72	64	0.8
LMICs	59	39	4.7
MICs	63	48	–
UMICs	67	57	–

Source: WDI.
Note: – = not available; ILO = International Labour Organization; LMICs = lower-middle-income countries; MICs = middle-income countries; and UMICs = upper-middle-income countries.

Figure 6.14 Youth Unemployment, Selected Countries and Groups, 2013

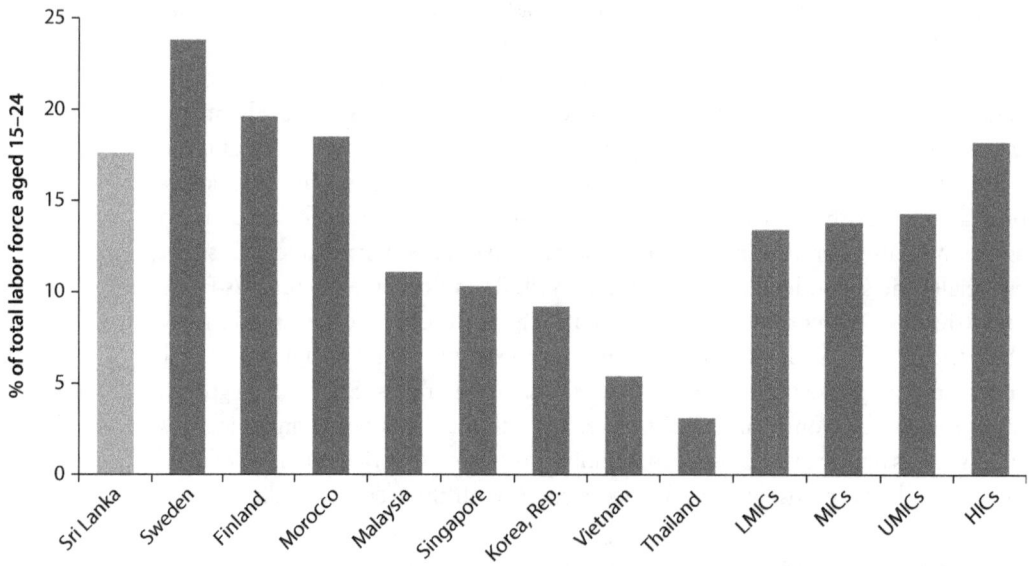

Source: WDI.
Note: Modeled ILO estimate. HICs = high-income countries; LMICs = low-income countries; MICs = middle-income countries; and UMICs = upper-middle-income countries.

Against this backdrop, the situation of individuals varies substantially, mainly depending on how much education they have. Those who hold a bachelor's or master's degree have a significantly higher LFPR than other groups, but only those with a master's degree reach close to 100 percent employment. Conversely, underemployment is far worse for holders of a master's or higher degree but about the same for those with a bachelor's as for all other categories (table 6.12). These complex patterns result from different individual strategies for employment and work.

A second measure of the success of graduates in the labor market is to compare their earnings with those of workers with less education. Although this does not tell the whole story about higher education performance—since gains also depend on experience, personal attitudes, and the sectors and firms where they are employed—it does give useful indications, especially when a clear pattern emerges. This is the case for Sri Lanka, where, as in most countries worldwide, higher education graduates have a hefty edge over nongraduates (figure 6.15). Based only on the aggregate figures, there is no obvious reason to be overly concerned about the labor market outcomes of the higher education sector in Sri Lanka.

Table 6.12 Labor Force Participation, Unemployment, and Underemployment, by Education Level and Gender, 2012–13
Percent

Education level and gender	Labor force participation	Unemployment	Underemployment
No education	61	8	26
Primary (G5)	65	3	18
Lower secondary (G9)	58	5	19
Passed GCE O levels	52	8	19
Passed GCE A levels	61	7	17
Bachelor's	84	8	18
Master's +	82	0	29
Females	43	10	22
Total	59	6	18

Source: Dundar et al. 2014, based on data from STEP survey.
Note: GCE = General Certificate of Education.

Figure 6.15 Monthly Earnings, by Level of Education, 2009–10

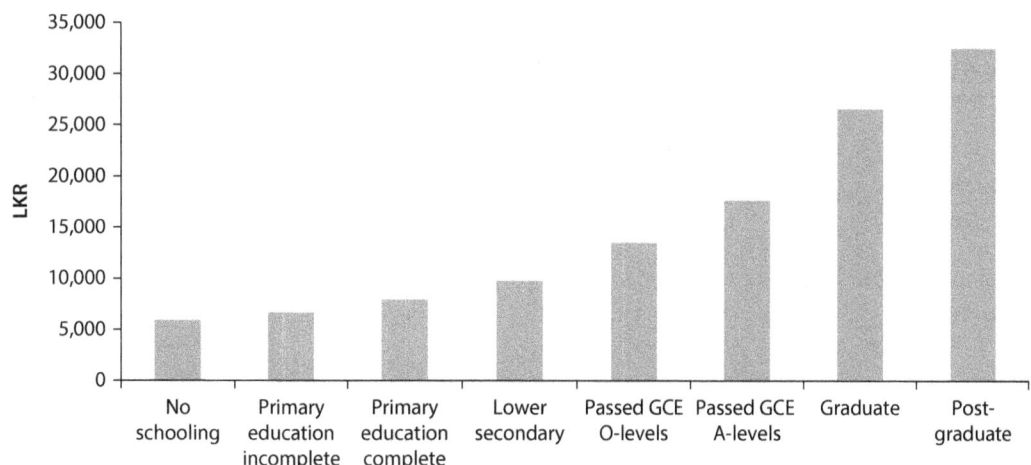

Source: HIES 2009/10.
Note: GCE = General Certificate of Education.

The Employability of Graduates

A few international comparisons help clarify the relationship between the supply of higher education graduates and the labor market (table 6.13). In 2013, of 111–113 countries, Sri Lanka had the highest proportion of graduates in the arts and the humanities—but one of the lowest proportions of graduates in engineering (ranking 92nd). This unique situation needs to be kept in mind during the following analysis of employability and fields of study.[20,21]

More detailed information specific to higher education graduates was gleaned from the Graduate Employment Study. In 2014, following convocation, 56 percent of university and 71 percent of SLIATE graduates were employed, but percentages varied widely by discipline—from 35 percent for arts to 97 percent for IT.[22] A small but stable proportion reported being underemployed (6 percent on average).[23] Looking at what happens at various times after graduation gives different figures, but a similar pattern. Three months after graduation, 58 percent of the IT graduates and 65 percent of the engineering graduates were employed, while only 13 percent of the arts and 20 percent of the management graduates were (figure 6.16). Another three months (i.e., six months after graduation) does not change the overall picture. Arts and management graduates improve their employment rates, but only to 20 percent for the former and 28 percent for the latter, while 62 percent of IT and 68 percent of engineers had found jobs. In all cases, employment rates plateau after six months, which indicates that the chances of finding a job then begin to shrink and that the risk of long-term unemployment is real for arts and management graduates.

A comparison of the proportion of graduates in various fields of study and enrollment in those fields also gives a clear picture: The larger the number of graduates in a given discipline, the lower the employment rate, and vice versa (figure 6.17). Graduates from the crowded arts and humanities fields have difficulty finding a job, and when they do, often end up in sectors only tangentially related to their field of study; engineering and IT graduates, who are relatively few,

Table 6.13 Graduates by Discipline, Selected Countries, 2013 or Closest Year

Discipline	Sri Lanka %	Sri Lanka world rank	World average %	World maximum Country	%	World minimum Country	%
Education	10.1	70/114	15.2	Antigua and Barbuda	78	Tunisia	0.8
Humanities and arts	35.2	**1/111**	10.9	**Sri Lanka**	**35.2**	Cuba	1.0
Social sciences, business, and law	22.5	106/114	37.1	Aruba	81.9	Antigua and Barbuda	9.4
Sciences	16.9	6/112	8.7	Myanmar	43.3	Lesotho	0.7
Engineering, manufacturing, and construction	6.9	**92/113**	11.9	Iran, Islamic Rep.	36.2	Lebanon	0.2
Agriculture	3.3	24/103	2.5	Eritrea	12	Nepal	0.02

Source: UIS.

Figure 6.16 Employment of Graduates Six and Three Months after Graduation, 2014

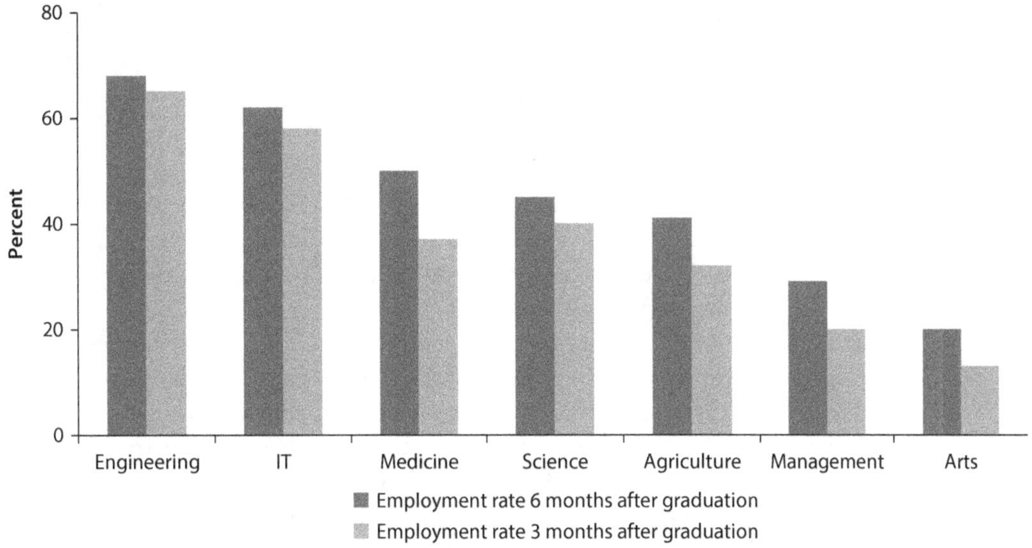

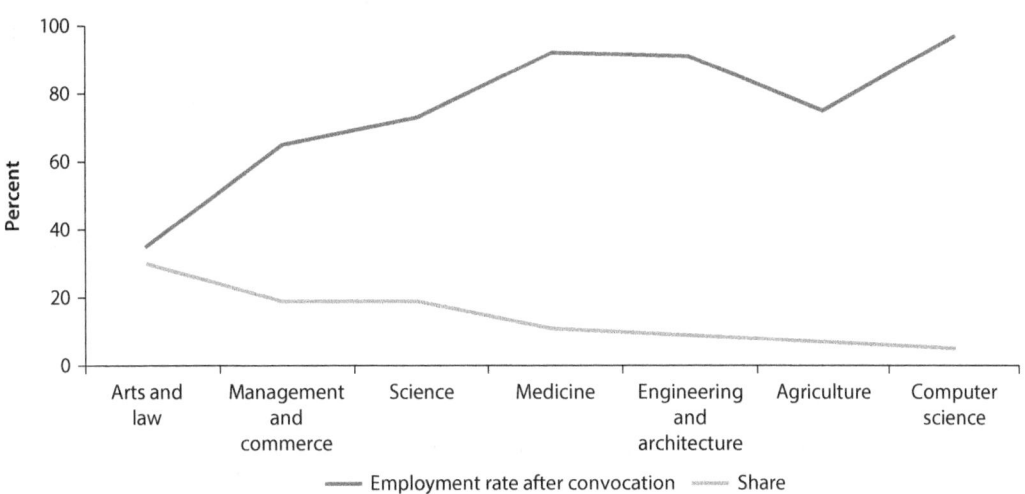

Source: World Bank–supported HETC Project Records.

Figure 6.17 Graduates and Employment Rate, by Discipline, 2012

Source: UGC 2014, World Bank-supported HETC project records.

have little difficulty in finding a job, and it usually corresponds to their discipline. These are signs of a major disconnect.

The Qualitative Side

What ultimately matters is whether employers find the skills they need and graduates find the jobs they want. The STEP survey has shown which kind of skills are most in demand, where the shortages are the most severe, and what are the most common problems employers have in finding workers. In Sri Lanka, as in a number of other countries, both job-specific and soft skills are hard to find for all types of jobs. English language proficiency is viewed as insufficient and employers expressed general dissatisfaction with HEIs and TVET institutions, which they see as irrelevant and not preparing students for the world of work (see figure 2.25).

The results of the 2014 survey of employers tend to confirm both the STEP survey results and opinions aired in focus groups. Satisfaction was highest for professional skills and lowest for personal skills. The largest skill gaps are in (a) communication; (b) desire and ability to learn; and (c) ability to work as a team (table 6.14). Because gaps in professional skills, such as proficiency in English, are clearly the responsibility of universities, there is a need to adapt curricula to give these skills more weight. Desire and ability to learn should also characterize university work, and HEIs can try to boost these traits. Finally, ability to work as a team is the type of skill that postsecondary study should encourage. In all these areas, the ability of faculty members to transmit the skills matters enormously, and this is why preservice and in-service training for lecturers is crucial to respond to the concerns of employers and better prepare graduates for the labor market.

The survey also gave students—the supply side—an opportunity to express their opinions on both the institution from which they graduated and their workplace (table 6.15). In general, graduates were quite satisfied with the quality of their instructors and the teaching methods. They almost all agree that practical training should be part of university education, and a small majority thought that was the case in reality. But they had reservations about how well the learning process relates to the job environment. In short, the perceptions of the graduates were not as somber as those of the employers.

In concluding this analysis of the labor market outcomes, it must be mentioned that closely linked to, and partly responsible for, the quantitative and qualitative mismatches is a serious communication gap between HEIs, students, and employers. This gap—mostly due to an information deficit—feeds false

Table 6.14 The Importance of Various Skills to Employers, 2014

Type of skills	Most important	Lowest satisfaction	Largest gaps
Professional skills	1. Subject knowledge 2. Ability to apply knowledge 3. Adaptability	1. Proficiency in English 2. Research skills 3. Adaptability	1. Communication skills 2. Proficiency in English 3. Adaptability
Personal skills	1. Loyalty and commitment 2. Self-confidence 3. Desire and ability to learn	1. Desire and ability to learn 2. Creative thinking 3. Loyalty and commitment	1. Desire and ability to learn 2. Loyalty and commitment 3. Self-discipline
Business skills	1. Ability to work as team 2. Work independently 3. Professional attitude	1. Knowledge of local affairs 2. Professional attitude 3. Initiative	1. Ability to work as team 2. Professional attitude 3. Initiative

Source: World Bank–supported HETC project records.

Table 6.15 Agreement of Graduates with Statements about Their Instruction, 2014
Percent

Measure	Teaching methods used at university are effective	The quality of lecturers/ instructors is good	Tutorials are used as learning tools	Practical training is part of university education	Practical knowledge is acquired through course work	The learning process is suitable for the current job environment
Average	81	83	79	77	66	59
Minimum	72	75	70	70	54	45
Maximum	95	91	92	94	88	80

Source: World Bank–supported project records.

expectations for all three groups. The fact that in job hunting, students rely more on social media (the opinions of peers) than on official channels or university career guidance centers suggests that the latter lack credibility.

Research

The intensity, quality, and applicability of research in HEIs are uneven. Research is essentially limited to public universities; private HEIs concentrate their resources on teaching. Sri Lanka has no hard data to gauge research performance, and the otherwise-detailed statistical yearbook issued by UGC does not monitor indicators commonly used for that purpose. The high proportion of academic staff with a doctorate suggests that, at least in terms of human resources, there could in principle be a solid research base. Typically, funds for research do not come solely from the public budget; current practice is for individual departments or even individuals to acquire funds for research without going through university channels or even without the knowledge of university management.

The general impression is that except for some outstanding but isolated cases, not much research is being done in HEIs. The most direct and obvious output of research is publication of the results, and the most reliable (though not flawless) measure is the number of articles published in international, peer-reviewed scholarly journals.[24] In 2014, Sri Lanka had six journals in the worldwide SCImago database; while the Philippines had 22, Thailand 26, and Malaysia 50.[25] The same database shows that between 2000 and 2013, Sri Lanka quadrupled the number of citable documents it produced. Yet during the same period, the country's rank regressed slightly, from 79th to 85th.[26] More worrying, the number of citations plunged over the last two years, although the period is too short to allow definitive conclusions about the reason for this.

When the number of citable documents is weighted by the population, at 133rd out of 204 countries, Sri Lanka ranks slightly lower than Pakistan and further down than India, let alone Thailand and Malaysia (figure 6.18). Using the number of cited articles per 1 million inhabitants, Sri Lanka's rank drops to 138th.

Recognizing the importance of research, the ministry has launched a number of initiatives. For instance, it has created a competitive fund to bolster innovation, which promotes postgraduate research; seven projects have

Figure 6.18 Citable Documents per Million Inhabitants, Selected Economies, 1996 to 2014

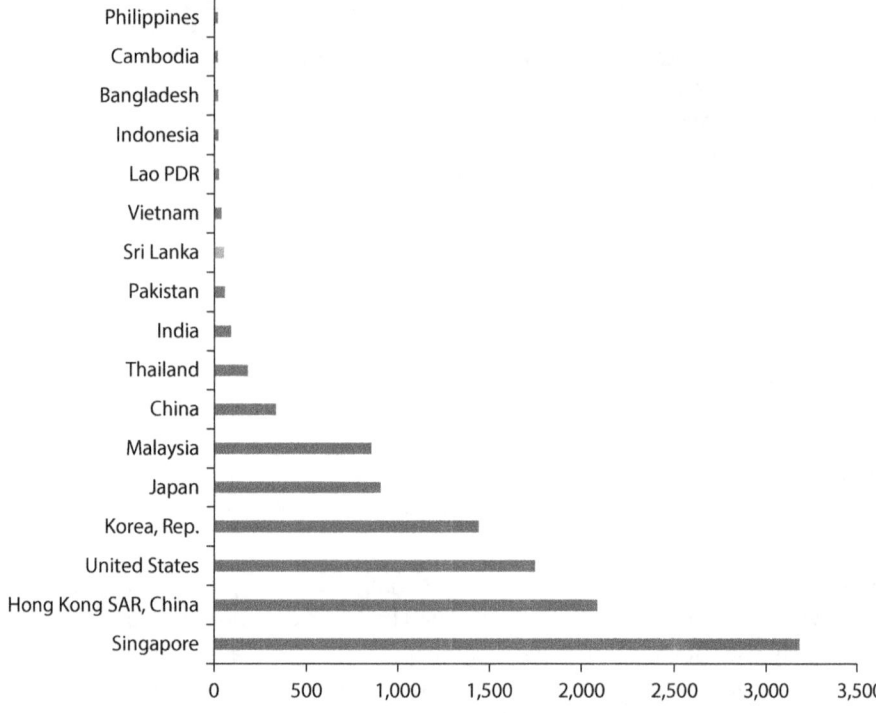

Sources: Scimago for citable documents; and WDI for population.

already been launched.[27] The main merit of the fund is that it has introduced a change in the academic mind-set by demonstrating that good ideas can attract funding. Other projects have taken off, such as the dengue research project (University of Jayewardenepura), projects cofinanced by the ministry and UGC, and the Encouragement Award Scheme. But although these initiatives are encouraging, they are few.

Not only is academic research still minimal in Sri Lanka, its relevance is elusive. In most cases, research is exclusively academic; its results are rarely publicized outside the Sri Lankan university arena. Among the reasons for this are (a) lack of staff interest in applying research to the "real world"; (b) a dearth of information about possibilities for commercializing results; (c) topics that are not aligned with national or regional priorities; and (d) tenuous university–industry links. Often these factors operate in combination.

A recent survey of academics and employers (MHEH 2016) gives a snapshot of university-industry collaboration and how the actors perceive it. There is considerable convergence on the diagnosis and even more on the remedies, with classic exceptions specific to each side: academics feel they lack time, and private employers perceive academics as lacking entrepreneurial spirit (table 6.16). A theme common to both sides is a shortage of information about the other.

Table 6.16 University-Industry Collaboration: Constraints and Perceptions, 2015

	Academic staff	Industry
Constraints on university–industry collaboration	1. Time constraints due to heavy teaching and administrative work load 2. Inadequate laboratory facilities 3. Inadequate infrastructure 4. Lack of proper procedures 5. Lack of autonomy to work with industry	1. No proper mechanism to collaborate with universities 2. Low commercialization potential of university research 3. University structure not adapted to the needs of industrial collaboration 4. No information on expertise / facilities available in universities 5. Lack of entrepreneurial spirit among academics
Promotional measures	1. Improve laboratory facilities 2. Encourage visits to businesses by students and faculty members 3. Publicize activities relevant to industry 4. Include industrial internships in the curriculum	1. Joint events to increase communication 2. Encourage visits to businesses by students and faculty members 3. Publicize activities relevant to industry 4. Include industrial internship in the curriculum

Source: MHEH 2016.

Several initiatives have tried to resolve some of these problems. One is designed to boost dissemination and commercialization of research; it has awarded Quality and Innovation Grants (QIGs) to 11 projects on a competitive basis.[28] The experience with the QIGs confirms that although commercialization and university-industry collaboration are still rare in Sri Lanka, measures to provide competitive funding to link performance and innovation have real potential.[29] Although the uncertainty regarding the regulatory framework within which universities can establish and operate a commercial arm has discouraged most of them, some have tried, and a few have been successful. Even though they are still waiting for a new, clearer, and more flexible university act, the universities of Colombo, Wayamba, and especially Moratuwa have demonstrated that there is room to establish mutually beneficial relationships with industry (box 6.1).

The number of patents submitted is often used to demonstrate how innovative research is and how its findings are brought to the outside world. The database of the World Intellectual Property Organization (WIPO) makes it possible to assess this number (table 6.17) and compare Sri Lanka's performance with other economies. In 2013, Sri Lanka submitted about the same number of international patents as Vietnam, and twice as many as Pakistan, but only a fifth as many as Malaysia (WIPO 2015). It ranked 56 out of 160 economies, the bottom of the first worldwide tier. Even though the number of Sri Lanka's patents has increased six-fold since 2000, that is a slower pace than India (seven times), Malaysia (10 times), or Vietnam (15 times). When controlling for the size of population, Sri Lanka's rank drops to 85th, with 22 patents per million inhabitants—well above Vietnam or Pakistan, but far behind Malaysia or Hong Kong SAR, China.

Box 6.1 University of Moratuwa UNI Consultancy Services

UNI Consultancy Services (UNIC) at the University of Moratuwa (UOM) has facilitated a number of university-industry partnerships. An association affiliated with the academic staff, UNIC is registered under the Company Act of 2007, as a Company Limited by Guarantee carrying on its business at the UOM; it is the commercial arm of the university. Here are three examples of activities it has facilitated.

Zone 24*7 and the Electronic Systems Research Laboratory

Zone 24*7 Inc., a leading provider of global technology innovation services headquartered in California, sponsors the Electronic System Research Laboratory operated by the UOM Department of Electronics and Telecommunication Engineering. The lab's main emphasis is to build the research competencies of the students and promote Sri Lanka's electronic systems expertise worldwide. Thanks to the support of Zone 24*7, graduates can contribute to innovative products while remaining in an academic environment. Its physical location is within the department, but equipment, furniture, and networking and teleconferencing facilities are provided by Zone 24*7. The lab is managed by a board chaired by the head of the UOM department and the manager of Zone 24*7. So far, products and services have been provided to government agencies free of charge.

SIL UOM Rubber Products and Process Development Incubator

To compete more efficiently on the global market, the rubber industry in Sri Lanka needs to be exposed to new research trends and advanced technical, analytical, and experimental technique that they do not have in-house but can find in UOM. SIL, a subsidiary of the D Samson group, has established the SIL UOM Rubber Product & Process Development Incubator through an agreement with UNIC to carry out joint R&D projects. The incubator funds a significant number of undergraduate and postgraduate research projects. Through a public-private partnership, the National Research Council and the National Science Foundation also provide grants to equip labs. Funding is shared 50/50 between SIL and UOM. The incubator draws academic experience from all UOM departments, giving research an interdisciplinary dimension. SIL/UOM has the right to use funds derived from product commercialization and pays 5 percent of the net sales to UOM. Management is entrusted to a board cochaired by the director of the SIL, UOM representatives, and a UNIC representative.

Dialog Mobile Communication Research Laboratory

The Dialog Mobile Communication Research Laboratory is the first industry-sponsored lab set up in Sri Lanka. It is the result of a long collaboration between Dialog Axiata PLC and UOM. It is fully funded by Dialog, based on a tripartite agreement between the company, UOM, and UNIC. The lab is managed by a board of executives from Dialog, representatives from UOM, and the head of the Department of Electronics and Telecommunication Engineering. Projects are managed by an Operations Committee consisting of senior research engineers in the lab and personnel of the New Product and Service Innovation Department of Dialog. The lab has produced two patents.

Source: MHEH 2016.

Table 6.17 Number of Resident Patents Submitted, Selected Countries, 2013

Country	Total patents 2013	World rank (*)	Increase in total patents, % 2000–2013
Bangladesh	84	88	20
Brazil	6,850	23	81
Chile	807	47	218
Egypt, Arab Rep.	760	48	42
India	20,923	14	625
Indonesia	755	49	349
Iran, Islamic Rep.	11,343	21	2,667
Korea, Rep.	223,532	4	161
Luxembourg	2,653	32	226
Malaysia	2,303	35	919
Mexico	2,139	38	177
Pakistan	207	73	350
Philippines	350	63	122
Saudi Arabia	3,124	31	1,580
Singapore	5,474	27	676
Sri Lanka	*445*	*56*	*518*
Thailand	1,911	39	229
Turkey	5,793	25	1,483
Vietnam	497	53	1,362

Source: WIPO statistics database. Last updated: December 2015. http://ipstats.wipo.int/ipstatv2/IpsStatsResultvalue.
Note: Number of countries ranked = 160.

Higher Education in International Rankings

Despite shortcomings inherent in their methodology (especially an excessive emphasis on research rather than learning outcomes), international university rankings give some global perspective on HEIs. The coverage of the three most popular rankings—Times Higher Education (THE), Quacquarelli Symonds (QS), and Academic Ranking of World Universities (ARWU)—although increasing every year, is still mostly focused on high- and middle-income countries; the top 400 universities are concentrated in 47 countries in the QS ranking and in 40 in the ARWU and THE rankings. Thus it may not be surprising that Sri Lankan HEIs do not show up in any of the three. However, Sri Lanka's future East Asia competitors are present in each, if only modestly.[30] Similarly, poorer, though larger, countries manage to have a few universities in the top 500 (table 6.18). The same is true of the Leiden League (also heavily focusing on research), which ranks 750 universities from 48 countries, including the Arab Republic of Egypt, India, Malaysia, and Thailand, but not Sri Lanka.[31] No Sri Lankan university is in the slightly more inclusive Multirank League, which covers some 60 countries, including four from the ASEAN that together have 12.

Nor are Sri Lankan universities very visible on the Web. In the Webometrics ranking, which looks at HEI Internet visibility and covers more than 20,000 HEIs, Sri Lanka has 6 in the "top" 5,000, again trailing comparators in East Asia (table 6.19).

Table 6.18 Universities Represented in Three International Rankings, Selected Countries, 2014–15

Country	THE					QS					ARWU				
	Top 100	101–200	201–300	301–400	401–500	Top 100	101–200	201–300	301–400	401–500	Top 100	101–200	201–300	301–400	401–500
Korea, Rep.	3	1	3	6	6	6	6	2	3	6	0	1	10	6	3
Singapore	2	0	0	0	0	3	0	0	0	0	0	2	0	0	0
India	0	0	3	3	3	0	0	6	3	3	0	0	0	1	0
Thailand	0	0	0	1	0	0	0	3	0	0	0	0	0	0	0
Malaysia	0	0	0	0	0	0	1	3	3	0	0	0	0	1	1
Indonesia	0	0	0	0	0	0	0	0	1	1	0	0	0	0	0
Philippines	0	0	0	0	0	0	0	0	1	1	0	0	0	0	0
South Africa	0	1	3	0	0	0	1	0	3	3	0	0	3	1	3
Colombia	0	0	1	0	0	0	0	1	3	1	0	0	0	0	0
Pakistan	0	0	0	0	0	0	0	0	0	1	0	0	0	0	0
Egypt, Arab Rep.	0	0	0	0	0	0	0	0	0	0	0	0	0	0	1
Sri Lanka	0	0	0	0	0	0	0	0	0	0	0	0	0	0	0

Sources: http://www.topuniversities.com/university-rankings/world-university-rankings/2014#sorting=rank+region=+country=+faculty=+stars=false+search=; http://www.timeshighereducation.co.uk/world-university-rankings/2014-15/world-ranking; http://www.shanghairanking.com/ARWU2014.html.

Note: THE = Times Higher Education; QS = Quacquarelli Symonds; and ARWU = Academic Ranking of World Universities.

Table 6.19 Webometrics Rankings, Selected Countries, 2014–15

Web hits	Sri Lanka	Indonesia	Malaysia	Philippines	Singapore	Thailand	Vietnam
1–999	1	4	6	0	2	11	1
1,000–4,999	5	68	23	10	5	48	22
5,000–9,999	0	70	19	12	10	50	37

Source: http://www.webometrics.info/en/world.

Table 6.20 U21 Rankings, Selected Countries, 2014 and 2015

Country	2015	2014
Singapore	9	10
Korea, Rep.	22	21
Malaysia	27	28
South Africa	39	45
Thailand	46	42
Indonesia	48	48
India	50	50

Source: http://www.universitas21.com/article/projects/details/158/overall-2015-ranking-scores.

One major problem with the university rankings analyzed is that by definition, they do not provide information on the health of the entire sector. That is why the Universitas Group launched U21: Instead of ranking universities, U21 ranks countries on the basis of how their entire higher education sector is faring. Of the 50 countries selected in 2014 and 2015, four ASEAN countries are represented (Thailand, Singapore, Malaysia, and Indonesia). Among other countries in this more holistic league are South Africa and India, but not Sri Lanka (table 6.20).

A final word about rankings: It would be imprudent to base a national strategy on being represented in international rankings or moving up in the league tables: Even if (hopefully, when) Sri Lanka's performance improves, so will that of other countries, so progress may not translate into better rankings; methodological pitfalls limit the significance of the rankings; and some institutions "game" the statistics to gain better rankings. Nevertheless, it is still informative to see how a country is doing in relation to its peers. In that regard, for government decision makers, system rankings are far more strategic than university rankings, although they still do not encompass all the dimensions of higher education systems (see, e.g., Hazelkorn 2015; and Millot 2015).

Financial Resources

The twofold challenge of expanding access to higher education and ramping up the quality of HEIs has obvious financial implications. Sri Lanka's government has expressed its commitment to dramatically increasing allocations to the entire education sector (6 percent of GDP), especially higher education (1.5–1.75 percent).

The current situation needs to be analyzed to ascertain where these new resources would have maximal effect. This section reviews the higher education financial situation, estimates how it translates to the institution and student levels, analyzes the composition and destination of public spending on higher education, and attempts to assess private contributions.

In the last decade, public funding for higher education in Sri Lanka has shot up in real terms—faster than in general education. The growth of funding has even outpaced the growth in enrollment. However, most of the increase went to investments in physical facilities; the increase in recurrent expenditures—those that matter most for delivery of services—was more modest, and most indicators suggest that higher education is in fact severely underfunded. All international comparisons of higher education budget allocations confirm that Sri Lanka is dangerously underinvesting in the subsector that is most crucial to propelling the country to become a knowledge-based economy. Whether in the aggregate or in per-student terms, Sri Lanka's public funding for higher education is far less than what is invested by the middle-income countries with which Sri Lanka aspires to compete. Its allocations to HEIs are not only small by international standards; they are also largely based on inputs rather than on how an institution performs and the relevance of its programs. Yet these institutions depend for at least 80 percent of their resources on government grants. There is very limited cost recovery, and fees from external and foreign students subsidize national and internal students who pay nothing to attend courses. As higher education expands and strives to boost quality (especially by dramatically raising the number of qualified staff), this situation will become unsustainable. Private financing will become a necessity. It will come from users—combined with student aid schemes to ensure equity—and from investment by private providers.

Aggregates

Within Sri Lanka's entire education sector, how is higher education faring? Public spending on higher education more than doubled between 2003 and 2013 (114 percent in constant terms) while spending on general education had a much less steep upward trend (38 percent; figure 6.19). Notably, during that decade capital spending surged by 450 percent; recurrent expenditures grew less, with periods of stagnation punctuated by sudden bumps due to sharp increases in benefit packages.

Weighted against either GDP or total public spending, however, Sri Lanka devotes a relatively small share of its wealth and total government spending to higher education (table 6.21, left panels).[32] However, relative to total government spending on education, this share, while far lower than in some East Asian countries or even India, is closer to that of several ASEAN countries (table 6.21, right panel). It seems that, within the entire underinvested education sector, higher education is a relative priority. This is a logical consequence of the fact that the foundations for primary and secondary education are already in place (at least in quantitative terms), making room to inject more sectoral resources at the summit of the pyramid.

Figure 6.19 Spending on General and Higher Education, 2003–13

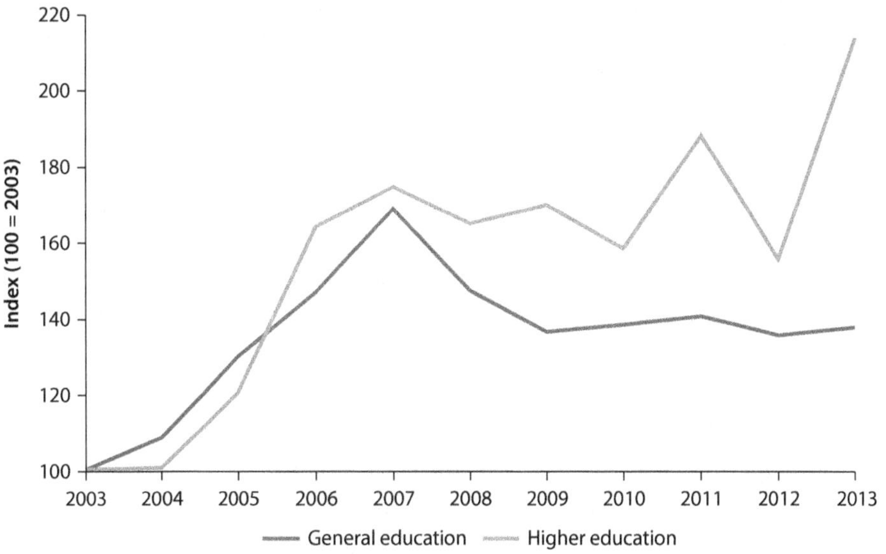

[Figure: Line chart with x-axis years 2003–2013 and y-axis "Index (100 = 2003)" from 100 to 220. Two lines labeled "General education" and "Higher education".]

Source: Aturupane et al. 2014.

Table 6.21 Government Spending on Tertiary Education, Selected Economies, 2012 or Closest Year
Percent

World rank[a]	Tertiary education spending, % of GDP		World rank[b]	Expenditures on tertiary as % of total government expenditures (%)		World rank[c]	Expenditures on tertiary as % of government expenditures on education (%)	
5	Tunisia	1.75	2	Singapore	7.95	2	Singapore	38.0
15	India	1.28	4	Hong Kong SAR, China	6.16	3	Malaysia	37.0
18	Singapore	1.19	5	Tunisia	5.98	5	India	33.2
19	Hong Kong SAR, China	1.16	14	Chile	4.07	6	Hong Kong SAR, China	33.0
24	Vietnam	1.05	21	Vietnam	3.57	62	*Sri Lanka*	*18.7*
46	Korea, Rep.	0.72	31	Indonesia	3.11	74	Indonesia	17.2
48	Thailand	0.71	34	Thailand	2.99	75	Vietnam	16.7
52	Indonesia	0.61	60	Japan	1.91	79	Korea, Rep.	15.6
61	*Sri Lanka*	*0.32*	64	*Sri Lanka*	*1.64*	81	Thailand	14.4

Source: Edstats.
a. Number of economies ranked is 69.
b. Number of economies ranked is 74.
c. Number of economies ranked is 105.

The indicators discussed relate only to public higher education spending. The value of private investment is not known. With only 20 percent of total enrollment in private institutions, the spending of nonstate HEIs probably accounts for less than 20 percent of total spending. For instance, in Argentina, where the share of private enrollment is close to Sri Lanka's (26 percent), spending by private HEIs accounts for 13 percent of total higher education spending. Similarly, in the Russian Federation, the ratios are 14 percent private enrollment and 11 percent (OECD 2014). In general, though, wealthy countries (e.g., Japan, Korea, and the United Kingdom) compensate for low levels of public spending on higher education by high private contributions. This is usually not the case for lower-income countries, and certainly not for Sri Lanka.

Before going more deeply into details, two general points need to be reiterated: (1) The association between level of development (as measured by GDP per capita) and spending on higher education is not strong. Still, Sri Lanka's public spending is clearly below where it "should" be, compared to other countries with the same per capita income (figure 6.20).

And (2) the relationship between the amount spent on higher education and its performance is even more tenuous; great quantities of monies poured in do not guarantee high outcomes in terms of quality or even quantity (see, e.g., World Bank 2012). This is illustrated by two countries whose governments spend a similar percentage as Sri Lanka: In Bermuda the GER is 29.6 percent and in Hungary it is 56.7 percent, against less than 20 percent for Sri Lanka (figure 6.21). What counts more is how the spending translates at the micro-level, how it is distributed and used—and indeed, how much the private sector is contributing; in Israel, 86 percent of higher education students are in private institutions, and in Latvia, 93 percent are.

Unit Costs

Public funds available per student give a reasonable approximation of the unit costs in a country like Sri Lanka, where so much of the cost is borne by the

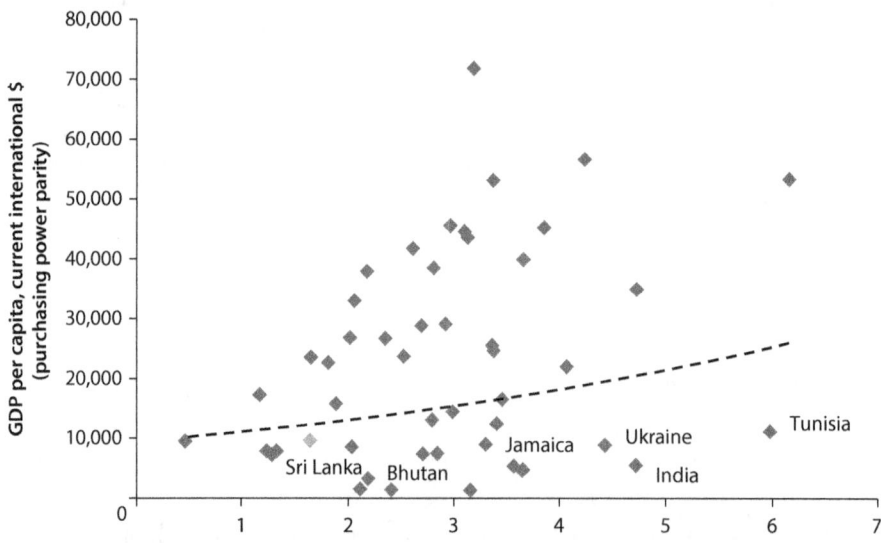

Figure 6.20 Tertiary Education Spending as a Share of Total Government Spending and GDP per Capita, Selected Countries, 2012/13

Sources: UIS and WDI.

Figure 6.21 Gross Enrollment Rate and Tertiary Education as a Share of Total Government Spending, 2012–13

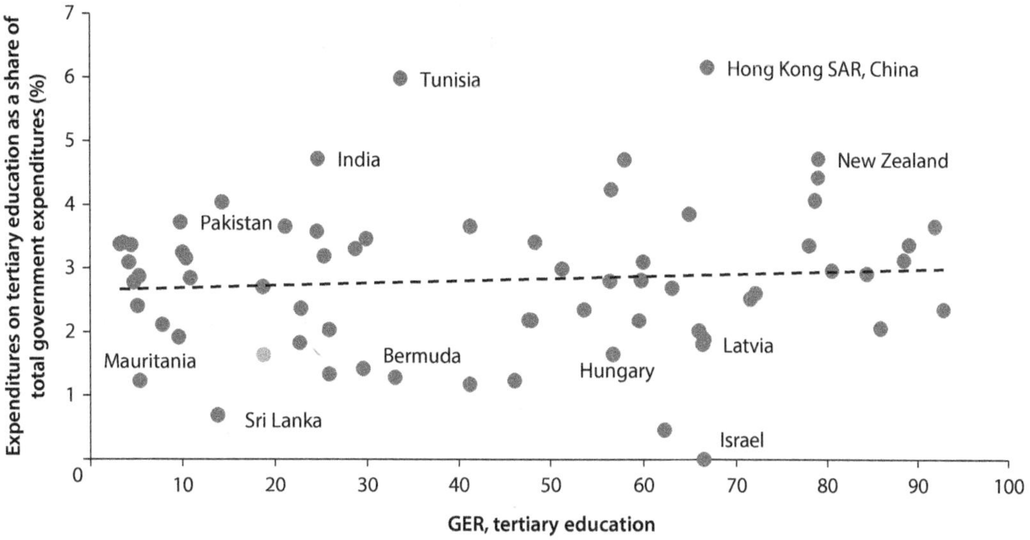

Source: UIS.
Note: GER = gross enrollment rate.

state (mostly by taxpayers). Estimates vary depending on what total cost covers and the student population benefiting. The estimates presented in table 6.22 apply to the budget allocated to universities, and, as is customary, only the recurrent budget has been retained. Students enrolled in EDPs are excluded because they use practically no university resources. Two scenarios were tested, with and without Open University students (although not full-time, they do benefit from the support of a full faculty). Unit cost estimates based on UGC data for 2012/13 range from US$1,200 to US$1,600—substantially higher than the UIS estimate (US$706) but much lower than the NHRDC estimate (US$2,300)—which demonstrates how hard it is to make precise estimates with imprecise data.[33]

From an international perspective, and using the UIS database, Sri Lanka not only spends less in dollar terms than high-income countries like Singapore or richer countries such as Chile or Malaysia, but also less than many poorer countries (table 6.23, left panel). It also spends less than a number of both poorer and richer countries as a percentage of GDP (table 6.23, right panel).

Budget Composition

Unlike in primary and secondary education and TVET, the higher education budget is entirely financed by the central government; provinces have no responsibility for higher education. Most of the budget allocated to the MOHE goes to the UGC, which dispatches it to each university.

Table 6.22 Per-Student Expenditures on Higher Education, Sri Lanka, 2012 and 2013

Year	Measure	H1[a]	H2[b]
2012	Per student (US$)	1,200	1,493
	% GDP per capita	41	51
2013	Per student (US$)	1,302	1,622
	% GDP per capita	40	49

Sources: UGC 2014; and NHRDC 2015 data.
a. Includes Open University students.
b. Excludes Open University students.

Table 6.23 Government Spending per Tertiary Student, Selected Economies, 2012 or Closest Year

US$ and percent of per capita GDP

World rank[a]	Government spending per student (US$)		World rank[b]	Government spending per student, percent of GDP per capita	
13	Singapore	13,774	17	Malaysia	60.9
28	Malaysia	6,130	18	India	54.9
44	Chile	2,289	26	Vietnam	41.2
62	Thailand	1,070	43	Hong Kong SAR, China	30.4
71	Indonesia	862	48	Singapore	26.1
73	India	828	54	Indonesia	24.3
76	Vietnam	724	55	Italy	24.2
77	*Sri Lanka*	*707*	*56*	*Sri Lanka*	*24.2*
88	El Salvador	413	70	Thailand	19.5

Source: Edstats.
a. Number of economies ranked is 93.
b. Number of economies ranked is 89.

Recurrent Expenditures

UGC allocates monies to universities for recurrent expenditures, based on the estimates submitted by universities and the following formula:

$$\text{Modified Cost per Student (MCPS)} * \text{Student Enrollment}$$

In turn, the MCPS is computed on the basis of the following factors: (a) annual salary increment on the actual cadre; (b) inflation of other recurrent costs; (c) capacity expansion of other recurrent costs; and (d) policy factors.

The policy factor (also referred to as the "funding ratio") leaves room for negotiation and introduces a discretionary element into the computation of allocations. Even though universities are required to have key performance indicators (KPIs), they are not strictly linked to the allocations, and are only supposed to contribute to effective and efficient utilization of funds. Therefore, allocations are mainly made as they have been historically rather than on any performance-based formula, combined with ad hoc decisions. Expressed in per-student terms, the e allocation varies substantially by university (figure 6.22), and the rationale for the variations, and the negative correlation with enrollment, is not clear.[34]

At 50 percent, the weight of remuneration in Sri Lanka is about 10 points below the average and the median estimated for the 39 countries for which this indicator was available in 2012 (table 6.24).[35] Most countries where remuneration has a heavier weight are middle- or even high-income countries, though there are some low-income country outliers. This suggests that the salary bill is not yet unbearable and that there will be room to add faculty as the system expands (assuming no major wage revalorizations), thus slowly bringing down the STR.

Figure 6.22 Recurrent Block Grant per Student and University Enrollment, 2016

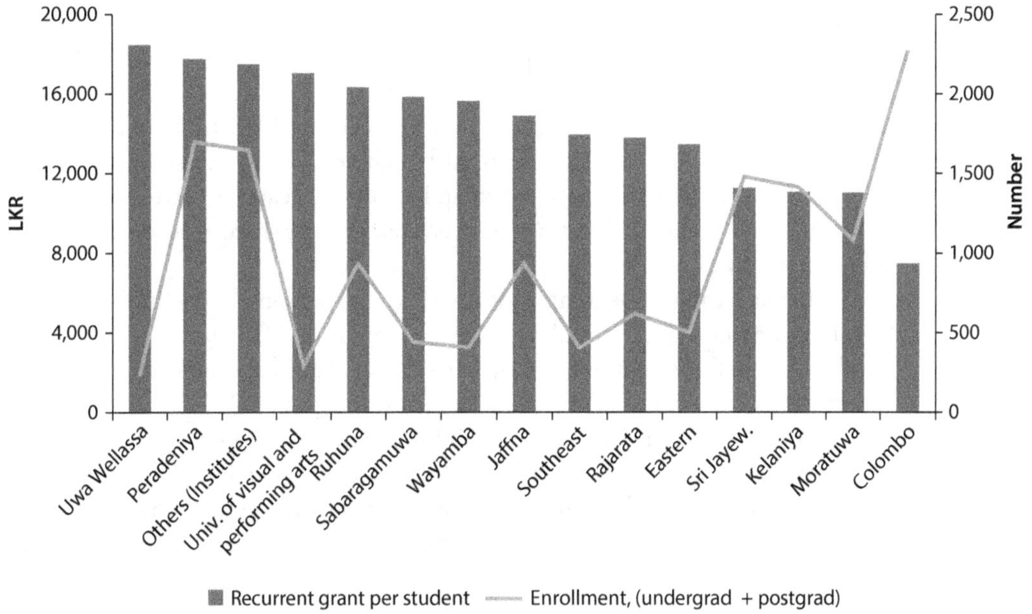

Sources: UGC Statistical Yearbook (enrollment); and UGC Finance Circular Letter No. 08/2015.

Table 6.24 Staff Compensation in Public Higher Education Institutions as a Share of Total Spending, Selected Economies, 2012

Country	Percent	Rank[a]		Percent	Rank[a]
Spain	66.7	13	Japan	49.2	28
Burundi	65.8	14	Colombia	46.6	30
Netherlands	61.7	18	Korea, Rep.	42.0	32
Moldova	60.6	19	Niger	29.6	34
Peru	60.4	20	Thailand	28.3	35
Finland	60.0	21	Mali	24.5	36
Sri Lanka	**50.5**	27	Indonesia	22.8	37

Source: EdStats.
a. Number of countries ranked is 39.

The relatively comfortable financial situation of the faculty in Sri Lanka substantiates this possibility. Based on 2013 figures, apparently though the salaries themselves are on the low side, they account for only 40–43 percent of total staff remuneration, the main component being a combination of academic and research allowance—the latter paid regardless of whether any research actually takes place. The ratio between the basic remuneration of a lecturer on probation and a senior professor is of the order of 1:2.5, which reflects a moderate lifetime raise, but is compensated for by the fact that promotion is automatic. Finally, the gross remuneration of faculty in Sri Lanka represents 170 percent (junior lecturer) to 430 percent (senior professor) of per capita GDP—a high proportion for a middle-income country.

Capital Spending

The hike in capital spending over the last eight years has not been steady. Linked to separate investment decisions, there have been steep rises, plateaus, and drops. The share of capital spending reached 40 percent in 2013 (table 6.25), and is projected to maintain its momentum. Although heavy spending on infrastructure is typical of countries that need to expand facilities to cater to a growing student population, Sri Lanka is devoting a higher than average share of its higher education budget to capital spending.

Sri Lanka's capital spending is of three types: spending by institutions, transfers to institutions, and "special development initiatives." The last category is relatively new; it allows central authorities to allocate funds at their discretion while avoiding the constraints of the allocation formula. Since 2012 its share of the capital budget has soared from 11 to 39 percent. An unallocated fund for new initiatives gives the center flexibility to influence HEI activities. However, it can achieve its full potential when allocations are made only on the basis of the progress of an HEI toward its own defined objectives. This, however, does not appear to be the case.

The next level of analysis is the institution itself. As can be expected, data are available only for public universities, and they vary depending on the source.

Table 6.25 Capital Spending in Tertiary Public Institutions, as a Share of Total Spending, Selected Economies, 2010–13

Economy	2010	2011	2012	2013
Hong Kong SAR, China	19.5	27.3	39.6	–
Indonesia	27.1	25.4	28.3	–
Malaysia	33.4	23.4	–	–
Singapore	6.7	6.3	1.7	7.0
Sri Lanka	**36.4**	**43.1**	**35.8**	**40.3**
Thailand	10.8	17.3	12.0	–
Vietnam	15.1	–	18.2	–

Source: EdStats.
Note: – = not available.

In 2014, transfers from the MOHE through the UGC (government grants) constituted 84 percent of total university revenues. Of the 16 percent generated by the universities themselves, 33 percent come from registration, tuition, and examination fees and 67 percent from a basket of other items, such as fees paid by foreign students (figure 6.23). Tuition fees are paid by national postgraduate and foreign students. Sri Lanka has no system for recovering costs from Sri Lankan undergraduates, whose trade unions respond vociferously to any hint of introducing fees. Paradoxically, while internal undergraduates do not pay for university teaching and other services, EDP students pay for services they do not receive, thus subsidizing the former group without receiving the benefit it enjoys.

Universities use their incomes to finance both capital and recurrent expenditures. More than half of the former are funneled to facility maintenance, and about 60 percent of the latter are for academic services (table 6.26), mainly wages for academic staff. Almost 20 percent of university spending is for general services. This is indeed a high proportion, which may be amenable to revision should savings or reallocations be needed. Similarly, the amounts spent on maintenance might be reduced if universities were to enter into PPPs and concentrate on their core academic functions. There is little information on which to base international comparisons of spending by institutions. As an illustration, in the United States, public 4-year universities spend 25 percent of their budget on instruction and 12 percent on research.

Figure 6.23 Revenues Generated by Public Universities, 2014

- Examination fees, 3%
- Tution fees, 25%
- Registration fees, 5%
- Others, 67%

Source: MOHE 2014.

Table 6.26 Expenditures by Category, Public Universities and Institutes, 2012

Recurrent	%	Capital	%
General administration and staff services	19	Construction	45
Academic services	59	Equipment, furniture, library books, periodicals, and vehicles	30
Welfare services	5	Rehabilitation and maintenance of capital assets	17
Maintenance services	6	Other	8
Other	11%		
Total	100%	Total	100%

Source: UGC Statistical Yearbook.

Private Financing

Private contributions to higher education essentially come from two sources: investment by private providers and student contributions. Based on the experience of OECD members and partners, it is unlikely that the first source accounts for more than 20 percent of total domestic higher education funding. As for the second source, much depends on the status of the institution where a student is enrolled. In public universities, undergraduates pay only examination fees. Only graduate students pay registration fees, and the only cost-recovery scheme is for the 700 or so foreign students enrolled in public universities. There are fees for dormitory meals, but these are minimal because meals are also subsidized. Private institutions obviously charge fees, which are their main source of funds, but there is not much reliable information about those.

Fees are only the most visible cost of education. Students, and their families, must also pay for learning materials and their living expenses while attending university.[36] According to the most recent household survey, the out-of-pocket cost of higher education represents only a tiny fraction of total household spending. Although rising moderately, in 2012/13 it was less than 0.2 percent of nonfood expenditure, corresponding to about US$30 a month. The amount does not vary significantly by HEI type (university or other). However, location and socioeconomic background make a huge difference; households from the richest quintile spend about 13 times more on children in higher education than the poorest quintile, and households from the Western Province spend about 6 times more than those from the Eastern Province. Gender has no significant impact on student disbursements (figure 6.24). Altogether, fees account for about half of all HE-linked private pending.

Despite the policy of free higher education, the real cost of HEI attendance is far from being equally distributed. The state could help to reduce the cost for lower-income students, perhaps through targeted scholarships or vouchers. By targeting students on the basics of their economic background and disciplines on the basis of national priorities, the system could become more relevant by channeling more students into priority fields of study while promoting equity.

Figure 6.24 Average Monthly Household Spending per Student in Higher Education, by Quintile, Location, and Gender, 2012–13

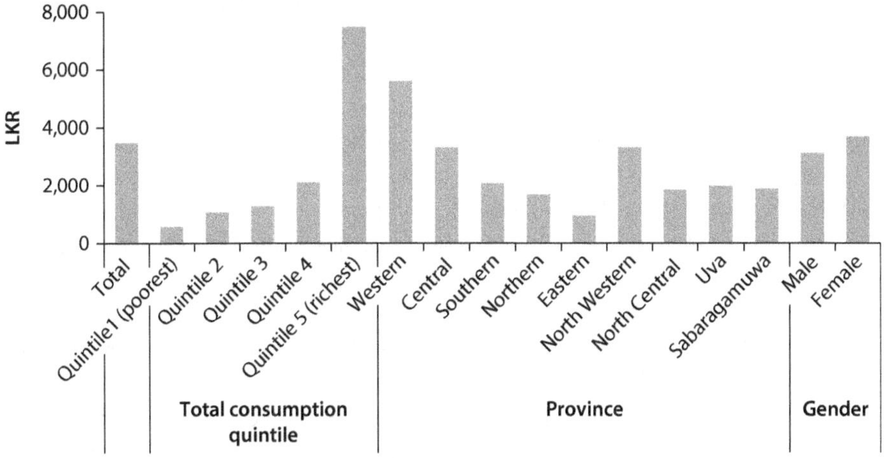

Source: HIES 2012/13.

Stewarding the Higher Education Sector

If higher education is to be a powerful driver of Sri Lanka's entry into the club of knowledge-based upper-middle-income countries, it will need more and better-trained secondary school graduates who opt for HE, more and better-qualified faculty, more relevant curricula, modernized teaching methods, competitive research, additional resources, and better use of them. But there is another dimension that encompasses and affects all the other factors: how the system is governed at every level. This section tackles three main aspects of governance: the relationship between central government agencies, management of HEIs, and the status of private providers.

Higher education in Sri Lanka is governed by the 38-year-old University Act, passed when there were fewer than 20,000 students enrolled. Public higher education is administratively fragmented without being functionally diversified. It is paradoxically characterized both by strong institutional autonomy and tight central control—a situation that promotes neither accountability nor performance. Central constraints on admissions, political interference in the recruitment of senior university managers, and ambiguity about the creation of commercial arms illustrate the encroachments on the independence of public HEIs. Severe bureaucratic inefficiencies, such as long delays in issuing graduate certificates, are damaging for students. The coexistence of the ministry and the UGC results in role confusion and a lack of clear lines of responsibility. Entrusting one single institution both with QA and accreditation on the one hand and resource allocation on the other is a breeding ground for conflicts of interest. Finally, the ill-defined way the private sector is treated from regulatory, financial, and QA perspectives slows its development, even though its contribution to the expansion of higher education will be critical. A common feature of all these issues is a sense of uncertainty, which tends to dampen both public and private initiatives. The positive new government attitude to these issues is encouraging, but it must be followed by action.

Systemwide Level

Higher education in Sri Lanka is a mosaic of institutions that differ in status, mission, age, quality, size, and student body. The Ministry of Higher Education and Highways (MHEH) "manages" 15 universities, 14 institutes,[37] and the SLIATE—(the only technical higher education institution).[38] Other ministries control other public degree-awarding institutions (e.g., academies). This kind of fragmentation, not unusual in most countries regardless of their administrative system, need not necessarily be a source of problems if there are mechanisms for coordination and qualification.

Sri Lanka's system follows the traditional Commonwealth model of a buffer body between the ministry and universities. In South Asia, for instance, Pakistan, Sri Lanka, India, and Bangladesh all have a Higher Education Commission or a UGC. These commissions, which allocate funds to HEIs, are largely responsible for their development, and in particular for their quality. Although sound in principle, sometimes the delineation of responsibilities between the apex body and the ministry is unclear.

In Sri Lanka, according to the 1978 University Act (Part I), UGC is responsible for:

- the planning and coordination of university education so as to conform to national policy;
- apportionment to HEIs of funds voted by Parliament for university education, and the control of each HEI's spending;
- maintaining academic standards in HEIs;
- regulating administration of HEIs; and
- regulating admission of students to each HEI.

This leaves little traction on the ministry's side, and there are numerous possibilities for duplication or tensions. There are also some oddities. As an example, UGC produces a detailed statistical yearbook that covers only HEIs established under the University Act but does not provide data for the SLIATE because this institution reports directly to the ministry.[39]

Higher education is a central government function. In Sri Lanka the central government (the ministry and UGC) is responsible for national policy; financing for public HEIs; allocation of staff and students to universities; and QA and accreditation. Provincial authorities have no say. The strongly centralized organization of the sector—which makes it politically dependent—is ensured by the fact that, in addition to being monitored by a line minister, it is de facto run by the UGC, whose chairman, vice chairman, and five other members are appointed by the president under the University Act.

Universities are established by the minister, in consultation with UGC. In theory they are autonomous; according to the University Act, Part V, they can do the following, among other things:

- Purchase, sell, hypothecate, or lease properties.
- Admit students.
- Hold examinations.
- Grant and confer degrees, diplomas, and other academic distinctions.
- Erect, equip, and maintain for the purpose of the university, libraries, laboratories, and other buildings whether for instructional or residential purposes.
- Recommend to the commission the institution of professorships, associate professorships, senior lectureships, and lectureships, and other posts as may be required for the purposes of the university.
- Demand and receive fees in accordance with any regulation providing for the same.

Public HEIs thus seem to enjoy procedural, academic, and financial autonomy. In fact, however, most of these powers are constrained by regulations and by strict oversight by the UGC (e.g., ceilings on admission of external students). The present practice of tight control carries the following risks:

- Delays while central institutions make decisions
- A burdensome workload for the MHEH and UGC because they have to make so many operational decisions
- Delays in awarding degrees, with negative consequences for graduates
- A risk of poor-quality decisions because some civil servants may not be familiar with the university culture and some HEIs are geographically remote[40]
- Frustration with the university system that may drive some individuals to use their personal authority or political relationships to bypass regulations and make decisions in contravention to official policy
- Political interference by the central authorities in, for example, appointments to university governance structures and to administrative and academic positions or promotions
- Uncertainty about the creation and operation of university business arms.

Institution Level
Sri Lankan universities have adopted the classic British Commonwealth governance structures, consisting of a University Council, a Senate (Academic Board), and deans who are responsible for faculties. A vice chancellor accountable to the University Council is responsible for academic and financial management. A registrar is responsible for administration. The Council, which is the governing authority of the university, varies in size depending on the number of deans.

The president of Sri Lanka appoints the vice chancellor from three candidates put forward by the Council. The UGC appoints a majority of Council members and all senior academic staff. There are very few if any senior university-wide posts, such as provost, between the vice chancellor and the deans, placing the latter under the direct authority of the former. If the vice chancellor and the Senate wish to alter the academic structure, for example, by creating a new faculty or merging faculties, they must secure the endorsement of the Council, which requires the approval of the UGC. Universities draft their own business plans, but these often lack operational relevance, are rarely costed, and are only loosely monitored.

In theory, as noted, Sri Lankan public universities are autonomous. However, legal constraints and various encroachments seriously limit this autonomy, among them:

- The admissions system (student quotas)
- How the vice chancellor is appointed
- Promotion of academic staff
- Decisions about new courses, departments, and faculty
- Remuneration of staff, both permanent and temporary.

Although such limitations infringe on their managerial freedom, it is also true that some universities do not make full use of the autonomy granted to them, particularly in the financial area. It has been reported, for instance, that universities do not always exercise the right to use funds generated through their own activity. Apparently accountability sometimes reduces the appetite of universities to fully embrace autonomy. Substantial efforts to ramp up university management capacity are needed to allow autonomy to fully play out.

Until recently, the politicization of university life, influenced by both radicalized trade unions and political interference from central government, has strained internal governance. One of the most contentious issues that is still unresolved is the lack of autonomy of the QAAC and its dependence on the UGC, which is also tasked to allocate funds to universities. Likewise, a recurrent theme in the academic community is the appointment of university officials more on the basis of political and personal factors than professional criteria. Within universities themselves, there is often an unhealthy divide between administrators and academic staff. Among the latter, it is often said that age and seniority carry more authority than competence. Internal governance is undermined by administrators who lack management experience because they are selected based on academic credentials, inefficient and bureaucratic procedures, and poor information systems.[41] Finally, strategic planning at the university level is rare.

SLIATE's activities are currently governed by a council, which defines the mandate of 11 ATIs and their admissions policies, program offerings, program content and course structure, academic staff workload, and other academic management matters. The ATIs overseen by the MHEH clearly have less autonomy than universities overseen by UGC.

Private Sector

The role of private providers in Sri Lanka has been controversial for many years, and in some cases still is.[42] Given the ideological opposition to private universities within Sri Lanka, some private HEIs have established themselves as businesses under the Company's Act and prepare students for degrees from overseas universities. The Board of Investment is in favor of promoting private HEIs to full campuses or foreign university franchises as a promising area for future growth.

There are, however, no legal barriers to establishing private HEIs. The MHEH has the power to certify a private HEI as a university, and it has indeed recognized 13. An unknown number of other HEIs are operating without any special educational status. Entry is close to a laissez-faire situation; there are no quality standards, protocols, or processes.

While QA protocols and mechanisms are well-tuned and meticulously implemented for public institutions, that is not true for private ones, which are within the purview of the ministry but outside the authority of the UGC. Consequently, the QAAC does not deal with private providers, which do not have to meet the same criteria as public "HEIs." Yet, external quality reviews of private and international providers could benefit students, governments, HEIs, and employers. They assure students and governments that the programs delivered meet certain standards and would give employers useful information on the quality of job-seeker degrees. Finally, accreditation is a useful instrument upon which governments can base institutional registration, funding, and regulatory decisions. These benefits are largely foregone when the playing field between the two subsectors is uneven.

Given the lack of recognition of private providers and lack of clarity about conditions for their establishment and operation, it is not surprising that they do not benefit from governmental support, either technical or financial. The reliance on nonstate training institutions to deliver on the EDPs is minimal, and very few partnerships have yet been recorded.

In addition to teaching, the private sector can also greatly contribute to the relevance of the higher education sector as a whole, and of public HEIs in particular, through many other channels: For instance: (1) Representatives of the productive sector can help update curricula by making them more relevant to the rapidly changing needs of the economy. (2) Public universities can benefit from the recruitment of adjunct professors from industry. (3) Research and the commercialization of its results can be significantly enhanced through partnerships with private firms. (4) Internships in private companies are invaluable for introducing students to the world of work, and are often a step to their employment. Yet these various types of collaboration are still rare.

Views about the role of the private sector are changing rapidly. The new government is adamant about the importance of the private sector in revamping and modernizing higher education and has repeatedly pointed out the need to establish parity for the mutual benefit of public and private providers. This new, positive attitude bodes well for the future.

Conclusion and Policy Options

If Sri Lanka is to join the group of upper-middle-income countries, it will have to broaden access to higher education while enhancing its quality and relevance. Reaching this ambitious but inescapable objective requires that the authorities take a series of synchronized actions, particularly in the areas of higher education human and financial resources, academic practices, and governance. These interlinked actions must all be coordinated not only within higher education but also with the other parts of the education system and with the economic sector. All necessary public and private initiatives must be taken collegially. The following measures should be seen as a package rather than in isolation. Similarly, while measures are categorized here as short term (ST), medium term (MT), or long term [LT], most will ultimately take a long time. While access can be increased relatively quickly, shepherding quality improvement requires continuous efforts over time. In rehabilitating the higher education sector, balancing quantity, quality, access, and excellence will often require careful trade-offs.

Access
a) Unclog the pipeline of candidates for higher education. This means essentially that more students pass both the GCE O/L and the GCE A/L exams, which implies that teaching in secondary schools must be boosted so that quality is not sacrificed for quantity [MT].
b) Release GCE exam results promptly [ST].
c) Reinforce the policy of channeling large numbers of students toward short technical higher education programs (ISCED 5). Gradually opening technological faculties would be a positive move in that direction [ST].
d) Open up horizontal and vertical pathways in conformity with the SLQF so that students have as many options as possible for moving up the academic ladder [ST].
e) Encourage the private sector to invest in higher education through financial incentives and arrangements such as PPPs for construction and ancillary services, and through regulation to facilitate the accreditation of providers [ST].
f) Upgrade campuses currently attached to the 15 public universities to universities in their own right [MT].
g) Identify alternatives to the centralized UGC system for selecting students for public universities [ST].
h) Introduce merit scholarships that target priority disciplines for students in remote areas but allow them to choose their university [MT].

Quality
a) Introduce English instruction early and mandate that scientific disciplines be part of all streams starting at grade 9 [ST].
b) Mandate in-service training to boost teachers' subject knowledge [LT].

University Faculty
c) Aggressively promote PhD scholarships (preferably split-type) with bonds to increase the number of faculty members in priority disciplines, especially STEM fields [ST].
d) Identify ways to reduce faculty vacancies, starting with priority disciplines [ST].
e) Bring in faculty members from neighboring countries in priority fields as a transitional solution to the severe shortage of qualified nationals [ST].

f) Upgrade in-service training so that academic staff are equipped with IT and student-centered pedagogical skills [MT].
g) Make the promotion and pay scale more flexible so as to increase opportunities to reach professorship status, link both promotion and pay to performance, and reduce the weight of seniority in career development criteria [MT].

Quality Assurance and External Degrees
h) Establish an independent Quality Assurance Council to deal with both public and private institutions, with power to accredit private HEIs (domestic, foreign, or franchised) based on criteria similar as those used for public HEIs [ST].
i) Resume the consultation initiated by UGC on the issue of EDPs and pilot measures to remedy the low quality of services rendered to external students, with special attention to using accredited private HEIs to complement overwhelmed public universities and exploring inexpensive MOOC courses in the fields of study most in demand [ST].

Research
j) Ensure continuity of the competitive scheme for promoting doctoral and postdoctoral research, emphasizing applied research, priority economic and social topics, and collaboration between universities, research institutes, and businesses [ST].
k) Promote partnerships between national HEIs themselves, national and reputable foreign HEIs, including exchange of students and faculty, and national HEIs and national or foreign companies to encourage dissemination and commercialization of research results [LT].
l) Make it easier for universities to retain revenues from providing services and establishing partnerships [LT].

Relevance
m) Promote collaboration between government, businesses, and universities to identify the skills best suited to the job market, emphasizing priority sectors, and adapt university offerings to these needs [LT].
n) Involve private professionals in curriculum design and appoint them to adjunct professorships [ST].
o) Intensify the use of internships to familiarize students with the workplace and make them more readily employable [ST].
p) Introduce soft skills in the curricula in all streams [ST].
q) Reduce the time it takes to release examination results [ST].

Finance
a) Cost out the new reform measures envisaged, using alternative scenarios for enrollment expansion, private sector participation, and cost-recovery / student aid schemes [ST].
b) Revise the formula used for allocating recurrent funds to public universities to make it more results-oriented [LT].

c) Leverage UGC discretionary funds to introduce performance-based financing and encourage universities to emphasize priority fields of study [LT].
d) Use PPPs systematically to provide noncore ancillary services in which universities do not have any comparative advantage and pilot PPPs for academic services [LT].
e) Partially delink the academic staff salary and promotion grid from general public service scales to introduce incentives linked to performance and hardships [LT].
f) Pilot portable scholarships targeted to priority disciplines that allow students to select their universities [MT].
g) Pilot cost-recovery programs for nonacademic services and products and for new undergraduate academic programs (coupled with student aid) [LT].

Governance
a) Establish a reliable and user-friendly higher education management information system with all public and private HEIs, using a uniform template that is accessible by all stakeholders, while preserving personal privacy [ST].
b) Set up a coordination and steering committee (with representatives of the private sector) to oversee all components of education and training and link with national planning authorities and with the business community [ST].
c) Allow public universities to set up their own processes for selecting students as long as they are consistent with parameters defined by UGC to protect equality of access and promote STEM disciplines [LT].
d) Reinforce the accountability of public universities by introducing performance-based funding [LT].
e) Identify KPIs that reflect national and individual public HEI priorities, with scorecards to monitor performance [ST].
f) Eliminate the interference of central authorities in the appointment of university council members [ST].
g) Eliminate the interference of central authorities in the appointment and promotion of senior faculty members [ST].
h) Revisit the rules governing the size and composition of university senates to make them more efficient [LT].
i) Create an independent Quality Assurance Council (linked to, but not under, the MHEH) operating for both public and private HEIs and empowered to accredit private HEIs [ST].
j) Delink responsibilities for resource allocation and accreditation [LT].
k) Review options for reducing university disruptions and closures for political reasons [LT].

Notes

1. Data are not available to estimate the full enrollment in higher education in Sri Lanka. Although efforts have been made to improve the production and dissemination of data, only the 15 public universities and the 18 UGC institutes have benefited, which

leaves out significant segments of the sector, in particular the private entities. Moreover, there are discrepancies between UCG and Ministry of Higher Education (MOHE) data, and neither dataset matches the figures published by the UNESCO Institute of Statistics (UIS)—even though those figures come from UGC.

2. This is the figure used by UIS, which excludes the much larger group of students who are enrolled in private institutions that are not officially recognized.
3. Since 2003, the number of pupils who sat for the GCE O-level exam has declined, though in an erratic way. The number of those who sat for the A-level exam rose, but the trend was smoother.
4. ISCED 5, which refers to short-term tertiary education, is described by UNESCO as "often designed to provide participants with professional knowledge, skills and competencies. Typically, they are practically based, occupationally specific and prepare students to enter the labor market." ISCED 6 refers to BA, ISCED 7 to master's, and ISCED 8 to doctoral programs.
5. In figure 6.3, which shows the close correlation between GDP per capita and the higher education GER in 2012 ($R^2 = 0.76$), Sri Lanka is below the trend line. For 2013 Sri Lanka would be even further below, but because there are fewer countries for which the correlation can be estimated, the correlation is weaker ($R^2 = 0.35$).
6. Figures published by MOHE/UGC and those collected by UIS do not correspond exactly because program definitions differ.
7. In the plantations, it did not reach even 3 percent (HIEs).
8. However, the gap seems to have narrowed somewhat since 2010/11. Based on the household survey, at that time tertiary NERs were 24 percent for students from the wealthiest households and 4 percent for those from the poorest.
9. Across the entire public higher education subsector, the total number of academic staff reaches 7,500.
10. Compared with 46 percent in public 4-year colleges and 55 percent in public 2-year colleges in the United States (*Chronicle of Higher Education*, August 21, 2015).
11. See the sub-section titled "Labor Market Outcomes" of the section, "Performance: Input, Processes, Outputs, and Outcomes" in this chapter.
12. As an example, in the United States, 29 percent of university faculty members are professors, 24 percent are associate professors, 26 percent are assistant professors, and 15 percent are instructors (*Chronicle of Higher Education*, August 21, 2015).
13. Although purely focused on the United States, Harcleroad (2011) offers an interesting discussion of QA modalities (approval/authorization/certification/registration/licensing) and how they are dealt with in a highly decentralized system, though there is currently a debate between forces advocating even more independence from federal control and others pushing for "recentralization."
14. The "credit" value in the SLQF is based on the Carnegie-Unit definition.
15. E.g., the Council for Higher Education Accreditation in the United States.
16. This is a 2008 study, discussed in World Bank 2009.
17. Household surveys and the ILO method use different definitions and are not directly comparable. The former allow comparisons within the country, and the latter allow international comparisons.
18. Sri Lanka ranks 151th of 187 countries for this indicator (WDI).
19. This rate has been stagnating for the last 10 years and does not show any sign of rising.

20. The relatively high share of graduates in sciences and low share of graduates in social sciences partially make up for the strongly contrasted figures for arts and engineering.
21. There are huge variations behind the world averages presented in table 6.13. A number of "odd couples" can be noted. For instance, in the humanities, Egypt and Korea (18 percent share); in the social sciences, Burundi and the Netherlands (40 percent share); in the sciences, Botswana and Ireland (12 percent share); and in engineering, Vietnam and Qatar (24 percent share). Definition problems notwithstanding, these variations suggest that there is room for specialization.
22. Differences between universities similarly range from 24 to 93 percent.
23. These figures cannot be compared with those from the household survey.
24. Other indicators such as the number of publications in university-housed, non-peer-reviewed journals or the number of conferences attended are either too "soft" (the former) or too easily manipulated (the latter) to be dependable.
25. Of the six journals, one was published by the National Science Foundation; three were dedicated to medical studies; and the other two journals were published by the International Water Management Institute (IWMI), a nonprofit organization.
26. On average, for the 1996-2014 period, Sri Lanka ranked 40th, between Tunisia and Georgia.
27. It is supported by a World Bank-financed higher education project (see World Bank 2010).
28. Assisted by the World Bank–supported HETC project.
29. The "triple helix" model associates universities, industry, and government. Experience shows that close collaboration by these three actors is essential for the success of partnerships (e.g., Penang in Malaysia).
30. Sri Lanka does not fare better, even in the separate QS Asia ranking. In this regional ranking, which covers 300 HEIs, only one is in Sri Lanka (University of Colombo), while Pakistan has 10 and Malaysia 21.
31. The CWTS Leiden Ranking uses the Web of Science database of Thomson Reuters, http://www.leidenranking.com/ranking/2015.
32. Revenues (excluding grants) as a percent of GDP are also lower in Sri Lanka (14.3 percent in 2010) than in middle-income countries (18.1 percent).
33. The higher NHRDC estimates may include capital spending.
34. $R^2 = -0.80$.
35. Values for this indicator range from 10 percent (Guatemala) to 100 percent (South Africa). There is no clear explanation of the reason for this huge dispersion.
36. Full-time students also forgo earnings, an opportunity cost estimated on the basis of earnings of secondary school graduates.
37. One institute is exclusively for undergraduates, nine are exclusively for postgraduates, and four cater to both.
38. Until September 2015, these institutions were under the MOHE.
39. The National Human Resource Development Committee provides statistics on a larger spectrum of institutions, but they are not always consistent with those produced by UGC, and even less consistent with those published by the ministry.
40. This risk is partially mitigated by the practice of recruiting UGC members from the academic community.

41. The report of the workshop organized by the "University of Colombo on University Governance, Autonomy, and Accountability" in November 2015 offers a comprehensive view of the concerns of the academic community about the issues discussed in the text.
42. The private school of medicine is exemplary in that respect.

References

Aturupane, H., Y. Savchenko, M. Shojo, and K. Larsen. 2014. "Sri Lanka: Investment in Human Capital." South Asia Human Development Unit Discussion Paper Series 69, World Bank, Washington, DC.

Dundar, H., B. Millot, Y. Savchenko, T. A. Piyasiri, and H. Aturupane. 2014. *Building the Skills for Economic Growth and Competitiveness in Sri Lanka*. Washington, DC: World Bank.

Harcleroad, F. 2011. *Quality Assurance in Higher Education in the Twenty-First Century and the Role of the Council for Higher Education Accreditation*. Washington, DC: Institute for Research and Study of Accreditation and Quality Assurance.

Hazelkorn, E. 2015. *Rankings and the Reshaping of Higher Education. The Battle for World-Class Excellence*. London: Palgrave Macmillan.

IPS (Institute of Policy Studies of Sri Lanka). 2015. *Sri Lanka State of the Economy 2015: Economic Reforms—Political Economy and Institutional Challenges*. Colombo: IPS.

Millot, B. 2015. "International Rankings: Universities vs. Higher Education Systems." *International Journal of Educational Development* 40: 156–65.

MHEH (Ministry of Higher Education and Highways). 2016. *Promoting University-Industry Collaboration in Sri Lanka: Status, Case-Studies and Policy Options*. Colombo: MHEH.

MOHE (Ministry of Higher Education). 2014. *Review of Activities*. Colombo: MOH.

OECD (Organisation for Economic Co-operation and Development). 2014. *Education at a Glance*. Paris: OECD.

UGC (University Grants Commission). *Statistical Yearbook*. Various Issues. Colombo: UGC.

WIPO (World Intellectual Property Organization). 2015. *World Intellectual Property Indicators*. Geneva: WIPO.

World Bank. 2009. *The Towers of Learning. Performance, Peril, and Promise of Higher Education in Sri Lanka*. Colombo: World Bank.

———. 2010. *Higher Education for the Twenty-First Century (HETC) Project Appraisal Document*. Washington, DC: World Bank.

———. 2012. "Are Countries' Investment in Tertiary Education Making a Difference?" South Asia Human Development Unit Discussion Paper Series 53, World Bank, Washington, DC.

APPENDIX A

Sri Lanka Education Sector Assessment: Main Issues, Strategic Directions, and Policy Actions

Area	Objectives	Short-term initiatives	Medium- / long-term initiatives
Early childhood development			
Access	• Enhance access to ECD programs. • Direct more policy attention to access of poor households and regions to ECD programs.	• Raise parental awareness through outreach campaigns on the benefits of ECD using a variety of media. • Expand the scope of current ECD programs to incorporate nutrition and cognitive stimulation, with special attention to poor households and regions.	• Provide poverty-targeted scholarships to children from poor households to attend ECD centers. • Provide matching grants and performance grants for enrolling poor children. • Establish ECD centers using public resources in locations not served by the nonstate sector.
Quality	• Enhance the quality of inputs, processes, and outcomes.	• Draw up a high-quality curriculum and establish standards for early childhood learning outcomes. • Set minimum quality standards for ECD centers. • Provide support so that ECD centers can achieve minimum quality standards. • Formulate a teacher professional development plan. • Support the development of ECD personnel capacity at all administrative levels.	• Roll out the curriculum framework and child learning standards. • Adopt minimum quality standards for ECD centers. • Support ECD centers for reaching the minimum quality standards through loan/matching grants. • Roll out the teacher professional development plan. • Continue regular capacity development for ECD personnel at all administrative levels.
Investment	• Increase sustainable financing for ECD programs	• Enable nonstate providers to establish ECD centers in underserved and unserved provinces through PPP mechanisms.	• Increase public financing of ECD to reach universal coverage.

table continues next page

Area	Objectives	Short-term initiatives	Medium- / long-term initiatives
Governance	• Adopt a National Policy on ECD. • Clarify central and provincial roles and better coordinate between government agencies. • Establish a Quality Assurance Framework. • Make available regular, comprehensive, and reliable data on ECD.	• Enact a National Policy on ECD consistent with the Constitution. • Formally delineate the responsibilities of central and provincial authorities for implementing ECD programs. • Develop a Quality Assurance Framework covering both public and nonstate ECD providers. • Establish mechanisms for the regular collection and analysis of ECD data.	• Adopt and implement the National Policy. • Establish coherent intersector coordination between government authorities responsible for early childhood development (MOE, MOH, MWCA, and others). • Roll out the Quality Assurance Framework. • Use data to make evidence-based ECD policy.
Primary and secondary education			
Access	• Increase opportunities in senior secondary schools for equitable access to science, math, and technology streams, and strengthen English language learning.	• Ensure the full functioning of 1,000 new senior secondary schools throughout the country with high-quality principals and teachers.	• Further identify opportunities throughout the country for students to enroll in all GCE A-level streams.
Quality	• Modernize and diversify the school curriculum. • Strengthen the teacher management and performance system. • Modernize the examination system. • Internationally benchmark student learning.	• Introduce an effective Career Guidance program for GCE O-level and GCE A-level students. • Benchmark and revise the school curriculum in line with high-quality international education systems. • Map teacher vacancies in schools by subject area to identify whether vacancies are due to shortages or deployment practices. • Benchmark and revise the examination system in line with the curriculum revision to align with high-performing international education systems. • Participate in international assessments (e.g., TIMMS, PISA, or PIRLS).	• Conduct career guidance activities in all schools with specially trained guidance teachers. • Roll out the modernized curriculum to promote student learning and socio-emotional skills. • Use results of national and international assessments to design education programs. • Roll out a continuous teacher professional development program for all teachers centered on schools and using resources such as teacher training colleges, national colleges of education and universities. • Move to an all-graduate teacher cadre. • Roll out a modernized examination system to complement curriculum reforms to promote student learning and socio-emotional skills.
Investment	• Improve the efficiency and equity of public financing.	• Increase the share of public education resources for the provinces. • Create a package of generous incentives for teachers to relocate to schools in difficult areas.	• Implement a school grants scheme with special focus on rural and plantation schools. • Enhance the teacher compensation package to attract qualified and capable individuals into the profession. • Revise teacher promotion criteria to incorporate rewards for teacher effectiveness.

table continues next page

Area	Objectives	Short-term initiatives	Medium-/long-term initiatives
Governance	• Enhance empowerment of schools and strengthen accountability.	• Modernize school monitoring based on internal and external quality assurance processes. • Recruit teachers to respond to the needs of the education system and transfer teachers based on transparent criteria applied impartially. • Appoint school principals and education administrators solely on merit. • Regulate private tuition effectively and impartially.	• Roll out quality assurance activities on a continuous cycle, reflecting international good practice. • Promote school-based management by devolving more power to schools and local communities.
Higher education			
Access	• Broaden and expand access to higher education.	• Increase university intake capacity in degree programs that have priority for economic development. • Expand higher education institutions. • Introduce PPPs to attract accredited national and international private higher education institutions to invest in Sri Lanka.	• Introduce new university degree programs important for economic development. • Establish new universities and faculties in disciplines important for economic development. • Introduce scholarships for qualified students from poor households to attend private higher education institutions.
Quality	• Enhance the quality and economic relevance of higher education.	• Introduce a scholarship scheme for young academics in priority disciplines (e.g., STEM) to qualify for PhD programs. • Appoint qualified international academic staff to reduce vacancies in universities. • Involve private sector representatives in program design and delivery, especially in professional programs. • Launch pilot schemes to improve the quality of EDPs (e.g., MOOCs). • Establish an autonomous Quality Assurance and Accreditation Agency for both public and private HEIs.	• Put in place a system for the continuous professional development of university academic and managerial staff. • Integrate soft-skills development in all higher education programs. • Expand the academic staff cadre in priority disciplines with high faculty-student ratios. • Promote partnerships between universities and national and foreign firms to stimulate research and development. • Roll out a system of internationally benchmarked quality assurance and accreditation programs for all public and private HEIs.
Investment	• Promote efficiency.	• Cost out human resources reforms based on alternative scenarios. • Adopt a competitive funding plan to promote research and innovation in universities.	• Insist on multiyear strategic development planning based on the QA system in universities. • Adopt performance-based funding linked to the strategic development plans of universities.

table continues next page

Area	Objectives	Short-term initiatives	Medium- / long-term initiatives
Governance	• Strengthen stewardship and management.	• Ensure that all HEI managerial and academic appointments are based on transparent procedures and merit-based criteria.	• Strengthen the link of promotion and academic compensation and performance in teaching and research. • Implement the Sri Lanka Higher Education Qualification Framework for horizontal and vertical mobility in public and private HEIs. • Reform the EDPs to focus on labor-market-oriented programs. • Promote mission differentiation among HEIs in line with global developments.

Technical and vocational education and training (TVET)

Area	Objectives	Short-term initiatives	Medium- / long-term initiatives
Access	• Broaden access to job-relevant training.	• Promote private sector provision of preemployment and on-the-job training, for instance through employment-linked training agreements. • Carry out a study on the design and implementation of voucher programs to target disadvantaged groups or for specific priority jobs.	
Quality	• Improve the quality and relevance of skills development programs.	• Ensure that all ISSCs are operational and assess their incentives for continued business engagement and sustainability. • Review and update TVET curricula regularly with inputs from employers. • Expand opportunities for the professional development of industry experts and instructors in new and emerging skills. • Initiate performance-linked compensation for TVET instructors. • Upgrade the quality of equipment and instructional materials for public TVET institutions. • Strengthen and expand QA mechanisms to cover both public and private providers.	• Review and update the NVQ framework periodically, with the full participation of the ISSCs.
Investment	• Ensure the adequacy and effectiveness of public spending on TVET.	• Ensure that the TVET sector has adequate resources to reach the objectives set out in the SSDP 2014. • Adopt performance-based financing to promote quality improvement.	• Support internal generation and retention of revenue by public TVET institutions.

table continues next page

Area	Objectives	Short-term initiatives	Medium- / long-term initiatives
Governance	• Better coordinate TVET policy. • Improve the use and dissemination of aggregate skills information. • Increase the autonomy and accountability of TVET institutions.	• Strengthen coordination between ministries and institutions providing TVET through the Inter-Ministerial Skills Coordination Committee (IMSCC) and ensure that the IMSCC is at the center of government, overseen by the prime minister. • Continue to build up labor market information systems and ensure that they are centrally coordinated and managed by the IMSCC. • Strengthen the M&E of system performance for TVET institutions, especially labor market analysis. • Regularly disseminate information on career opportunities, returns to TVET, and labor market changes to all stakeholders (youth, parents/ community, employers).	• Delegate greater financial and administrative power to public TVET institutions. • Use data on skills demand and supply s for evidence-based decision making.

Environmental Benefits Statement

The World Bank Group is committed to reducing its environmental footprint. In support of this commitment, we leverage electronic publishing options and print-on-demand technology, which is located in regional hubs worldwide. Together, these initiatives enable print runs to be lowered and shipping distances decreased, resulting in reduced paper consumption, chemical use, greenhouse gas emissions, and waste.

We follow the recommended standards for paper use set by the Green Press Initiative. The majority of our books are printed on Forest Stewardship Council (FSC)–certified paper, with nearly all containing 50–100 percent recycled content. The recycled fiber in our book paper is either unbleached or bleached using totally chlorine-free (TCF), processed chlorine–free (PCF), or enhanced elemental chlorine–free (EECF) processes.

More information about the Bank's environmental philosophy can be found at http://www.worldbank.org/corporateresponsibility.

www.ingramcontent.com/pod-product-compliance
Lightning Source LLC
Chambersburg PA
CBHW081809300426

44116CB00014B/2296